Computable Models

Raymond Turner

Computable Models

 Springer

Raymond Turner
University of Essex
UK

ISBN 978-1-84996-818-8   e-ISBN 978-1-84882-052-4
DOI 10.1007/978-1-84882-052-4

British Library Cataloguing in Publication Data
A catalogue record for this book is available from the British Library

Printed on acid-free paper

Springer Science+Business Media
springer.com

Preface

I take the central task of *theoretical computing science* (TCS) to be the construction of mathematical models of computational phenomena. Such models provide us with a deeper understanding of the nature of *computation* and *representation*. For example, the early work on computability theory provided a mathematical model of computation. Later work on the semantics of programming languages enabled a precise articulation of the underlying differences among programming languages and led to a clearer understanding of the distinction between semantic representation and implementation. Early work in complexity theory supplied us with abstract notions that formally articulated informal ideas about the resources used during computation. Such mathematical modeling provides the means of exploring the properties and limitations of languages and tools that would otherwise be unavailable.

The aim of this book is to contribute to this fundamental activity. Here we have two interrelated goals. One is to provide a logical framework and foundation for the process of specification and the design of specification languages. The second is to employ this framework to introduce and study *computable models*. These extend the notion of specification to the more general arena of mathematical modeling where our aim is to build mathematical models that are constructed from specifications.

During the preparation of this book, every proper computer scientist at the University of Essex provided valuable feedback. Some provided quite detailed comments. I will not single out any of you; you know who you are. But to all who contributed, thank you. Referees on the various journal papers that led to the book also provided valuable advice and criticism. But my greatest debt is to my wife, Rosana. Over the years, she has read draft after draft and made innumerable (not literally) suggestions for change and improvement. Without her, the size of the set of errors that remains would be much greater than it is.

Contents

Chapter 1
What is a Computable Model?

As a first approximation, a *computable model* is a mathematical model constructed from data types using operations and relations that are computable relative to those types. But what do we understand by the terms *mathematical model* and *data type* and what is it to be *computable* relative to the latter? As a preliminary to formalization, in this chapter we aim to clarify how we intend to use these notions. The rest of the book will provide mathematical substance to these more informal considerations.

1.1 Mathematical Models

The term *mathematical model* is often used to mean a model of a system built from mathematical structures and their associated notions. Such models are employed throughout engineering, the natural sciences, and the social ones. Typical examples range from models constructed from sets, number systems of various kinds, algebraic structures, especially categories, topological spaces through to probabilistic and statistical models, etc. Very common examples employ the real and complex number systems and, in particular, consist of differential equations such as the following.

$$m \frac{d^2}{dt^2} f(t) = - \operatorname{grad}(g(f(t))$$

$$\frac{dS}{S} = \mu dt + \sigma dX$$

The first is the model of a particle in a potential field and the second is the Black–Scholes partial differential equation for a derivative price. The exact meaning of the terms involved need not detain us; our only concern is that they illustrate how mathematical notions (in these cases differential equations) are used to model natural or artificial phenomena. This very general notion of modeling partly illustrates how we intend to use the term *mathematical modeling*.

However, our primary use of the term is closer to that found in logic and set theory [5, 11, 13] where sets, relations, and functions (conceived of as sets of

R. Turner, *Computable Models*, DOI 10.1007/978-1-84882-052-4_1, tuples) are the basic building blocks for the construction of mathematical models of axiomatic systems. While this kind of modeling may be seen as a special case of the more general notion, it is distinguished by the central role it gives to sets. For example, in the denotational semantics [19] of programming languages, programs are modeled as set-theoretic functions acting upon some set-theoretic representation of the underlying abstract machine. In formal ontology, a typical representation of time will model instants as certain sets of events [22]. And modal notions such as necessity and possibility are unpacked in terms of sets of possible worlds [4]. Such modeling is ubiquitous in mathematical logic and theoretical computer science. Indeed, if one takes set theory as a foundation for mathematics, to which everything can be reduced, then ultimately all mathematical models are set-theoretic.

In very general terms, we shall often follow the structure of these set-theoretic models. However, we shall not build our models from sets. Instead, we shall employ *data types* and *computable relations* and *functions* operating on them. And in their fundamental guise, these are not to be interpreted as sets but taken as *sui generis*. In particular, our notion of *type* has its origins in computer science [16] and our notion of relation/function has its origin in computability theory [6], intensional logic [20, 21], and specification [23].

This is the general picture of our enterprise. We now look at matters in more detail.

1.2 Specifications, Programs, and Models

While our models will not be set-theoretic, neither will they be programming models, where the latter consists solely of programs written in some programming language. There is a crucial distinction between mathematical models and programming ones. For while it is true that the process of programming results in the construction of *models* from programs and data types, and so fits our desiderata for being computable, they are not, by themselves, mathematical models. In isolation, a programming language is just that, i.e., a language. And without some mathematical interpretation of its constructs, aside from the formal nature of its grammar, it has no mathematical content. And neither do the programs written in it. Such content has to be imposed upon it via a semantic account (of some kind) and it is this that renders it amenable to mathematical analysis.

In fact, computable models are closer to specifications [23, 12] than programs. Indeed, specifications form the building blocks of computable models, which take the form of suites of interrelated individual relation and function specifications. However, our models are taken to include a much broader class of phenomena than the usual description of a software engineering system. While we are not aiming to exclude such systems, quite the contrary, eventually we shall take matters somewhat further and consider the construction of computable models that have more theoretical interest. In particular, many are best seen as providing a computational makeover of some standard set-theoretic models such as the modelling of events and time.

1.3 Data Types and Programming Languages

Natural numbers, characters, tuples of numbers, lists of numbers, finite sets of characters, classes of objects, and stacks of characters are all examples of types of data. In particular, they are the kinds of things that occur as data types in programming languages [7]. This provides some insight into what we intend by the term *data type*. More specifically, we might use programming languages themselves as the characterization of such structures; i.e., a data type is one that occurs as a data type in some programming language. For example, Miranda™ admits numbers, lists, and functional operations among its data types, while object-oriented languages such as Smalltalk employ objects and classes as their main modeling notions. Older languages (e.g., members of the ALGOL family) focus on stacks, arrays, and, more generally, the structures that support imperative programming. Indeed, imperative languages such as ALGOL and C can be seen as implicitly containing some notion of *state* as a basic type. This programming language perspective captures something about what we intend by the term *data type*. But it does not characterize the abstract notion. It is too contingent a definition. In particular, it captures only the data types of existing languages and says nothing about new ones that may occur in future languages. Are we to count the sets of extensional higher-order logic (with the natural number type) or those of standard Zermelo–Fraenkel set theory as data types? Presumably not, but why exactly? The answer that they do not occur as types in any existing language is neither conceptually nor mathematically informative.

We might generalize matters by not demanding that a data type occur as a type in an existing language, but only require it to have an interpretation in one. But what does this amount to? Presumably, that the structure has an interpretation in such a language. For example, finite sets can be implemented in any language that supports lists. But being a model usually means being a model of some set of axioms. In this particular example, the axioms of finite sets need to come out true under the interpretation that is induced by the implementation. Of course, to check that the axioms for finite sets are sound, we shall need the axioms for lists in place. Consequently, without some notion of what the theory of lists is, we are back to square one; without some axiomatic theory to measure it against, we have no mathematical characterization.[1] But this changes the central question: It is not which syntactic structures are data types but which axiomatic theories determine them.

---

[1] It will do no good to suggest that an implementation on a physical machine is all we need to establish soundness. The best that this can achieve is some form of empirical verification. A physical machine cannot provide a mathematical account, at least not unless the machine has a precise characterization. Indeed, without the latter, we cannot even carry out any empirical testing, since, without some independent characterization, the actual propositional content of the testing is unclear.

1.4 Theories of Data

We shall refer to theories that involve the axiomatization of one or more type constructors as *theories of data types* (**TDT**). Indeed, an informal data type comes
equipped with some basic relations and functions that operate over them; i.e., they
are not naked collections of things [7]. For example, the type of natural numbers usually comes equipped with successor, addition, and the numerical ordering relations.
Similarly, lists are constructed and manipulated by operations such as concatenation
($*$), *head* (h), and *tail* (t). Finally, any account of classes might make reference
to an *inherit* relation. It is the defining characteristics of these operations and their
types that are articulated in any axiomatization. So, for example, they might be given
by rules of the following form that govern the notions of type and their membership.
The first informs us that N forms a type (the type of natural numbers), while the next
two tell us that 0 is a number and that numbers are closed under addition; i.e., if n
and m are numbers, so is $n + m$. The second three are parallel ones for lists: If T is
a type, then $List(T)$ is a type, the empty list is a list, and lists are closed under the
concatenation.

$$N \; type \qquad 0 : N \qquad \frac{a : N \quad b : N}{a + b : N}$$

$$\frac{T \; type}{List(T) \; type} \qquad empty : List(T) \qquad \frac{a : T \qquad l : List(T)}{a * l : List(T)}$$

These form part of the rules that govern the type. However, they only provide rules
of *type inference*. They have meager logical content. In particular, they do not tell
us how to compute with the operators of addition and concatenation. For this we
need rules that govern the relationships between the operators. For example, the
following govern the relationship between addition and successor and among head,
tail, and concatenation.

$$\frac{a : N \qquad\qquad b : N}{a + succ(b) = succ(a + b)} \tag{1}$$

$$\frac{a : T \qquad l : List(T)}{head(a * l) * tail(a * l) = a * l} \tag{2}$$

These give more semantic content to the operators. Such principles reflect and un-
derpin how we program with numbers and lists, and indeed, what we take them to
be. More generally, a set of such principles for a type determines the *data type*. Of
course, for any given informal data type, there is no unique set of rules and axioms.
While (1) and (2) will almost certainly form part of any theory of numbers/lists,
we have some freedom to decide on which further axioms and rules we take to
determine the type. For example, there is no single theory of natural numbers.

Indeed, for the construction of mathematical models, we need to go beyond the
simple systems of type inference that, for type-checking purposes, are often taken

to determine a data type. Any mathematically useful account must also include an induction principle of the form

$$\frac{\phi(0) \qquad \forall x : N \cdot \phi[x] \to \phi[succ(x)]}{\forall x : N \cdot \phi[x]}$$

where ϕ is a proposition of the formal language in which the axioms and rules are expressed. Without induction it is not possible to reason about numbers. Similarly, the parallel principle for lists takes the following form.

$$\frac{\phi[empty] \qquad \forall u : T \cdot \forall v : List(T) \cdot \phi[v] \to \phi[u * v]}{\forall x : List(T) \cdot \phi[x]}$$

Clearly, such principles depend upon the class of propositions that ϕ ranges over. Different classes of propositions determine different induction principles, which leads to different axiomatic theories. So there will always be a normative aspect to the choice of axioms and rules. Consequently, every informal data type gives rise to many axiomatic theories, and consequently, any programming language gives rise to many **TDT**.

1.5 Recursive Models

But do all axiomatic theories determine **TDT**? Or do such theories form a natural subclass, and can we characterize it? One possible mathematical characterization insists that a **TDT** is any axiomatic theory that has a finite model. After all, in any implementation of an actual programming language on a physical machine, there is a finite upper bound on the number of elements in a data type and on their individual size. So why is this not the answer to the characterization problem; i.e., **TDT** are those theories that have finite models. Unfortunately, this is not consistent with the notion of a Turing complete programming language, where the basic data type of numbers is unbounded. And it is the latter that gives mathematical support for the idea of a machine-independent language.

The natural numbers not only form a very basic data type (or several), but they come equipped with the paradigm notion of *computability* for relations and functions. Consequently, a better mathematical characterization insists that a **TDT** has a model in the natural numbers in which its types and its basic operations and relations, and in particular its notion of equality, are Turing computable. More exactly, any basic operations must be Turing computable and any basic relation and any type are to be recursively enumerable.[2] Put more succinctly, it must have a *recursive model*. This appropriately generalizes the idea that it has a finite one.[3]

But what does this sanction and what does it rule out; i.e., which theories have recursive models? Certainly, any standard axiomatic theory of the numbers with $+, \times, <$ as its basic function and relation symbols with their standard first-order axiomatizations has one. And the standard theory of lists has one. And so does the first-order theory of finite sets with membership and the basic operations of union, difference, and intersection. Indeed, every structure that functions as a data type in an existing programming language has one.

Conversely, it rules out the structures that intuitively cannot so function. For example, extensional higher-logic with a natural number type [1] has no recursive model. In particular, equality for its underlying theory of sets is not even semidecidable. More explicitly, on the assumptions that N, the set of natural numbers, is a type and that we can form the type of all subsets of a given type, $P(N)$ is a type. However, membership and equality for such infinite extensional sets are not semidecidable.

So we shall use the notion of a recursive model to determine our notion of **TDT**. Indeed, our recursive model constructions will employ a version of formal arithmetic and establish that our theories are conservative extensions of it. But there are other characteristics of our theories that support the construction of such recursive models.

1.6 Intensional Models

In our theories, *types*, *relations,* and *functions* are *intensional* objects.[4] That is, their criterion of equality is not *extensional*. Consequently, two types will not be taken to be equal simply because they share all elements. Similarly, two relations will not be taken to be the same just because they apply to the same objects, and two functions will not be taken to be identical when they have the same graphs. Types are not intended to be notational variants of sets and relations and functions are not taken to be sets of ordered pairs, triples etc. Instead, they are to be taken as primitive notions that are determined by their axiomatic theories. They are *intensional* notions. This

---

[2] We shall use *computable function* to mean Turing computable function. Semi-decidable relations are also called recursively enumerable ones. These have Turing computable characteristic functions.

[3] While finiteness may explain why finite sets may be taken to be data structures, and while infinite sets given in extension may not be, it does not explain why sets given intensionally can be. For example, consider the recursively enumerable sets given via their Gödel codes. We can compute their union via their codes. In this way the codes act as the vehicles of the computation.

[4] In respect of their intensional character, the traditional notion of *property* would be a close cousin of these notions [20].

is all consistent with the demand that our theories have recursive models where the primary notion of function is operational and algorithmic.[5]

1.7 A Logical Foundation for Specification

The given set constructors of Zermelo–Fraenkel set theory (union, power set, pairing, separation, etc.) will not suffice for many applications. Clearly, one cannot develop set-theoretic models without the development of some set-theoretic notions, i.e., pure Zermelo–Fraenkel set theory has to be enriched by the conservative definition of new notions expressed within the language of set theory [13]. For example, at some point, one has to define new set constructors. Indeed, the reconstruction of mathematics inside set theory is an activity of this very kind. And it requires a massive build-up of mathematical infrastructure.

Similarly, a bare **TDT** will seldom suffice for the construction of a computable model. The theory will need to be supplemented by the definition of new notions, i.e., new types, relations, and functions. In a computable setting, such definitions will take the form of *specifications* of new relations and functions [23, 12].

Consequently, much of the book will involve not only the development of **TDT**, but also the development, construction, and mathematical investigation of specifications expressed within them. This will yield a *logical foundation* for specification. Indeed, one of our aims is to unpack the logical content of specifications: What are the rules that govern their introduction and use? How do we reason about them? How do we treat them as mathematical objects?

1.8 Implementable Models

Many set-theoretic models have no recursive interpretation. However, it is often possible to replace the set-theoretic model with a computable counterpart. Of course, such a replacement does not entail mathematical equivalence. But computable models have the advantage that they can be implemented in the sense that they have a recursive interpretation. Indeed, more directly, a computable model could be coded in a version of Prolog, i.e., one with the appropriate type structure [17]. Such interpretations offer the possibility of building a prototype implementation of the mathematical model.

In contrast, the formal and conceptual relationships between set-theoretic models and actual implementations are often obscure and/or complicated [15]. Mostly one can only implement an approximation or simulation of the mathematical model. Both theoretically and practically, this is far from satisfactory. Computable models are implementable specifications, and so there is a precise and direct connection

---

[5] Here we assume the standard recursive model where algorithms are representable as codes of Turing machines and their criterion of equality is the one inherited from this representation.

between the specification and the implementation. Indeed, at least in our case studies, we suggest that the computable model is often a more *faithful*, in the sense of [3, 8], reflection of practice.

1.9 The Logical Setting

Informally at least, we have now settled the nature of our theories and our models; now we need to examine how to formally formulate them. To this end, we shall exploit some of the central disciplines of mathematical logic, namely, recursion theory [18, 6], formal arithmetic [10], and admissible set theory [2].

First, the language of formal arithmetic provides a (albeit very impoverished) paradigm **TDT** and we shall employ it as a yard-stick in the construction of our more complex and applicable theories. There are several reasons for this. Not only are numbers a fundamental notion of data in computer science, but formal number theory provides a paradigm for the investigation of our theories: In it one can specify or define functions and relations in much the same way as with more complex and expressive theories. Indeed, much of formal number theory can be productively seen as an exercise in formal specification for numerical relations and functions. This will furnish us with a framework in which the various important mathematical and metamathematical questions are presented and investigated in stark form, and so provide us with a road map for the investigation of more elaborate theories. Much the same is true of admissible set theory. In particular, the elementary parts of the latter provide a detailed study of the definition of new relation and function symbols over hereditarily finite sets.

Second, all the aforementioned theories furnish us with a precise notion of *computability* for relations and functions. For instance, in formal arithmetic the Σ *definable* wff characterize the *recursively enumerable* relations in that every recursively enumerable relation is Σ definable and vice versa. This will guide us in formulating explicit notions of definability/computability for our theories. Indeed, we shall generalize these notions of Σ *definability* to **TDT**. In this way we shall provide a generalized notion of computability for arbitrary **TDT**.

However, unlike these theories, which are single type theories, we are concerned with theories with very rich and expressive notions of type. So in the formulation of our rather grammatically complex theories of types, we shall borrow heavily from recent work in constructive type theory [14, 3] and, more generally, the type theories developed in theoretical computer science. The latter, with its emphasis on type checking, presents us with a very flexible way of formulating syntax.[6] Indeed, modern logical systems also display such grammatical flexibility, and the present logical framework follows suit.

In the next chapter we shall develop our basic logical framework, called *typed predicate logic* (**TPL**), within which we shall articulate our **TDT**. Once that is in

---

[6] This was itself inspired by early work in combinatorial logic.

place, we shall develop a general theory of specification based upon **TPL**. This will yield a very general approach to specification that will automatically apply to all **TDT** articulated within it. We shall then begin the development of a sequence of **TDT**. The first concentrates on the natural numbers as a paradigm theory of data. This is followed by the development of a typed theory of finite sets. The rest of the book will cover topics such as higher-order specifications, specifications as data, subtypes, polymorphic specifications, abstract types, and various examples of computable models including examples from theoretical computer science, computable real analysis, philosophical logic, and formal ontology. And every theory and model cast within it will have a recursive interpretation.

References

1. Andrews, P.B. An Introduction to Mathematical Logic and Type Theory. Academic Press, New York, 1986.
2. Barwise, J. Admissible Sets and Structures. Springer-Verlag, Berlin, 1975.
3. Beeson, M.J. Foundations of Constructive Mathematics, Springer-Verlag Berlin, 1985.
4. Blackburn, P., de Rijke, M., and Venema, Y. Modal Logic. Cambridge Univ. Press, Cambridge, 2001.
5. Bridge, J. Beginning Model Theory: The Completeness Theorem and Some Consequences. Clarendon Press, Oxford, 1977.
6. Cutland, N. Computability: An Introduction to Recursive Function Theory. Cambridge Univ. Press, Cambridge, 1990.
7. Dale, N., and Dale, H.M.W. Abstract Data Types: Specifications, Implementations, and Applications. Jones and Bartlett Publishers, Boston, 1996.
8. Feferman, S. Constructive theories of functions and classes. In: M. Boffa, D. van Dalen, and K. McAloon (Eds.), Logic Colloquium '78, pp. 159–225, North-Holland, Amsterdam, 1979.
9. Gordon, J.C. The Denotational Semantics of Programming Languages. Springer-Verlag, New York, 1970
10. Havel, P. Metamathematics of First Order Arithmetic. Springer-Verlag, Berlin, 1991.
11. Hodges, W. Model theory. Cambridge University Press, Cambridge, 1993.
12. Jones, C.B.. Systematic Software Development Using VDM. Prentice-Hall, Inc., Englewood Cliffs, NJ, 1986.
13. Krivine, J.L. Introduction to Axiomatic Set Theory. Springer-Verlag, New York, 1971.
14. Martin-Lof, P. An intuitionistic theory of sets, predicative part. In Logic Colloquim, 73. North-Holland, Amsterdam, 1975.
15. Mulmuley, K. Full Abstraction and Semantic Equivalence. MIT Press, Cambridge, MA, 1986.
16. Pierce, B.C. Types and Programming Languages. MIT Press, Cambridge, MA, 2002.
17. Pfenning, F. (Ed.). Types in Logic Programming. MIT Press, Cambridge, MA, 1992.
18. Rogers, H. Theory of Recursive Functions and Effective Computability. McGraw Hill, New York, 1967; 1988.
19. Stoy, J.E. Denotational Semantics: The Scott Strachey Approach to Programming Language Theory. MIT Press, Cambridge, MA, 1977.
20. Turner, R. A theory of properties. J. Symb. Log. 52(2): 455–472, 1987.
21. Turner, R. Logics of truth. Notre Dame Journal of Formal Logic, 31(4): 308–329, 1990.
22. Van Benthem, J. Tense logic and time. Notre Dame J. Formal Logic 25(1): 1–16, 1984.
23. Woodcock, J. and Davies, J. Using Z- Specifications, Refinement and Proof, Prentice Hall, Englewood Cliffs, NJ, 1996.

Chapter 2
Typed Predicate Logic

In this initial technical chapter we develop the logical framework within which to articulate our theories of data types (**TDT**). It is also to form our basic language of specification and provide the host for the construction of computable models. It is important to note that we are not advocating a single theory of types, but a broad framework in which a rich variety of theories can be easily and elegantly formulated.

Generally in logic and theoretical computer science, type theories are inductively generated from some basic types via type constructors. Our framework needs to be sufficiently flexible to elegantly support a wide range of such constructors, including dependent types, subtypes, and polymorphism. In addition, it must support a *type of types*; i.e., it must facilitate a natural formulation of theories where objects used to classify data become themselves items of data. However, the standard approach to the syntax of logical languages, where the syntax is given via some context-free grammar, does not easily support the expression of such a wide variety of notions. Nor does the traditional approach to simple type theory, i.e., where the types are hard-wired to the terms.

However, computer science with its emphasis on types [4, 1] and type checking, presents us with a more flexible way of formulating a typed syntax.[1] Indeed, modern logical systems also display such grammatical flexibility, e.g., the type theories of Martin Löf [3, 2]. The present logical framework follows suit. In the next few sections we shall present it and explore its simple properties.

2.1 Judgments and Contexts

We employ a system of natural deduction that we shall call *typed predicate logic* (**TPL**). This will form the logical skeleton of all our theories. However, unlike standard logical systems, where there is only one judgment form in conclusions, we admit several. More exactly, it is a many-sorted natural deduction system with the following four judgment forms:

---

[1] This was itself inspired by early work in combinatorial logic.

R. Turner, *Computable Models*, DOI 10.1007/978-1-84882-052-4_2,
© Springer-Verlag London Limited 2009

$$T \; type$$
$$\phi \; prop$$
$$t : T$$
$$\phi$$

The first asserts that T is a *type,* the second that ϕ is a *proposition,* the third that t is an object term of type T, and the fourth that ϕ is true. We shall refer to the first three as type-inference judgments.

These judgments are formed from a syntax of terms that are built from variables ($x_0, x_1, x_2, x_3...$), constant, function, and relation symbols, including equality ($=$), and the logical connectives ($\Omega, \wedge, \vee, \neg, \rightarrow, \forall, \exists$). As metavariables for strings on these alphabets, we employ the Roman and Greek alphabets, where we reserve x, y, z, u, v, w to range over the object-level variables of the language. While this is the stuff of the syntax, the actual grammar is determined not by a traditional BNF or context-free syntax, but by a type-inference system that is constituted by the *membership* and *formation* rules for types and propositions [6, 3, 5]. The rules for this rule-based grammar will form part of the overall proof system.[2]

Generally, judgments in the logic are made relative to a *context* Γ that is a finite sequence of terms. In the logic, these take one of the following two forms:

$$x : T$$
$$\phi$$

i.e., a *declaration* that a variable has a given type or the assumption that a proposition, ϕ, is true. Thus, sequents in the theory have the shape,

$$\Gamma \vdash \Theta$$

where Θ is one of our four judgment forms and Γ a context. Such sequents are the basic carriers of meaning in the logic. They determine not only what follows from what, but also what is grammatically legitimate. We shall call contexts that contain only type assignments, i.e., ones of the form $x : T$, *declaration contexts*. We shall

---

[2] This background syntax may be further refined via the following BNF grammar.

$$t ::= F(t_1, . - ., t_n) | R(t_1, . - ., t_n) | O(t_1, . - ., t_n) \; | \; t =_t t$$
$$t \vee t | t \wedge t | \neg t | \forall x : t \cdot t | \exists x : t.t$$

Similarly, the raw syntax of contexts might also be made explicit as follows.

$$\Gamma ::= t \; | \; t, \Gamma$$

However, such BNF style definitions do not play too much of a role, since they sanction way too much nonsense. They only provide the background strings for the actual grammar, which is rule-given, i.e., by the rules of the logic itself.

use c, c', d, d', etc., as variables for these contexts and c_Γ for that part of the context Γ that consists of just its type assignments.

2.2 Structural Rules

We begin with the structural rules, i.e., *assumption, thinning,* and *substitution.* The first two permit the addition of new (grammatically acceptable) assumptions. The next allows weakening under the same grammatical constraints. The final rule is a substitution rule. Note that it respects the fact that, in contexts, the order of the occurrence of assumptions is significant.

$$\mathbf{A_1} \qquad \frac{\Gamma \vdash T \; type}{\Gamma, x : T \vdash x : T} \qquad\qquad \mathbf{A_2} \qquad \frac{\Gamma \vdash \phi \; prop}{\Gamma, \phi \vdash \phi}$$

$$\mathbf{W_1} \qquad \frac{\Gamma, \Delta \vdash \Theta \quad \Gamma \vdash T \; type}{\Gamma, x : T, \Delta \vdash \Theta}$$

$$\mathbf{W_2} \qquad \frac{\Gamma, \Delta \vdash \Theta \quad \Gamma \vdash \phi \; prop}{\Gamma, \phi, \Delta \vdash \Theta}$$

$$\mathbf{Sub} \qquad \frac{\Gamma, y : S, \Delta \vdash \Theta \quad \Gamma \vdash s : S}{\Gamma, \Delta[s/y] \vdash \Theta[s/y]}$$

where in $\mathbf{A_1}$ and $\mathbf{W_1}$, x is fresh (i.e., it is not declared in Γ, Δ) and $\Theta[s/y]$ indicates the substitution of the term s for the variable y. Grammatical constraints play a significant role. For example, in $\mathbf{A_1}$ we are only permitted to add type assignments involving terms that are types, whereas $\mathbf{A_2}$ only sanctions assumptions that are propositions. Note that we do not have an exchange rule. This is a consequence of the fact that, in general, contexts will be dependent, i.e., the grammatical status of later assumptions may depend upon earlier ones. For example, the status of a purported proposition may depend upon the types of its free variables, and so may depend upon previous type declarations. A simple illustration of such dependence is generated by the equality rules. We shall see this shortly. The **Sub** rule could be avoided (it is partly covered by the universal elimination rule), but it will often prove convenient for the statement of our theories.

2.3 Types

As we have previously emphasized, types, relations, and functions are the basic building blocks of computable models. However, our treatment is not standard. They are to be taken as intensional and primitive notions whose content is given by the rules of the system. This will become clear as we proceed.

The types of any particular theory will be given in terms of some basic types and closed under a collection of type constructors. More explicitly, in their most elementary guise, the formation rules for types will take the following shape.

$$\mathbf{O_1} \quad B \ type \qquad \mathbf{O_2} \quad \frac{\Gamma \vdash T_1 \ type, \ ..., \Gamma \vdash T_n \ type}{\Gamma \vdash O(T_1, \ ..., T_n) \ type}$$

The first rule allows for the inclusion of basic types such as Booleans and numbers. In addition, there will be a type rule for each type constructor O of the language. For example, the rule for Cartesian products has the following formation rule.

$$\frac{\Gamma \vdash T \ type \qquad \Gamma \vdash S \ type}{\Gamma \vdash T \otimes S \ type}$$

Such a rule might be expressed in standard context-free style as follows.

$$type ::= ...| \ type \otimes type$$

But this approach is limited in that it does not easily support dependency. Later, we shall consider generalizations of such type formation rules as $\mathbf{O_2}$, rules that permit types to depend upon propositions and other types, i.e., dependent types.[3] We shall discuss these notions in more detail when we get to them. Our rule-based account of the grammar of types will really come into its own when we consider a type of types and, subsequently, consider the types themselves as items of data. Here we indicate their possibility to give the reader a sense of what is to come and that this is a much more flexible approach to type formation than any standard context-free style grammar. One cannot easily generalize the latter to cater for such notions of type.

The alert reader might think that we also need rules of type equality. We shall get to these when types are themselves taken to be objects in the theory. At this point, suffice it to say that, whatever type equality is taken to be, it will not be extensional; i.e., we shall not identify two types on the basis of shared membership.

---

[3] For example, in the following the first rule generalizes Cartesian products to allow for the second type to depend on the first one. The second introduces separation or sub-types. Here proposition formation may depend upon type formation, and subsequently, type formation may depend upon proposition formation.

$$\frac{\Gamma \vdash T \ type \qquad \Gamma, x : T \vdash S \ type}{\Gamma \vdash \Sigma x : T \cdot S \ type} \qquad \frac{\Gamma \vdash T \ type \qquad \Gamma, x : T \vdash \phi \ prop}{\Gamma \vdash \{x : T \cdot \phi\} \ type}$$

2.4 Relations and Functions

A relation is introduced by its grammatical rule, which takes the following shape.

$$\mathbf{R} \quad \frac{\Gamma \vdash t_1 : T_1, ..., \Gamma \vdash t_n : T_n}{\Gamma \vdash R(t_1, ..., t_n) \, prop}$$

This informs us of its grammatical territory, its intended domain and range. Of course, in any theory there may be many such relations, given by such rules.

This notion of relation is to be seen in contrast to the standard set-theoretic one in which a relation is taken to be a set of ordered tuples i.e.,

$$R \subseteq T_1 \otimes, ..., \otimes T_n$$

where now $T_1, ..., T_n$ are sets. This is a fundamentally different notion of relation. And while ours has a set-theoretic interpretation, it is not the intended one. As we have said before, our relations are not taken to be extensional; i.e., they are not taken to satisfy any axiom of extensionality that insists that relations that hold of the same objects are the same relation. This is forced by the set-theoretic interpretation.

Similar remarks apply to functions. In the rule for function symbols, the resulting type is tied to a type constructor of the language; i.e., we assume that rule **O** governs the formation of the type $O(T_1, ..., T_n)$. Thus, the types themselves are introduced via rules and the function symbols follow suit.

$$\mathbf{F} \quad \frac{\Gamma \vdash t_1 : T_1, ..., \Gamma \vdash t_n : T_n}{\Gamma \vdash F(t_1, ..., t_n) : O(T_1, ..., T_n)}$$

In line with the generalization of type formation, the rules for functions and relations will admit parallel generalizations. But we shall explain these in context.

2.5 Equality

The formation rule for equality is a special case of the formation rule for relations. $\mathbf{E}_1$ insists that equality forms a proposition when the terms flanking it have the same type. In addition, distinguished symbols such as equality are given content by their associated axioms and rules. $\mathbf{E}_2$ and $\mathbf{E}_3$ are the standard rules of introduction and elimination; i.e., every element of every type is equal to itself and equal objects can be substituted for each other in all contexts.

$$E_1 \quad \frac{\Gamma \vdash t : T \qquad \Gamma \vdash s : T}{\Gamma \vdash t =_T s \; prop} \qquad\qquad E_2 \quad \frac{\Gamma \vdash t : T}{\Gamma \vdash t =_T t}$$

$$E_3 \quad \frac{\Gamma \vdash t =_T s \qquad \Gamma \vdash \Theta[t/x]}{\Gamma \vdash \Theta[s/x]}$$

The equality rules illustrate how dependency in contexts can occur. For instance, a provable sequent such as

$$x : T, y : T, z : T, x =_T y, y =_T z \vdash x =_T z$$

demonstrates how the occurrences of equality in the context (as well as the conclusion) are legitimate (i.e., form propositions) only where their constituent terms have the same type. Observe that, as a suffix, the type of the equality symbol is explicitly marked. However, where the context determines matters, we shall often drop the subscript on the equality relation; i.e., we shall just write:

$$x : T, y : T, z : T, x = y, y = z \vdash x = z$$

This principle of parsimony will be adopted generally.

2.6 Propositional Rules

We next provide the rules for the propositional connectives. The formation rules for these connectives capture their standard closure conditions, i.e., the ones normally given in a context-free style, while the introduction and elimination rules are their standard introduction and elimination logical rules.

$$L_1 \quad \frac{\Gamma \vdash \phi \; prop \qquad \Gamma \vdash \psi \; prop}{\Gamma \vdash \phi \wedge \psi \; prop} \qquad\qquad L_2 \quad \frac{\Gamma \vdash \phi \qquad \Gamma \vdash \psi}{\Gamma \vdash \phi \wedge \psi}$$

$$L_3 \quad \frac{\Gamma \vdash \phi \wedge \psi}{\Gamma \vdash \phi} \qquad\qquad L_4 \quad \frac{\Gamma \vdash \phi \wedge \psi}{\Gamma \vdash \psi}$$

$$L_5 \quad \frac{\Gamma \vdash \phi \; prop \qquad \Gamma \vdash \psi \; prop}{\Gamma \vdash \phi \vee \psi \; prop}$$

$$L_6 \quad \frac{\Gamma \vdash \phi \vee \psi \qquad \Gamma, \phi \vdash \eta \qquad \Gamma, \psi \vdash \eta}{\Gamma \vdash \eta}$$

$$L_7 \quad \frac{\Gamma \vdash \phi \qquad \Gamma \vdash \psi \; prop}{\Gamma \vdash \phi \vee \psi} \qquad\qquad L_8 \quad \frac{\Gamma \vdash \psi \qquad \Gamma \vdash \phi \; prop}{\Gamma \vdash \phi \vee \psi}$$

$$\mathbf{L_9} \quad \Gamma \vdash \Omega \; prop \qquad\qquad \mathbf{L_{10}} \quad \frac{\Gamma \vdash \phi \quad \Gamma \vdash \neg\phi}{\Gamma \vdash \Omega}$$

$$\mathbf{L_{11}} \quad \frac{\Gamma \vdash \phi \; prop \qquad \Gamma \vdash \Omega}{\Gamma \vdash \phi}$$

$$\mathbf{L_{12}} \quad \frac{\Gamma \vdash \phi \; prop \quad \Gamma \vdash \psi \; prop}{\Gamma \vdash \phi \to \psi \; prop} \qquad \mathbf{L_{13}} \quad \frac{\Gamma, \phi \vdash \psi}{\Gamma \vdash \phi \to \psi}$$

$$\mathbf{L_{14}} \quad \frac{\Gamma \vdash \phi \to \psi \quad \Gamma \vdash \phi}{\Gamma \vdash \psi}$$

$$\mathbf{L_{15}} \quad \frac{\Gamma \vdash \phi \; prop}{\Gamma \vdash \neg\phi \; prop} \qquad \mathbf{L_{16}} \quad \frac{\Gamma, \phi \vdash \Omega}{\Gamma \vdash \neg\phi} \qquad \mathbf{L_{17}} \quad \frac{\Gamma, \neg\phi \vdash \Omega}{\Gamma \vdash \phi}$$

There are additional grammatical assumptions in some of the rules. For instance, in the disjunction introduction rules ($\mathbf{L_7}$, $\mathbf{L_8}$), we include the assumption that the alternate constituent of the disjunction has to be a proposition. These grammatical side conditions, as we shall see, are to ensure that only grammatically legitimate objects (i.e., propositions) are provable. Note that the underlying logic is classical logic. Unless overridden by parentheses, we shall assume that negation takes precedence over conjunction and disjunction, which take precedence over implication. But most of the time we shall use brackets.

2.7 Quantifier Rules

Aside from their generalized grammatical setting, the rules for the quantifiers are also classical. In particular, we assume the normal side conditions for the quantifier rules; i.e., in $\mathbf{L_{20}}$, x must not be free in Γ, T, or η, and in $\mathbf{L_{22}}$, x must not be free in any proposition in Γ.

$$\mathbf{L_{18}} \quad \frac{\Gamma, x : T \vdash \phi \; prop}{\Gamma \vdash \exists x : T \cdot \phi \; prop}$$

$$\mathbf{L_{19}} \quad \frac{\Gamma \vdash \phi[t/x] \quad \Gamma \vdash t : T \qquad \Gamma, x : T \vdash \phi \; prop}{\Gamma \vdash \exists x : T \cdot \phi}$$

$$\mathbf{L_{20}} \quad \frac{\Gamma \vdash \exists x : T \cdot \phi \qquad \Gamma, x : T, \phi \vdash \eta}{\Gamma \vdash \eta} \qquad \mathbf{L_{21}} \quad \frac{\Gamma, x : T \vdash \phi \; prop}{\Gamma \vdash \forall x : T \cdot \phi \; prop}$$

$$\mathbf{L_{22}} \quad \frac{\Gamma, x : T \vdash \phi}{\Gamma \vdash \forall x : T \cdot \phi} \qquad \mathbf{L_{23}} \quad \frac{\Gamma \vdash \forall x : T \cdot \phi \quad \Gamma \vdash t : T}{\Gamma \vdash \phi[t/x]}$$

We shall assume that the scope of the quantifier in $\forall x : T \cdot \phi$, $\exists x : T \cdot \phi$ is the whole of ϕ. It is only overridden by explicit parentheses.

This concludes the rules of **TPL**. We shall often indicate matters explicitly and write

$$\Gamma \vdash_{\textbf{TPL}} \Theta$$

if the sequent $\Gamma \vdash \Theta$ is derivable using the rules of **TPL**.

The system may appear to be somewhat nonstandard, especially for the reader accustomed to first-order predicate logic. Hence, we provide some example derivations.

2.8 TPL Derivations

There is little here that is not a straightforward generalization that flows from the additional rules that replace the standard context-free grammar of a typed logic. However, given the slightly novel nature of **TPL**, we illustrate its notion of deduction with some simple examples. Of course, we shall see many more throughout the book. However, they will be somewhat less completely and formally presented.

Example 1 We deduce

$$\forall x : B \cdot \forall y : B \cdot x =_B y \rightarrow y =_B x$$

By the first equality rule, $\textbf{E}_1$, we have

$$\frac{x : B, y : B \vdash x : B \qquad x : B, y : B \vdash y : B}{x : B, y : B \vdash x =_B y \ prop} \tag{1}$$

In the following, (2) is an instance of the structural rule, $\textbf{A}_2$.

$$\frac{x : B, y : B \vdash x =_B y \ prop}{x : B, y : B, x =_B y \vdash x =_B y} \tag{2}$$

Step (3) is an instance of the second equality rule $\textbf{E}_2$.

$$\frac{x : B \vdash x : B}{x : B \vdash x =_B x} \tag{3}$$

The conclusion of (3) may be enriched to (4). This follows by a judicious use of $\textbf{A}_1$ and $\textbf{A}_2$.

$$\frac{x : B \vdash x =_B x}{x : B, y : B, x =_B y \vdash x =_B x} \tag{4}$$

By the third equality rule, the conclusions of (2) and (4), we may deduce the following

$$\frac{x : B, y : B, x =_B y \vdash x =_B y \quad x : B \vdash x =_B x}{x : B, y : B, x =_B y \vdash y =_B x} \tag{5}$$

By the implication introduction rule L_{13} and the conclusion of (5), we can deduce (6).

$$\frac{x : B, y : B, x =_B y \vdash y =_B x}{x : B, y : B \vdash x =_B y \to y =_B x} \tag{6}$$

By L_{21} and the conclusion of (6), we may conclude

$$\frac{x : B, y : B \vdash x =_B y \to y =_B x}{x : B \vdash \forall y : B \cdot x =_B y \to y =_B x} \tag{7}$$

By the conclusion of (7) and L_{21}, we arrive at the following

$$\frac{x : B \vdash \forall y : B \cdot x =_B y \to y =_B x}{\forall x : B \cdot \forall y : B \cdot x =_B y \to y =_B x} \tag{8}$$

Example 2 We deduce

$$\forall x : B \cdot \exists y : B \cdot x =_B y$$

By the first structural rule, A_1, we have

$$\frac{B \; type}{x : B \vdash x : B} \tag{1}$$

By the first equality rule, E_1, we have

$$\frac{x : B, y : B \vdash x : B \qquad x : B, y : B \vdash y : B}{x : B, y : B \vdash x =_B y \; prop} \tag{2}$$

The conclusion (3) is an instance of the equality rule E_2

$$\frac{x : B \vdash x : B}{x : B \vdash x =_B x} \tag{3}$$

By the existential introduction rule, L_{19}, and conclusions of (1), (2), and (3), we may deduce the following

$$\frac{x : B \vdash x =_B x \qquad x : B \vdash x : B \quad x : B, y : B \vdash x =_B y \; prop}{x : B \vdash \exists y : B \cdot x =_B y} \tag{4}$$

By the conclusion of (4) and universal introduction, we obtain

$$\frac{x : B \vdash \exists y : B \cdot x =_B y}{\forall x : B \cdot \exists y : B \cdot x =_B y} \tag{5}$$

We shall not see a great many examples worked out in such great detail. But these should be enough for the reader to grasp the dynamics of deduction in the system.

Example 3 Given

$$\phi \; prop \; and \; \psi \; prop$$

i.e., we can derive these in some context, we may define, in that context,

$$\phi \leftrightarrow \psi \; \triangleq (\phi \rightarrow \psi) \wedge (\psi \rightarrow \phi)$$

These is a new defined connective that illustrates the way that new notions are introduced via specification. But more of this later.

2.9 Type Inference

A distinctive aspect of **TPL** is its underlying type-inference system. As mentioned at the outset, we have inherited our approach to typed systems from the type-checking approach to syntax developed by computer scientists to ensure the type correctness of programs. It is a flexible approach in which types are not attached to terms. Instead, terms receive their types via type declarations.

This type-inference system constitutes the real grammar of **TPL**. We shall refer to it as **TI**. It is populated by the formation and type membership rules for the theory. Such a grammatical framework not only supports a very elegant and syntactically sensitive way of expressing a wide range of theories of data, but also has some conceptual significance. Types in our theories are meant to be vehicles for carving up the world in ways that can assist the computational model builder. As such, they play somewhat the same role as dimensional analysis in physics, a role that is isolated in the following subsystem.

Definition 4 *The subtheory* **TI** *is that sub theory of* **TPL** *whose rules are those of* **TPL** *but restricted to instances of the form*

$$\frac{c_1 \vdash \Theta_1, ..., c_n \vdash \Theta_n}{c \vdash \Theta}$$

where the contexts are type declarations and the conclusions (Θ, Θ_i) *are type-inference judgments, i.e., of the form*

$$T \ type$$
$$\phi \ prop$$
$$t : T$$

We write

$$c \vdash_{\textbf{TI}} \Theta$$

if the sequent follows in **TI**.

A quick glance shows that only the rules O_1, O_2, R, F, E_1, E_3, A_1, W_1, W_2, Sub, L_1, L_5, L_9, L_{12}, L_{15}, L_{18}, and L_{21} furnish possible instances of such type-inference rules.

We first establish that this system is independent of the main one; i.e., it is a genuine subsystem.

Proposition 5 *(Independence) If* $\Gamma \vdash_{\textbf{TPL}} \Theta$, *where* Θ *is a type-inference judgment, then* $c_\Gamma \vdash_{\textbf{TI}} \Theta$.

Proof By induction on the rules with type-inference conclusions. Observation of these demonstrates that they only require declaration contexts and type-inference premises. For example, consider the structural rule

$$\frac{\Gamma \vdash T \ type}{\Gamma, x : T \vdash x : T}$$

By induction, $c_\Gamma \vdash T \ type$. By the rule itself, $c_\Gamma, x : T \vdash T \ type$. Similarly, for the following rule, i.e., if only type-inference is used in the premises, it is only used in the conclusion.

$$\frac{\Gamma, \Delta \vdash \Theta \quad \Gamma \vdash T \ type}{\Gamma, x : T, \Delta \vdash \Theta}$$

This style of argument succeeds for all cases.∎

The following provides the basis for a type-checking algorithm.

Proposition 6 *(Type Checking) In TI we have:*

1. $c \vdash R(t_1, ..., t_n) \ prop$ iff $c \vdash t_1 : T_1$ and...and $c \vdash t_n : T_n$,
2. $c \vdash O(T_1, ..., T_n) \ type$ iff $c \vdash T_1 \ type$ and...and $c \vdash T_n \ type$,
3. $c \vdash F(t_1, ..., t_n) : O(T_1, ..., T_n)$ iff $c \vdash t_1 : T_1$ and...and $c \vdash t_n : T_n$,
4. $c \vdash \phi \circ \psi \ prop$ iff $c \vdash \phi \ prop$ and $c \vdash \psi \ prop$, where $\circ = \vee, \wedge, \rightarrow$,
5. $c \vdash \neg\phi \ prop$ iff $c \vdash \phi \ prop$,
6. $c \vdash Qx : T.\phi \ prop$ iff $c, x : T \vdash \phi \ prop$ where $Q = \exists$ or $\forall$
7. $c \vdash t =_T s \ prop$ iff $c \vdash t : T$ and $c \vdash s : T$

Proof The directions from right to left follow immediately from the rules. For the other direction, we use induction on the structure of derivations. Consider part 1. If the conclusion follows from the formation rule

$$\mathbf{R} \quad \frac{c \vdash t_1 : T_1, ..., c \vdash t_n : T_n}{c \vdash R(t_1, ..., t_n)\ prop}$$

the result is immediate. If the conclusion is the result of a structural rule, the result follows from using the structural rule itself. Consider part 4. If the conclusion follows from the introduction rules for the connective, the result is immediate. If the conclusion is the result of a structural rule, the result follows from using the structural rule itself. For example, suppose the last step in the derivation is the following instance of an application of W_1.

$$\frac{c \vdash T\ type \quad c \vdash \phi \wedge \psi\ prop}{c, x : T \vdash \phi \wedge \psi\ prop}$$

Consider the premises. By induction, we may suppose that $c \vdash \phi\ prop$ and $c \vdash \psi\ prop$. By induction, $c, x : T \vdash \phi\ prop$ and $c, x : T \vdash \psi\ prop$.

The other rules follow exactly the same pattern of argument.∎

Using the left-to-right directions, we obtain an obvious recursive algorithm for type checking. The next result is significant for the coherence of the logic. It guarantees that what is provable is grammatical.

Theorem 7 *(Coherence)*

1. If $\Gamma \vdash \phi$, then $\Gamma \vdash \phi\ prop$,
2. If $\Gamma \vdash t : T$, then $\Gamma \vdash T\ type$,
3. If $\Gamma, x : T, \Gamma' \vdash \Theta$, then $\Gamma \vdash T\ type$,
4. If $\Gamma, \phi, \Gamma' \vdash \Theta$, then $\Gamma \vdash \phi\ prop$

Proof By induction on the structure of derivations. Most of the cases are routine. We illustrate part 1 with the cases of disjunction elimination, universal introduction, and existential quantification introduction. Consider

$$\frac{\Gamma \vdash \phi \vee \theta \quad \Gamma, \phi \vdash \eta \quad \Gamma, \theta \vdash \eta}{\Gamma \vdash \eta}$$

By induction, and using type checking, we obtain

$$c_\Gamma \vdash \eta\ prop$$

Next, consider the existential introduction rule

$$\frac{\Gamma \vdash \phi[t/x] \quad \Gamma \vdash t : T \quad \Gamma, x : T \vdash \phi\ prop}{\Gamma \vdash \exists x : T \cdot \phi}$$

By induction, $c_\Gamma, x : T \vdash \phi$ *prop*. By the formation rule for the existential quantifier, we are finished. Finally, consider the existential elimination rule in the following case.

$$\frac{\Gamma \vdash \exists x : T \cdot \phi \qquad \Gamma, x : T, \phi \vdash \eta}{\Gamma \vdash \eta}$$

By the premises $\Gamma, x : T, \phi \vdash \eta$. By induction and type checking, and the fact that x is not free in η, $c_\Gamma \vdash \eta$ *prop*. For part 2, we illustrate with rule **F**; i.e., suppose that the last step is

$$\frac{\Gamma \vdash t_1 : T_1 \qquad \Gamma \vdash t_n : T_n}{\Gamma \vdash F(t_1, ..., t_n) : O(T_1, ..., T_n)}$$

By induction and the assumptions, T_1 *type*, T_2 *type*,...,T_n *type*. Hence by the rule **O**, $O(T_1, ..., T_n)$ *type*. For part 3, the substantial case is

$$\mathbf{W}_1 \quad \frac{\Gamma, \Gamma' \vdash \Theta \qquad \Gamma \vdash T \; type}{\Gamma, x : T, \Gamma' \vdash \Theta}$$

It follows immediately that $\Gamma \vdash T \; type$. The same argument works for part 4 and

$$\mathbf{W}_2 \quad \frac{\Gamma, \Gamma' \vdash \delta \qquad \Gamma \vdash \phi \; prop}{\Gamma, \phi, \Gamma' \vdash \delta}$$

The rest of the rules can be established using similar observations.■

TPL is a generalization of a standard many-sorted logic in two ways. First, the types may be inductively generated, and so it generalizes the simple fixed structure of standard many-sorted logic. Second, and more importantly, the variables of the theory range freely over the types. This has the knock-on effect that the grammatical legitimacy of the various syntactic constructs not only depends upon the types, but also depends dynamically on them; i.e., the expressions are only well formed relative to an assignment of types to the variables. This is a *Curry* (after Haskell Curry) approach to typing [1]. And for the natural and elegant development of our quite rich range of theories, we need all this flexibility. So the slightly complex nature of our logical framework will eventually reap its rewards.

References

1. Barendregt, H.P. Lambda Calculus With Types. In: S. Abramsky, D.M. Gabbay, and T.S.E. Maibaum, (Eds), Handbook of Logic in Computer Science. Oxford Science Publications. Abramsky, S., Gabbay, D.M. and Maibaum, T.S.E., pp. 118–310, Oxford University Press, Oxford, 1992.
2. Beeson, M.J. Foundations of Constructive Mathematics, Springer-Verlag Berlin, 1985.

3. Martin-Lof, P. An intuitionistic theory of sets, predicative part. In Logic Colloquim, 73. North-Holland, Amsterdam, 1975.
4. Pierce, B.C. Types and Programming Languages. MIT Press, Cambridge, MA, 2002.
5. Thompson, S. Type Theory and Functional Programming. Addison-Wesley, Reading, MA, 1991.
6. Turner, R. Type inference for set theory. Theor. Comput. Sci. 266(1–2): 951–974, 2001.

Chapter 3
Data Types

In this chapter we shall study the general structure of theories of data types (**TDT**) and provide some elementary examples. While the whole book will be taken up with the introduction and study of such theories and their application to specification and the construction of computable models, before we begin we need to clear the way a little.

In first-order logic a *theory* is any consistent set of sentences of the underlying language [8, 3]. Much the same is true of simple type theory and higher-order logic [1]. But with **TPL**, matters are a little more complicated due to the way that the formation rules for types and propositions are intermingled with the logic itself. Types and propositions are generated from some basic types, and most often one or more type constructors, together with their associated function and relation symbols. In particular, the various formation rules provide part of the grammatical backlog to proposition formation. It is their types and type constructors that determine interesting **TDT**. This is similar to the situation in the Curry approach to types [2] and constructive type theory [5].

But in order to more precisely introduce matters, we need some building blocks, i.e., some actual type constructors. Here we shall not provide any analysis; our objective is to introduce some constructors in order to provide some concrete examples and illustrate the general structure of **TDT**. For type inspiration, we shall call upon some simple standard resources [7, 4, 6]. Some of the types will be used later and some will not. Nor should the axiomatizations provided be taken as definitive. They are here for illustrative purposes.

3.1 Booleans

The type of *Booleans* is found in the majority of programming languages and it is simple. Hence, it is an appropriate type with which to start. The following rules provide a standard, axiomatic account.

R. Turner, *Computable Models*, DOI 10.1007/978-1-84882-052-4_3,
© Springer-Verlag London Limited 2009

Definition 8 (Booleans)

$$\mathbf{B_0} \quad Bool\ type \qquad \mathbf{B_1}\ true : Bool \qquad \mathbf{B_2}\ false : Bool$$

$$\mathbf{B_3} \quad \frac{b : Bool \qquad\qquad t : Bool \qquad\qquad s : Bool}{cond(b, t, s) : Bool}$$

$$\mathbf{B_4} \quad \frac{t : Bool \qquad\qquad s : Bool}{cond(true, t, s) =_{Bool} t} \qquad\qquad \mathbf{B_5} \quad \frac{t : Bool \qquad\qquad s : Bool}{cond(false, t, s) =_{Bool} s}$$

The first rule informs us that *Bool* is a type of the theory. The other rules are the standard ones for Booleans. The first two are the introduction rules: They tell us that *true* and *false* are members of the type. $\mathbf{B_3}$ introduces the conditional expression. The last two provide the normal equality rules that govern the conditional. In the above, we have left all contexts implicit; in the future, this will be the norm. Where the context disambiguates matters, we shall frequently drop the subscripts.

In isolation there is not much more one can do with this type. But once ensconced as a type of **TPL**, we can define other operators as new functional operators of our logic.

Example 9 (Logical Connectives) Given

$$a, b : Bool$$

we can define the standard Boolean connectives.

$$and(a, b) \triangleq cond(a, b, false)$$
$$or(a, b) \triangleq cond(a, true, b)$$
$$neg(a) \triangleq cond(a, false, true)$$

These are new defined operators. This heralds the way that new relations and operations are introduced via specification. But more of this later. Alternatively, these could be taken as primitive with the obvious derived rules. For example, conjunction would be governed by the following axioms and rule.

$$\frac{t : Bool \qquad\qquad s : Bool}{and(t, s) : Bool}$$

$$and(true, true) = true$$
$$and(true, false) = false$$
$$and(false, true) = false$$
$$and(false, false) = false$$

Of course, such rules add nothing to the mathematical content of the theory in that, as the above definitions demonstrate, such additions yield definitional extensions. This will be a feature of our basic notion of specification.

Actually, when other types are present in a **TDT**, then we can generalize matters to allow for a conditional operating over arbitrary types of the theory. In the following, T is any type of the underlying theory.

$$\mathbf{B_3} \quad \frac{b : Bool \qquad t : T \qquad s : T}{cond(b, t, s) : T}$$

$$\mathbf{B_4} \quad \frac{t : T \qquad s : T}{cond(true, t, s) = t} \qquad \mathbf{B_5} \quad \frac{t : T \qquad s : T}{cond(false, t, s) = s}$$

It is in this form that *Bool* will find its main application. We shall also frequently adopt the convention of writing $cond(a, b, c)$ as $a \rightarrow b, c$.

3.2 Products

In some form or other, Cartesian products occur in most programming and specification languages. Usually some generalization that supports tuples rather than simple pairs is included. Equally often, these tuples are labeled or decorated, leading to the notion of a *labeled product*. In this section we explore various incarnations of products in order to put more flesh on our notion of a type constructor. We shall get to the variations shortly, but first we deal with the standard one.

Definition 10 (Cartesian Products)

$$\mathbf{P_0} \quad \frac{A\ type \qquad B\ type}{A \otimes B\ type} \qquad \mathbf{P_1} \quad \frac{a : A \qquad b : B}{(a, b) : A \otimes B}$$

$$\mathbf{P_2} \quad \frac{a : A \otimes B}{\pi_1(a) : A} \qquad \mathbf{P_3} \quad \frac{a : A \otimes B}{\pi_2(a) : B}$$

$$\mathbf{P_4} \quad \frac{(a, b) : A \otimes B}{\pi_1(a, b) = a \wedge \pi_2(a, b) = b} \qquad \mathbf{P_5} \quad \frac{a : A \otimes B}{a = (\pi_1(a), \pi_2(a))}$$

The first rule is the type formation rule. The next three rules are the rules for pairing (written in the standard infix notation) and selection. $\mathbf{P_1}$ is the introduction rule and introduces pairs. The next two ($\mathbf{P_2}$, $\mathbf{P_3}$) are the rules for selection (i.e., the elimination rules for the type). There are no special relation symbols. The special equality axioms ($\mathbf{P_4}$, $\mathbf{P_5}$) demand that the selection functions behave appropriately on pairs and support surjective pairing. We shall often write $\pi_1(x)$ as x_1, etc.

Within any theory containing products, we define

$$T_1 \otimes T_2 \otimes T_3 \triangleq T_1 \otimes (T_2 \otimes T_3)$$
$$T_1 \otimes T_2 \otimes T_3 \otimes T_4 \triangleq T_1 \otimes (T_2 \otimes T_3 \otimes T_4)$$
$$= T_1 \otimes (T_2 \otimes (T_3 \otimes T_4))$$
$$\ldots$$

We shall use this convention (i.e., where the tail forms the current Cartesian product) throughout. With it, triple formation and selection can be specified as follows. Given

$$a : T_1, b : T_2, c : T_3$$

we define triples as follows.

$$(a, b, c) \triangleq (a, (b, c))$$

And for

$$a : T_1 \otimes T_2 \otimes T_3$$

we define

$$\pi_1^3(a) \triangleq \pi_1(a)$$
$$\pi_2^3(a) \triangleq \pi_1(\pi_2(a))$$
$$\pi_3^3(a) \triangleq \pi_2(\pi_2(a))$$

We shall later see these as specifications. And we shall be able to be a little more exact in the form that such specifications take.

This constructor can be modified/generalized in several ways. The first is a modification that employs labels rather than position to select elements. The type is defined by the following rules. Ordinary products can be viewed as a special case where the labels are the numerals 1 and 2.

Definition 11 (Labeled Products)

$$\mathbf{LP_0} \quad \frac{A \ type \quad B \ type}{[l : A, k : B] \ type} \qquad\qquad \mathbf{LP_1} \quad \frac{a : A \qquad b : B}{\langle l : a, k : b \rangle : [l : A, k : B]}$$

$$\mathbf{LP_2} \quad \frac{a : [l : A, k : B]}{\pi_l(a) : A} \qquad\qquad \mathbf{LP_3} \quad \frac{a : [l : A, k : B]}{\pi_k(a) : B}$$

$$\mathbf{LP_4} \quad \frac{\langle l : a, k : b \rangle : [l : A, k : B]}{\pi_l \langle l : a, k : b \rangle = a \wedge \pi_k \langle l : a, k : b \rangle = b}$$

$$\mathbf{LP_5} \quad \frac{a : [l : A, k : B]}{a = \langle l : \pi_l(a), k : \pi_k(a) \rangle}$$

Here l, k are labels or attributes that enable selection. $\langle l : a, k : b \rangle$ is a labelled tuple and $[l : A, k : B]$ the corresponding labelled product. This is the form that products take in relational databases. Also, when the Z notion of a schema is taken to be a set of bindings [9], it seems to be underpinned by this representation of products.

A third notion, and one that illustrates the idea of a dependent type formation, occurs when types can contain variables, and so the grammatical legitimacy of one type may depend upon the type of a contained variable. This leads to the following rules for generalized or dependent products.

Definition 12 (Dependent Products)

$$DP_0 \quad \frac{\Gamma, x : A \vdash B[x]\,type}{\Gamma \vdash \Sigma x : A \cdot B\,type} \qquad DP_1 \quad \frac{a : A \qquad b : B[a/x]}{(a, b) : \Sigma x : A \cdot B}$$

$$DP_2 \quad \frac{a : \Sigma x : A \cdot B}{\pi_1(a) : A} \qquad DP_3 \quad \frac{a : \Sigma x : A \cdot B}{\pi_2(a) : B[x]}$$

$$DP_4 \quad \frac{(a, b) : \Sigma x : A \cdot B}{\pi_1(a, b) = a \wedge \pi_2(a, b) = b} \qquad DP_5 \quad \frac{a : \Sigma x : A \cdot B}{a = (\pi_1(a), \pi_2(a))}$$

Again, simple products are a special case, i.e., where the variable x is not free in B. In these rules, the sequent

$$\Gamma, x : A \vdash B[x]\,type$$

indicates that the legitimacy of any instance of type B depends upon the indexing element in type A. Two cases that will support this kind of generalization involve the introduction of subtypes, generated by propositions, and a type of types. These we shall study in separate chapters.

3.3 Stacks

Our next type constructor is also to be found in some form in many procedural languages. Even where it is not present, for implementation purposes, it is often implemented; i.e., it is often represented in terms of the other types of the language. Although we shall not use this constructor in any application, it yields a worthy illustrative example. In one incarnation, it is governed by the following rules.

Definition 13 (Stacks)

$$St_0 \quad \frac{T\,type}{Stack(T)\,type} \qquad St_1 \quad emptystack : Stack(T)$$

$$St_2 \quad \frac{a : Stack(T)}{empty_T(a) : Bool} \qquad St_3 \quad \frac{a : T \qquad b : Stack(T)}{push_T(a, b) : Stack(T)}$$

$$St_4 \quad \frac{b : Stack(T)}{top_T(b) : T} \qquad St_5 \quad \frac{b : Stack(T)}{pop_T(b) : Stack(T)}$$

$$St_6 \quad \frac{a : T \qquad b : Stack(T)}{pop_T(push_T(a, b)) = b} \qquad St_7 \quad \frac{a : T \qquad b : Stack(T)}{top_T(push_T(a, b)) = a}$$

$$St_8 \quad \frac{a : T \qquad b : Stack(T)}{empty_T((push_T(a, b)) = false}$$

$$St_9 \quad empty_T(emptystack) = true$$

The first rule tells us that we can form the type of stacks of elements for any given type. The second allows for an empty stack. St_2 introduces a predicate that allows one to check whether the stack is empty. St_3 allows us to push an object onto a stack, St_4 to select the top element, and St_5 enables us to pop the top element. The next two relate pushing and popping: They inform us that *push*, *pop*, and *top* behave as we expect them to. The last two tell us that the empty stack is empty (St_9) and that any stack with a push is not (St_8).

3.4 Terms

We next examine a type whose elements are the expressions of a formal language where, following logical terminology, we shall call such expressions *terms*. Typically, they are constructed over a given alphabet, but we generalize matters to allow for an arbitrary underlying type.

Let T be any type with operators f_1, f_2, ..., f_m, where f_i has arity a_i (i.e., f_i takes a_i arguments from T) and where zero place operators are taken to be constants. We construct the type $Term(T, f_1, f_2, ..., f_m)$ of *terms on T* as follows. We shall abbreviate the type to $Term(T)$.

Definition 14 (Terms)

$$Term_0 \quad \frac{T\ type}{Term(T)\ type}$$

$$Term_1 \quad \frac{t_1 : T, ..., t_{a_i} : T}{f_i(t_1, ..., t_{a_i}) : Term(T)}$$

These rules spell out the form and nature of terms. The first is the type-formation rule and the second allows terms to be constructed via operators. We shall see many examples of this kind of type. The first example is given in the following.

3.5 Numbers

There is not one data type of numbers; there are many [3]. In this section we review some of them and informally point out how they differ and how they are related. We begin with a very rudimentary notion.

Definition 15 (Baby Numbers)

$$N_0 \quad Num\ type$$

$$N_1 \quad 0 : Num \qquad\qquad N_2 \quad \frac{a : Num}{a^+ : Num}$$

Here a^+ functions as the successor of a. $\mathbf{N_0}$ guarantees that Num is a type, while $\mathbf{N_1}$ and $\mathbf{N_2}$ insist that 0 is a number and the type of numbers is closed under successor. These are essentially the type-inference rules for numbers. Most type-checking systems for programming languages will contain a shadow of such rules.

But they are not enough for the purposes of specification and for the construction of computable models. We also require rules that determine the nature of successor; i.e.,

$$\mathbf{N_3} \quad \frac{a : Num}{a^+ \neq 0} \qquad\qquad \mathbf{N_4} \quad \frac{a^+ = b^+}{a = b}$$

i.e., zero is never a successor and the successor operation is injective. Any useful account of formal arithmetic will include constants and operations that satisfy these rules. Indeed, we cannot do much without some version of addition, determined by the following rules.

$$\mathbf{Add_1} \quad \frac{a : Num \qquad b : Num}{a + b : Num}$$

$$\mathbf{Add_2} \quad \frac{a : Num}{a + 0 = a}$$

$$\mathbf{Add_3} \quad \frac{a : Num \qquad b : Num}{a + b^+ = (a + b)^+}$$

Of course, any actual implementation on a physical machine will only implement a fraction of addition. But we are concerned with Turing complete languages and theories. We need such rules to reason about specifications that are by their very nature machine-independent. Indeed, the above equations guide any actual implementation and provide the criteria for correctness.

But even this is not enough to do arithmetic in the sense needed for specification and computable modeling. We need to reason about numbers and specifications written over numbers and establish their properties. And for this we need some form of numerical induction; i.e.,

$$\mathbf{N_{ind}} \quad \frac{\phi[0] \qquad \forall x : N \cdot \phi[x] \rightarrow \phi[x^+]}{\forall x : N \cdot \phi[x]}$$

Notice that the exact content of $\mathbf{N_{ind}}$ is only fixed when the language of the embedding theory is fixed; i.e., the induction rule depends upon the class of propositions that can function as the induction proposition ϕ. This may be the whole class or some subclass. And there are many possible type theories depending upon the class chosen and the embedding theory. We shall formulate more exact theories when we study the numbers in more detail in a later chapter.

3.6 Lists

The rules for lists form a component of the type theories of many programming languages and some specification languages. Let T be any type. One version of the lists on a type T parallels the rudimentary version of the numbers.

Definition 16 (Baby Lists)

$$\mathbf{L_0} \quad \frac{T \; type}{List(T) \; type}$$

$$\mathbf{L_1} \quad \frac{T \; type}{[]_T : List(T)} \qquad \mathbf{L_2} \quad \frac{a : T \quad b : List(T)}{a \star_T b : List(T)}$$

These are the type rules. The first rule is the formation rule. $\mathbf{L_1}$ introduces the empty list and $\mathbf{L_2}$ the *append* operation ($*$) that adds an element of the underlying type to a list of that type.

But any mathematically useful account of lists will also include operations for manipulating lists, together with rules for their associated properties.

$$\mathbf{L_3} \quad \frac{a : T \quad b : List(T)}{a \star_T b \neq []_T}$$

$$\mathbf{L_4} \quad \frac{b : List(T) \quad b \neq []_T}{head(b) : T} \qquad \mathbf{L_5} \quad \frac{b : List(T)}{tail(b) : List(T)}$$

$$\mathbf{L_6} \quad \frac{a : T \quad b : List(T)}{head(a \star_T b) = a} \qquad \mathbf{L_7} \quad \frac{a : T \quad b : List(T)}{tail(a \star_T b) = b}$$

$\mathbf{L_3}$ informs us that no complex list can be equal to the empty list, and $\mathbf{L_4}$ and $\mathbf{L_5}$ introduce operations that select the *head* and *tail* of a list, where $\mathbf{L_6}$ and $\mathbf{L_7}$ guarantee their content. There are many other options here. For example, we could introduce a Boolean function for equality rather than using the underlying equality of the type. This was the option we selected with stacks.

These rules are also pretty rudimentary. But they do describe one standard notion of a list constructor. But as with the numbers, we have no guarantee that only lists are so obtained. In particular, we have no induction principle, and so we cannot reason about them inductively. For this, we need the standard principle of list induction.

$$\mathbf{L_8} \quad \frac{\phi[[]_T] \quad \forall x : T \cdot \forall y : List(T) \cdot \phi[y] \rightarrow \phi[x \star_T y]}{\forall x : List(T) \cdot \phi[x]}$$

The induction principle is given relative to the language of the embedding **TDT.** More explicitly, as with numbers, it is envisaged that any such theory of lists will only form one component of a **TDT**, and so the class of ϕ's that may occur in the induction scheme will vary from theory to theory. Finally, we introduce a type whose members are binary trees.

Example 17 (Baby Binary Trees)

$$\textbf{Bt}_1 \quad \frac{A \; type}{Tree(A) \; type} \qquad \textbf{Bt}_2 \quad \frac{a : A}{Node(a) : Tree(A)}$$

$$\textbf{Bt}_3 \quad \frac{a : A \qquad b : Tree(A) \qquad c : Tree(A)}{Branch(a, b, c) : Tree(A)}$$

These are subject to exactly the same kinds of extensions and analysis. And the baby versions of numbers, lists, and trees all form examples of terms.

3.7 A Type of Types

Programming languages provide one source for data types. Indeed, any programing language gives rise to many **TDT**. But there are other sources: Our final type constructor emanates from logic and type theory and is a little more adventurous. It is a type whose elements are themselves types. It is governed by the following rules.

$$\textbf{type} \; type \qquad \qquad \frac{T \; type}{T : \textbf{type}}$$

These rules insist that every type is a type and that the type **type** is itself a type. This will later play a crucial role in our treatment of polymorphism. This is different to the previous examples in that we are now treating types (that characterize objects) as objects. Of course, if one has a too permissive underlying notion of type, adding such a type can cause problems. We shall get to this later. At this point, suffice it to say that all our types will be interpretable as recursively enumerable sets.

We allude to this type here, only to provide the reader with an early indication of the range of type constructors that we shall consider. We are not constrained by the existing ones of programming languages. It is the notion of recursive interpretation that determines matters.

Obviously, we could go on adding new types and type constructors. And many more will emerge as we proceed through the book. But we have done enough to illustrate our notion of **TDT**.

3.8 Theories of Data Types

A **TDT** will be made up from some basic types and type constructors, their associated function and relation symbols, and their governing rules. We shall display these theories by indicating their type, relation, and function symbols, viz.

$$\mathbf{Th}(O_1, ..., O_k, R_1, ..., R_n, F_1, ..., F_m)$$

Indeed, where matters are clear, we shall often suppress the relation and function symbols and only display the basic types/type constructors to identify a theory; i.e.,

$$\mathbf{Th}(O_1, ..., O_k)$$

With the above type constructors at hand, we can now introduce our first explicit theory of data types.

Example 18 The **TDT**

$$\mathbf{Th}(\mathbf{Bool, CP, List})$$

has **Bool** as its only basic type and Cartesian products and Lists as the type constructors, where we include all the rules for lists given above.

Observe that with the type of Booleans present, we might add a Boolean operator for equality:

$$\frac{a : A \qquad b : A}{Eq_A(a, b) : Bool} \qquad \qquad \textbf{(Eq)}$$

with rules such as the following:

$$\frac{a : A \qquad b : A}{Eq_A(a, b) = true \leftrightarrow a =_A b}$$

Indeed, as we shall see shortly, this may be specified.

If we add *type*, the above theory supports a version of polymorphic lists. In this case, types may contain variables, and so we can generalize the Cartesian products to allow dependent ones.

$$\mathbf{Th}(\mathbf{Bool, type, DP, List})$$

We shall explain all this in more detail in the chapter on the type **type**. Here we are only outlining some possibilities.

Definition 19 *The* **TDT** *theory*

$$\mathbf{Th}(\mathbf{N, CP, Stack})$$

has **N** *as its only basic type and Cartesian products and Stacks as the type constructors.*

Once again, we get a more traditional axiomatization [7] if we assume that the type of Booleans is present and we employ a Boolean operator for equality.

Of course, there are many permutations of the type constructors we have already introduced. But the general idea of the structure of a **TDT** ought now to be clear. We can now better grasp the following idea.

Definition 20 *For a* **TDT***,* **T***, we shall write*

$$\Gamma \vdash_\mathbf{T} \Theta$$

to indicate that the judgment Θ *is derivable in the theory* **T** *from the assumptions* Γ, *i.e., derivable from the rules of* **TPL** *plus the axioms and rules of* **T**.

In practice, we would need to extend the properties of **TPL** to each such theory; i.e., we would need to show how the independence, type checking, and coherence results extend. In particular, for the theory

$$\mathbf{T = Th(Bool, CP, List)}$$

we have the following extension to the second.

Proposition 21 (Type Checking) *For the above theory, we have*

1. *if* $\Gamma \vdash \Theta$, *where* Θ *is a type-inference judgment, then* $c_\Gamma \vdash_\mathbf{T} \Theta$,
2. *if* $c \vdash_\mathbf{T} O(T_1, ..., T_n)$ *type iff* $c \vdash_\mathbf{T} T_1$ *type and...and* $c \vdash_\mathbf{T} T_n$ *type, where* O *is any of the type constructors of the theory.*

Proposition 22 (Coherence) *The coherence theorem holds for the theory* **Th(Bool, CP, List)**

We shall leave the details to the reader. There are no new issues in the proofs. Indeed, in many cases this will be our general approach: We shall prove a theorem once and, where straightforward, we shall leave the details to the reader.

This completes our basic introduction to theories of data types. Much of the book will be taken up with their construction and investigation. Of course, we shall investigate the more substantial and central ones in some detail.

References

1. An Introduction to Mathematical logic and Type Theory. Academic Press, New York, 1986.
2. Lambda calculus with types. In S. Abramsky, D.M. Gabbay, and T.S.E. Maibaum, (Eds), Handbook of Logic in Computer Science. Oxford Science Publications. Abramsky, S., Gabbay, D.M. and Maibaum, T.S.E., pp. 118–310, Oxford University Press, Oxford, 1992.
3. Bell, J.L., and Machover, M. A Course in Mathematical Logic. North Holland, Amsterdam, 1977. 4th printing, 2003.
4. Dale, N., and Dale, H.M.W., Abstract Data Types: Specifications, Implementations, and Applications. Jones and Bartlett Publishers, Boston, 1996.
5. Martin-Lof, P. An intuitionistic theory of sets, predicative part. In Logic Colloquim, 73. North-Holland, Amsterdam, 1975.
6. Pierce, B.C. Types and Programming Languages. MIT Press, Cambridge, MA, 2002.

7. Thomas, P., Robinson, H. and Emms, J. Abstract Data Types: Their Specification, Representation. Oxford University Press, Oxford, 1988.
8. Van Dalen, D. Logic and Structure. Springer-Verlag, New York, 1983.
9. Woodcock, J. and Davies, J. Using Z- Specifications, Refinement and Proof, Prentice Hall, Englewood Cliffs, NJ, 1996.

Chapter 4
Definability

Our objective is to develop, within the confines of **TPL**, a notion of *computability* or *definability* that applies to any **TDT**. We aim to provide a notion that will service our discussion of specification and, in particular, the role played by computability.

For the type of natural numbers, we are well stocked with equivalent notions of computability [4, 17]. In the standard one based upon Turing machines, what is taken to be a computable relation or function is determined by a computation on a Turing machine. Extensionally equivalent notions employ other machine-like notions or are based upon programming language–oriented formalisms such as the lambda calculus [2]. We might try and apply these ideas to the current typed setting. Indeed, much energy has been invested in developing theories of computation on structures other than the natural numbers (e.g., [5]). In particular, efforts have been made to obtain analogues of the Church-Turing Thesis for various algebraic structures. And although many of these generalizations [11, 12, 13, 14, 15] have resulted in elegant theories, unfortunately, none seems quite suitable for our purposes.

Fortunately, there are ways of characterizing a notion of computability that, for the present purposes, are more appropriate and attractive. These are the logical approaches based upon the concept of *definability* cast within the axiomatic setting of formal arithmetic [7, 9]. In this setting, a certain subclass of wff of formal arithmetic, the so-called Σ definable wff (no negations, implications, or universal quantifiers), characterizes the recursively enumerable relations in that every recursively enumerable relation is Σ definable, and vice versa. Admissible set theory [3] also supplies us with a precise notion of definability for relations and functions acting on hereditarily finite sets. Again, the Σ *definable* wff characterize the appropriate notion.

A generalization of this idea to arbitrary structures was originally suggested by Montague [8], and more recently taken up by Hodges. This material and the approach of [6] will guide us in formulating explicit notions of definability/computability for our theories. Specifically, we shall generalize these notions of Σ *definability* to **TDT**. We shall then explore the notion of specification that is circumscribed by Σ *definability*.

R. Turner, *Computable Models*, DOI 10.1007/978-1-84882-052-4_4,
© Springer-Verlag London Limited 2009

4.1 Semidecidable Relations

The class of Σ propositions of a theory of types is restricted to propositions that may be constructed from the basic relations and functions of the theory via the logical connectives Ω, $\vee$, $\wedge$, and $\exists$. We take them to be central because any program with designated input and output types I and O implicitly describes an extensional relation between those types. Moreover, these relations can be expressed by the above logical connectives. More explicitly, let L be any programming language. Then the graph of any L-program determines an extensional relation as follows.

> For any x of type I and y of type O, $R_p(x, y)$ will be true precisely when p with input x terminates with value y.

In other words, the relation is constituted by all the input/output pairs.[1] In particular, in a Turing complete language, with the natural numbers as the only data type, such relations characterize the recursively enumerable sets of numbers (RE); i.e., the recursively enumerable relations are precisely those characterized by the numerical programs in a Turing complete language. Moreover, it is well known that this relation can be characterized via the Σ propositions. This leads to the following generalized notion that applies to any theory of data types.

Definition 23 *Let*

$$\mathbf{T} = \mathbf{Th}(O_1, ..., O_k, R_1, ..., R_n, F_1, ..., F_m)$$

be any theory of data types. Suppose that

$$c \vdash_{\mathbf{T}} \phi \; prop$$

where ϕ is a proposition that is built from the basic function and relation symbols $R_1, ..., R_n, F_1, ..., F_m$ but whose only connectives are Ω, $\vee$, $\wedge$, $\exists$. Then, relative to **T***, we shall say that ϕ is Σ.*

In intuitive terms, via their free variables, such propositions determine what we take to be *semidecidable* relations. Note that we allow all the basic relations/functions of the theory to occur in Σ propositions. In addition, the latter include absurdity and basic equality assertions and are closed under conjunction, disjunction, and existential quantification.

Example 24 In the **TDT**

$$\mathbf{Th}(\mathbf{Bool}, \mathbf{CP}, \mathbf{List})$$

---

[1] In general, this is a relation and not a function since for any given input there might be many possible outputs.

the Σ propositions include all the basic constants and function symbols and all the basic relations of **Bool**, **CP**, and **List**.

The inclusion of any such relations and functions must always be justified by providing a recursive model in arithmetic in which the interpretation of the relations and functions is Σ in arithmetic.

This account of Σ definability for arbitrary **TDT** will form our main account of computability for our theories. It will inform our main notion of relational specification and guide us in our construction of computable models.

4.2 Decidable Relations

If we take Σ propositions to characterize the semi decidable relations of a **TDT**, then the decidable ones are characterized as those Σ propositions whose negations are also Σ. Again, this is a standard approach to decidability in a logical setting and leads to the following notions.

Definition 25 *In a theory* **T**, *a* Σ *proposition given by*

$$x_1 : T_1, ..., x_n : T_n \vdash \phi[x_1, ..., x_n] \; prop$$

*is **decidable** if there exists a* Σ *proposition* $\overline{\phi}$ *(its internal negation) that satisfies the following.*

$$x_1 : T_1, ..., x_n : T_n \vdash \overline{\phi}[x_1, ..., x_n] \; prop$$
$$x_1 : T_1, ..., x_n : T_n \vdash \overline{\phi}[x_1, ..., x_n] \leftrightarrow \neg\phi[x_1, ..., x_n]$$

Thus, a proposition is taken to be decidable if it and its (internal) negation are semidecidable. This is a straightforward generalization of the numerical notion.

The concept of decidability is preserved by $\wedge$ and $\vee$. To see this, we have only to note that we may define

$$\overline{\phi \wedge \psi} \triangleq \overline{\phi} \vee \overline{\psi} \qquad \overline{\phi \vee \psi} \triangleq \overline{\phi} \wedge \overline{\psi}$$

i.e., the witnessing (internal negations) Σ propositions may be stipulated as above.

Of course, in any given theory, the class of decidable propositions is partly determined by the class of basic relations that we take to be decidable. For example, as things stand, we have not guaranteed that the equality relations of **Th(Bool, CP)** are decidable. Intuitively, they should be. But formally, we have to make them so by stipulation. In particular, where the relation of equality is taken to be decidable, we add an *internal negation* of equality, an inequality relation, written $\neq$, that is taken to be Σ and that satisfies the following.

Definition 26 (Decidable Equality) *Let* **T** *be any* **TDT**. *Equality is **decidable** in* **T** *if there exists a relation* $\neq_T$ *in* **T** *(the **internal negation** of* $=_T$*) such that*

$$x : T, y : T \vdash x \neq_T y \ prop$$
$$\forall x : T \cdot \forall y : T \cdot \neg(x =_T y) \leftrightarrow x \neq_T y$$

A simple example is afforded by Booleans.

Example 27 (Boolean Inequality) In the case of **Bool,** if we add the assumption

$$\forall x : T \cdot \forall y : T \cdot x = true \lor x = false$$

then we can define

$$x \neq_T y \triangleq cond(x, cond(y, false, true), y)$$

Of course, in general, one could just use $\neg(x =_T y)$ itself and assert that this case of negation is Σ. But conceptually, the above approach seems clearer. We can generalize matters to arbitrary relations.

Definition 28 (Decidable Relations) *Let* **T** *be any* **TDT.** *In* **T** *assume*

$$x_1 : T_1, \ \ldots\ldots\ , x_n : T_n \vdash R(x_1, .., x_n) \ prop$$

*Then R is **decidable** in* **T** *if there exists a relation* $\overline{R}$ *in* **T** *(the **internal negation** of R) such that*

$$x_1 : T_1, ..., x_n : T_n \vdash \overline{R}(x_1, ..., x_n) \ prop$$
$$\forall x_1 : T_1 \cdot ... \cdot \forall x_n : T_n \cdot \overline{R}(x_1, ..., x_n) \leftrightarrow \neg R(x_1, ..., x_n)$$

We shall often write

$$Dec(R)$$

to name the above pair of axioms.

More generally, if R is decidable as a proposition, as we shall see, we may conservatively add a new relation that can function as an internal negation. We shall return to this in the next chapter.

A very special class of decidable propositions is determined by the propositional connectives alone. Following tradition, we shall call these propositions Δ_0. Formally,

Definition 29 (Δ_0 Propositions) *Let* **T** *be any theory of data types. Suppose that*

$$c \vdash_\mathbf{T} \phi \ prop$$

where ϕ is a proposition that is built from decidable atomic relations by all the propositional connectives ($\Omega, \lor, \land, \neg, \rightarrow$). Then we shall say that ϕ is Δ_0.

The following is clear.

Proposition 30 *The Δ_0 propositions are decidable.*

In the case of arithmetic, the class of propositions that is generated from the decidable atomic relations by just the propositional connectives is often named the Σ_0^0 class of propositions.[2] Indeed, most presentations of the arithmetic hierarchy [9] start with this class and then layer it via the number of alternating quantifiers. In this connection, we have the following simple normal form result.

Proposition 31 *In* **TPL**, *suppose* $\Gamma \vdash \phi$ *prop. And let* ϕ *be* Σ. *Then there is a* Δ_0 *proposition* η *such that* $\Gamma \vdash \eta$ *prop and* $\Gamma \vdash T_1$ *type,...,* $\Gamma \vdash T_n$ *type such that*

$$\Gamma \vdash \phi \leftrightarrow \exists x : T_1 \cdot ... \cdot \exists x : T_n \cdot \eta$$

Proof We transform matters using the following rules.

$$(\exists x : T \cdot \zeta) \wedge \delta \text{ is transformed to } \exists x : T \cdot (\zeta \wedge \delta)$$
$$(\exists x : T \cdot \zeta) \vee \delta \text{ is transformed to } \exists x : T \cdot (\zeta \vee \delta)$$

We may assume that x is not free in δ if it is, rename it in ζ. In this way we move the existential quantifiers to their wide scope positions. The transformed propositions are then equivalent to the originals.■

As with the Σ relations, we cannot just select the relations of any theory and deem its basic relations to be decidable. They must have arithmetic representations that are decidable. And this has to be established for each such theory.

References

1. Barendregt, H.P. The Lambda Calculus: Its Syntax and Semantics, North Holland, Amsterdam,1981.
2. Barendregt, H.P. Lambda calculus with types. In S. Abramsky, D.M. Gabbay, and T.S.E. Maibaum, (Eds), Handbook of Logic in Computer Science, pp. 118–310, Oxford University Press, Oxford, 1992.
3. Barwise, J. Admissible Sets and Structures. Springer-Verlag, Berlin. 1975.
4. Cutland, N. Computability: An Introduction to Recursive Function Theory. Cambridge University Press, Cambridge, 1990.
5. Drake, F.R., and Wainer, S.J. Eds. Recursion Theory and Its Generalizations. London Mathematical Society Lecture Notes Series, no. 45, Cambridge University Press, Cambridge, 1980.
6. Ershov, Y.L. Definability and Computability. Nauka, Novosibirsk, 1996.
7. Havel, P. Metamathematics of First Order Arithmetic. Springer-Verlag, New York, 1991
8. Montague, R. Recursion theory as a branch of model theory. In: B. van Roostelaar et al. Ed., Logic, Methodogology and Philosophy of Science III. Proc. of the 1967 Congress., pp 63–86. North-Holland, Amsterdam, 1968.

---

[2] Together with the bounded quantifiers.

9. Rogers, H. Theory of Recursive Functions and Effective Computability. McGraw Hill, New York, 1967; 1988.

10. Smorynski, C. Logical Number Theory I: An Introduction. Springer-Verlag, Berlin, 1991.

11. Tucker, J.V. , and Bergstra, J.A. Equational specifications, complete term rewriting systems, and computable and semicomputable algebras, ACM, Volume 42, 1194–1230, 1995.

12. Tucker, J. V. and Stoltenberg-Hansen, V. Effective algebras. In: S. Abramsky, D.M. Gabbay, and T.S.E. Maibaum, (Eds), Handbook of Logic in Computer Science. Vol. 4. pp. 357–526, Oxford University Press, Oxford, 1995.

13. Tucker, J.V. and Stoltenberg-Hansen, V. Computable rings and fields, in E Griffor (Ed.), Handbook of Computability Theory, pp. 363–447. Elsevier, Amsterdam, 1999.

14. Tucker, J. V. and Zucker, J. I.Computable functions and semicomputable sets on many sorted algebras. In: S. Abramsky, D.M. Gabbay, and T.S.E. Maibaum, (Eds), Handbook of Logic in Computer Science. Vol. 5, pp. 317–523. Oxford University Press, Oxford, 2000.

15. Tucker. J.V. Zucker, J.I. Abstract computability and algebraic specification. ACM Trans. on Comput. Logic. 5: 611–668, 2004.

16. Turing, A.M. On computable numbers, with an application to the Entscheidungsproblem. Proceedings of the London Math. Soc., 42(2), 230–265; correction ibid. 43, 544-546 (1937).

17. Turing, A.M., Computability and Lambda-Definability, J. of Symbol. Log, 2, 1937.

Chapter 5
Specification

Computable models are built inside theories of data types. And specifications form
the main building blocks. In this chapter we provide our basic account of specification. This has its origins in the notion of a *representable relation* in logical number
theory [2, 3] and admissible set theory [1]. Furthermore, although its interpretation
will be quite different, in terms of the notation, our account is similar to the *schema*
notation pioneered by the Z specification language [4, 6]. Lastly, it has its more
recent roots in [5].

For us a specification consists of two parts:

- a declaration part,
- a predicate part.

In the declaration part the variables of the specification are declared and associated with their types. In the predicate part the properties of the intended objects and
their relationships are articulated. Symbolically, this gives the body of a specification the following two components.

$$x_1 : T_1, \dots, x_n : T_n$$
$$\phi[x_1, \dots, x_n]$$

where $x_1, \dots, x_n$ are variables and $T_1, \dots, T_n$ types and where the declaration provides the declaration context for the proposition. Given this, we take specifications
to have the following Z-like form.

$$R \triangleq [x_1 : T_1, \dots, x_n : T_n \mid \phi[x_1, \dots, x_n]] \qquad \textbf{Schema}$$

On our interpretation this is taken to introduce a new relation symbol R whose type
is given by the types in the declaration.

But how are specifications to be logically unpacked; i.e., how are we to understand their logical content? More exactly, what are the rules that govern their
introduction and use? The main aim of this chapter is to answer these questions.

R. Turner, *Computable Models*, DOI 10.1007/978-1-84882-052-4_5,
© Springer-Verlag London Limited 2009

5.1 A Logical Perspective

We adopt the logical perspective; i.e., relation specifications involve the conservative addition of new relation symbols. More exactly, we take **Schema** to introduce a new relation symbol R whose logical content is unpacked as follows.

Definition 32 (Schema Specifications) *Suppose that* **T** *is any* **TDT**. *Further suppose that*

$$x_1 : T_1, \ldots\ldots, x_n : T_n \vdash_{\mathbf{T}} \phi \ prop \qquad\qquad \mathbf{R_0}$$

where ϕ is Σ. Let $\mathbf{T^R}$ be the theory obtained from **T** *by the addition of a new Σ relation symbol (R) that is governed by the following axioms.*

$$x_1 : T_1, \ldots, x_n : T_n \vdash R(x_1, \ldots, x_n) \ prop \qquad\qquad \mathbf{R_1}$$

$$\forall x_1 : T_1 \cdot \ldots \cdot \forall x_n : T_n \cdot \phi[x_1, \ldots, x_n] \rightarrow R(x_1, \ldots, x_n) \qquad\qquad \mathbf{R_2}$$

$$\forall x_1 : T_1 \cdot \ldots \cdot \forall x_n : T_n \cdot R(x_1, \ldots, x_n) \rightarrow \phi[x_1, \ldots, x_n] \qquad\qquad \mathbf{R_3}$$

The first axiom is the formation rule. It informs us that R forms a proposition under the assumption of the declaration. The second is the introduction axiom, and provides the conditions necessary for the introduction of the relation, and the third, its rule of elimination, santions its removal.

Given R_0, **Schema** is taken to introduce a new relation R that is governed by R_1, R_2, R_3. This provides a general notion of specification that is applicable to any theory of data types. Note that in such a specification, because of the assumption that

$$x_1 : T_1, \ldots, x_n : T_n \vdash \phi \ prop$$

by coherence,

$$x_1 : T_1, \ldots, x_n : T_n \vdash T_i \ type$$

for $1 \leq i \leq n$.

Take note that specifications are restricted to Σ propositions. On the face of it, specifications are intended to delineate programs, and so the corresponding relation between its inputs and outputs will be Σ. For this reason, we take our principal notion of specification to be the specification of Σ relations. There are many subtle issues here, issues that we shall address as we proceed. These will motivate the introduction of *schema definitions* where the Σ constraint is lifted. But we shall reserve the term *specification* for the Σ ones.

Often we shall write these schema vertically as follows. This brings the notation even closer to that of Z notation.

$$
\begin{array}{|l}
\hline
R \\
\hline
x_1 : T_1, \dots, x_n : T_n \\
\hline
\phi[x_1, \dots, x_n] \\
\hline
\end{array}
$$

However, we are not claiming that schemata have the same meaning as in the Z notation. For one thing, our notion of schema is not wedded to any particular theory of data types and certainly not to standard set theory. For another, our logical account seems different. Despite this, we shall adopt some of the Z notational conventions. In particular, we shall often mark conjunctions with a new line. In addition, when defining operations, we shall sometimes indicate inputs with ? and outputs with !. Alternatively, we shall just as often simply write inputs on the first line and the output on the second.

5.2 Some Specifications

We first revisit some old examples. The following provides the definition of the Boolean connectives in terms of the conditional operator.

Example 33 (Conjunction)

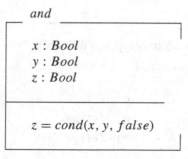

$$
\begin{array}{|l}
\hline
and \\
\hline
x : Bool \\
y : Bool \\
z : Bool \\
\hline
z = cond(x, y, false) \\
\hline
\end{array}
$$

Example 34 (Disjunction)

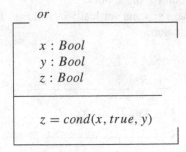

Example 35 (Negation)

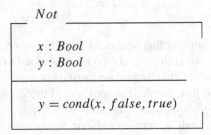

These examples provide the formal definitions of these notions. They are specifications within the framework of **TPL**. Our next examples deal with products. Recall that $T_1 \otimes T_2 \otimes T_3$ is an abbreviation for $T_1 \otimes (T_2 \otimes T_3)$.

Example 36 (Triples)

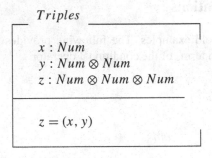

We may extend this to arbitrary types as follows.

Example 37 (Triples) Suppose that

$$c \vdash T_1 \; type$$
$$c \vdash T_2 \; type$$
$$c \vdash T_3 \; type$$

Then, relative to c, we may specify triples as follows.

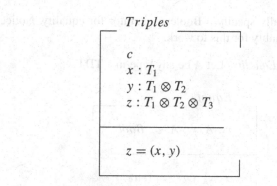

We shall often suppress the background declaration context and just write:

Suppose that T_1, T_2, and T_3 are types in a **TDT**. Then we may specify ....

This will often simplify the presentation. For example, the corresponding selection operations may be specified as follows.

Example 38 (Selection) Suppose that T_1, T_2, and T_3 are types. Then we may specify

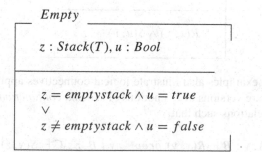

Here we have suppressed the context c. Our next example involves stacks. We can specify the empty test for stacks. This returns a Boolean. In our original account we took it to be a basic operation. But the following demonstrates that once the type is embedded in a **TDT**, there is no need to do so. Here we take $Stack(T)$ to have decidable equality.

Example 39 (Empty Test) Let T be a type. Then we specify

```
  Empty ─────────────────────────

    z : Stack(T), u : Bool

  ───────────────────────────────

    z = emptystack ∧ u = true
    ∨
    z ≠ emptystack ∧ u = false

  ───────────────────────────────
```

We may also formally specify a Boolean operator for equality. Notice that we need propositional equality for this to work.

Example 40 (Boolean Equality) Let A be any type in a **TDT**.

$$
\begin{array}{|l}
\hline
Equal_A \\
\hline
\quad x : A, y : A, z : Bool \\
\hline
\quad x =_A y \wedge z = true \\
\quad \vee \\
\quad x \neq_A y \wedge z = false \\
\hline
\end{array}
$$

This provides our basic notion of specification. Its formal content should now be clear. We shall now put some more infrastructure in place.

5.3 Operations on Schema

We shall further illustrate our specification style with some rather general strategies of specification. The following can be seen as a means of constructing complex specifications from simple ones. They apply to any theory of data types and provide the core of a simple algebra of schemata.

Example 41 (Schema Product) Let R, S be relations such that

$$x : A, y : B \vdash R(x, y) \, prop \quad u : C, v : D \vdash S(u, v) \, prop$$

Then we may specify the following new relation that introduces their product.

$$
\begin{array}{|l}
\hline
R \otimes S \\
\hline
\quad x : A, y : B, u : C, v : D \\
\hline
\quad R(x, y) \wedge S(u, v) \\
\hline
\end{array}
$$

Our next two examples also illustrate logical connectives applied at the level of schemata. They are versions of Z's notions of *schema conjunction* and *disjunction*.
Let R, S be relations such that

$$x : A, y : B \vdash R(x, y) \, prop \quad y : B, z : C \vdash S(y, z) \, prop$$

Then we may specify the following new relations that introduce their conjunction and disjunction.

Example 42 (Schema Conjunction)

$$\begin{array}{|l} \hline R \wedge S \\ \hline x : A, y : B, z : C \\ \hline R(x, y) \wedge S(y, z) \\ \hline \end{array}$$

Example 43 (Schema Disjunction)

$$\begin{array}{|l} \hline R \vee S \\ \hline x : A, y : B, z : C \\ \hline R(x, y) \vee S(y, z) \\ \hline \end{array}$$

Given some basic relations that are taken to be decidable, we can build up more decidable relations by conjunction and disjunction; i.e., products, conjunction and disjunction preserve decidable relations.

The next example continues the theme of logical operations applied at the level of schemata. It illustrates what Z calls *schema hiding*; i.e., information in the relation definition has been hidden via existential quantification. Clearly, this does not preserve decidability.

Example 44 (Composition) Let R, S be any relations such that

$$x : A, y : B \vdash R(x, y) \ prop \ \text{ and } \ y : B, z : C \vdash S(y, z) \ prop$$

Then we may specify their **composition** via the following schema.

$$\begin{array}{|l} \hline R \circ S \\ \hline x : A, z : C \\ \hline \exists y : B \cdot R(x, y) \wedge S(y, z) \\ \hline \end{array}$$

The next provides another example of the use of the existential to hide information.

Example 45 (Projection) Suppose

$$x_1 : T_1, \dots, x_n : T_n \vdash R(x_1, \dots, x_n) \; prop$$

Then the *ith* **projection** of R is given as

$$
\boxed{
\begin{array}{l}
Proj(R, i) \\[4pt]
\hline
x_1 : T_1, \dots, x_{i-1} : T_{i-1}, x_{i+1} : T_{i+1}, \dots, x_n : T_n \\[4pt]
\hline
\exists x_i : T_i \cdot R(x_1, \dots, x_n)
\end{array}
}
$$

The following pair of relation specifications are special cases. Let R be any binary relation such that

$$\frac{a : A \qquad b : B}{R(a, b) \; prop}$$

Then we may specify the *domain* and *range* of R as follows.

Example 46 (Domain)

$$
\boxed{
\begin{array}{l}
Dom\,R \\[4pt]
\hline
y : B \\[4pt]
\hline
\exists x : A \cdot R(x, y)
\end{array}
}
$$

Example 47 (Range)

$$
\boxed{
\begin{array}{l}
Ran\,R \\[4pt]
\hline
x : A \\[4pt]
\hline
\exists y : B \cdot R(x, y)
\end{array}
}
$$

These operations on relations form part of what may be thought of as a toolkit of strategies for building new specifications from old ones. We shall study them in a more mathematically elegant way when we study a type of schemata.

In the last chapter we alluded to the possibility of specifying the internal inverse of a decidable proposition; i.e., in the case where the defining proposition is decidable, we may also specify its *internal negation*. The new relation automatically satisfies the required conditions for being an internal negation.

Definition 48 *Suppose that*

$$R \triangleq [x_1 : T_1, ..., x_n : T_n \mid \phi]$$

where ϕ is decidable. Then we may specify $\overline{R}$, as

$$\overline{R} \triangleq [x_1 : T_1, ..., x_n : T_n \mid \neg\phi]$$

5.4 Conservative Extensions

Such introductions of new relations preserve the underlying theory of data. Technically, this means that their introduction is conservative. This is the content of the following. The link between specifications and conservative extensions will form a major theme of the book.

Theorem 49 *Suppose that Γ, Θ do not contain R. Then*

$$\Gamma \vdash_{\mathbf{T^R}} \Theta \ implies \ \Gamma \vdash_{\mathbf{T}} \Theta$$

This follows from the following compilation lemma.

Lemma 50 *(Compilation)*
There is a translation $*$ from $\mathbf{T^R}$ to $\mathbf{T}$ such that

1. if $\Gamma \vdash_{\mathbf{T^R}} \Theta$, then $\Gamma^* \vdash_{\mathbf{T}} \Theta^*$,
2. if $\Gamma \vdash_{\mathbf{T^R}} \Theta$, then, where Θ does not contain R, $\Theta^* = \Theta$,
3. if $\phi \ prop$ is Σ in $\mathbf{T^R}$, then $\phi^* \ is \ \Sigma \ in \ \mathbf{T}$,

where Γ^* is the translated context and Θ^* is the translated judgment.

Proof Let $*$ be the translation between the two theories obtained by replacing, in the expressions of $\mathbf{T^R}$, every occurrence of $R(t)$ by $\phi[t]$. This applies to all judgments and their constituents. Part 1 follows by induction on the derivations in $\mathbf{T^R}$. All the rules of **TPL** expressed in $\mathbf{T^R}$ remain in place because they translate across unchanged. Similarly, the translation does not affect any rule of any specific theory: Instances of the rules of the new theory will be translated to instances of rules of the old one. This leaves us to check the new axiom, and this is immediate. The proofs of 2 and 3 are by inspection.∎

This completes our preliminary account of relational specification. There is much more to be said. But much of this will have to wait for specific theories. Specifications, or rather suites of them, form the body of computable models and we shall eventually get to some interesting examples. But first we must put another building block in place.

References

1. Barwise, J. Admissible Sets and Structures. Springer-Verlag, Berlin, 1975.
2. Havel, P. Metamathematics of First Order Arithmetic. Springer-Verlag, Berlin, 1991
3. Smorynski, C. Logical Number Theory I: An Introduction. Springer-Verlag, New York, 1991.
4. Spivey, J.M. Understanding Z. Cambridge University Press, Cambridge, 1988.
5. Turner, R. The foundations of specification. J. Log. Comput., 15: 623–662, Oct. 2005.
6. Woodcock, J. and Davies, J. Using Z- Specifications, Refinement and Proof, Prentice Hall, Englewood Cliffs, NJ, 1996.

Chapter 6
Functions

In **VDM** [3, 2]) it is not relational specifications that take center stage but functional ones. In this chapter we provide our account of these [4]. But we shall do so in terms of our basic notion of relational specification. To set the scene, we recall that functions do not constitute a new kind of entity; they are special kinds of relations. More explicitly, a relation given by the formation rule

$$\frac{a : I \qquad b : O}{R(a, b) \; prop}$$

is a *function* if each input uniquely determines an output; i.e., it obeys the following rule.

$$\frac{R(a, b) \qquad R(a, c)}{b = c}$$

Furthermore, in line with relations, they are not taken to satisfy any principle of extensionality; i.e., from

$$\forall x : I \cdot \forall y : O \cdot R(x, y) \leftrightarrow S(x, y)$$

it does not follow that R and S are identical relations.

Consequently, functions are introduced as relations that are governed by a special operation of application. More explicitly, because they are single-valued, they can applied to arguments in their domain to yield a unique result; i.e., functions are single-valued, intensional, and computable (Σ) relations.

6.1 Totality and Functionality

Two special properties of relations will play a significant role in our account. We shall illustrate matters with the binary case; the use of products facilitates the extension to the case of many-place relations.

R. Turner, *Computable Models*, DOI 10.1007/978-1-84882-052-4_6,
© Springer-Verlag London Limited 2009

Definition 51 (Total Relations) *Suppose that* **T** *is any* **TDT**. *Assume that*

$$\frac{a : I \qquad\qquad b : O}{R(a, b) \ prop}$$

R will be said to be **total** *iff*

$$\forall x : I \cdot \exists y : O \cdot R(x, y) \qquad\qquad\qquad \textbf{Tot}$$

i.e., its domain is the whole of the input type. We shall write this as follows.

$$\textbf{Tot}(R, I, O)$$

Total relations are defined on the whole of their domain. Since it will give rise to total functions, this will be especially important in the case of relations that are also functional.

Definition 52 (Functional Relations) *Suppose that* **T** *is any* **TDT**. *Assume that*

$$\frac{a : I \qquad\qquad b : O}{R(a, b) \ prop}$$

We shall say that R is **functional** *iff*

$$\forall x : I \cdot \forall y : O \cdot \forall z : O \cdot R(x, y) \wedge R(x, z) \rightarrow y = z \qquad\qquad \textbf{Fun}$$

We shall write this as

$$\textbf{Fun}(R, I, O)$$

We shall write **TF**(R, I, O) *to indicate that R is total and functional; i.e.,*

$$\forall x : I \cdot \exists! y : O \cdot R(x, y) \qquad\qquad\qquad \textbf{TF}$$

where ! *indicates there is exactly one.*

With these notions at hand, we can deal with the introduction of functional application. To begin with, we treat the case where relations are both total and functional. The case where they are just functional leads to partial application and partial functions. We shall discuss this in the next chapter, where we introduce the notion of a specification with preconditions.

6.2 Functional Application

We shall not introduce functions as a new kind of specification but rather introduce a method that enables relations, that are proven to be functions, to be applied to their arguments. This enables such relations to operate as functions. For this we only require one new function symbol. We shall be guided by the treatment of the addition of new function symbols in [1].

Definition 53 (Apply) *Suppose that* **T** *is any* **TDT**. *Let* **T**^{apply} *be* **T** *with a new function symbol apply, governed by the following rules. For each total and functional relation,*

$$\frac{a : I \qquad b : O}{F(a, b) \; prop}$$

application satisfies the following rules.

$$\frac{a : I}{apply(F, a) : O} \qquad \mathbf{F_1}$$

$$\frac{a : I}{F(a, apply(F, a))} \qquad \mathbf{F_2}$$

In line with convention, we shall abbreviate apply(F, x) as $F(x)$.

$\mathbf{F_1}$ tells us that application returns a value in the target type, while $\mathbf{F_2}$ demands that the input, together with the output, satisfies the original relation given by $\mathbf{F}$.

This is more far-reaching than the introduction of relation symbols themselves. The addition of *apply* allows every total functional relation to behave as a new function symbol with all that entails; i.e., it can be applied to arguments to form new terms etc. And this can involve the construction of complex terms such as the following.

$$F(x, G(x, y))$$

Finally, note that application may be extended to many-place functions using Cartesian products; i.e.,

$$\frac{\mathbf{TF}(F, I_1 \otimes \dots \otimes I_n, O) \qquad a : I_1 \otimes \dots \otimes I_n \qquad b : O}{apply(F, a) : O}$$

In terms of its conservative justification, *apply* constitutes a more complex addition. But before we look into this, we illustrate its use. Our first example is a numerical one that we shall deal with in more detail in the next chapter.

Example 54 (Maximum)

$$
\begin{array}{|l}
\hline
Max \\
\hline
x? : N, y? : N, z! : N \\
\hline
x \leq z \wedge y \leq z \\
z = x \vee z = y \\
\hline
\end{array}
$$

Since there is only one maximum number, this is functional. Of course, to establish this formally, we need some more precise account and, in particular, we need to work in some version of formal arithmetic. That will come later. For the present, we note that, as a consequence, we may employ it as a function symbol that satisfies the following instances of $\mathbf{F_1}$ and $\mathbf{F_2}$.

$$\frac{a : N \qquad\qquad b : N}{Max(a, b) : N}$$

$$\frac{a : N \qquad\qquad b : N}{a \leq Max(a, b) \wedge b \leq Max(a, b) \wedge (Max(a, b) = a \vee Max(a, b) = b)}$$

In a parallel way we may introduce a minimum function; parallel remarks apply.

Example 55 (Minimum)

$$
\begin{array}{|l}
\hline
\quad Min \\\\
\hline
\quad x? : N, y? : N, z! : N \\\\
\hline
\\\\
\quad z \leq x \wedge z \leq y \\\\
\quad z = x \vee z = y \\\\
\\\\
\hline
\end{array}
$$

This is also functional and, as a function, it satisfies

$$\frac{a : N \qquad\qquad b : N}{Min(a, b) : N}$$

$$\frac{a : N \qquad\qquad b : N}{Min(a, b) \leq a \wedge Min(a, b) \leq b \wedge (Min(a, b) = a \vee Min(a, b) = b)}$$

In the future, we shall not always spell out such conditions. Enough is enough. Our next function is more general and applies to any **TDT** with Booleans. We assume equality is decidable. We have seen the following before, but not as a formal specification. It is clearly functional and returns a Boolean value.

Example 56 (Boolean Equality) Let A be any type.

$$
\begin{array}{|l}
\hline Eq_A \\
\hline
x : A, y : A, z : Bool \\
\hline
\\
x = y \wedge z = true \\
\vee \\
x \neq y \wedge z = false \\
\\
\hline
\end{array}
$$

6.3 Explicit Functions

Some specifications define functions by explicitly indicating their arguments; i.e., a function is explicitly defined via a term of the language [3]. Such specifications are so frequent that we consider them as a special case. In general, they take the following form.

Definition 57 (Explicit Functions) *Given types I and O and the fact that*

$$
x : I \vdash t[x] : O
$$

*we may introduce a new functional relation symbol, by **explicit function definition**, as*

$$
F \triangleq [x : I, y : O \mid y = t[x]]
$$

This is taken to satisfy

$$
\frac{a : I}{apply(F, a) : O} \qquad \mathbf{F_1}
$$

$$
\frac{a : I}{apply(F, a) = t[a/x]} \qquad \mathbf{F_2}
$$

We shall frequently write such explicit specifications using lambda notation; i.e.,

$$
F \triangleq \lambda x : I \cdot t[x]
$$

Our first example of such an explicit specification applies to any **TDT**. Suppose we have two functional operations such that

$$\frac{a : A}{F(a) : B} \qquad \frac{b : B}{G(b) : C}$$

Then the following specified function is their composition:

Example 58 (Composition)

$$
\boxed{
\begin{array}{l}
H \\
\hline
x : A, z : C \\
\hline
z = G(F(x))
\end{array}
}
$$

In lambda notation we would write

$$H \triangleq \lambda x : A \cdot G(F(x))$$

Once again, this is obviously functional. Thus, we may introduce it as a new function symbol H that satisfies the following rules.

$$\frac{a : A}{H(a) : C} \qquad \frac{a : A}{H(a) = G(F(a))}$$

In the following example we assume the underlying **TDT** contains the stack constructor.

Example 59 (Second) Let A be any type in the **TDT**. We may then specify:

$$
\boxed{
\begin{array}{l}
Second \\
\hline
x : Stack(A),\ y : A \\
\hline
y = top(top(x))
\end{array}
}
$$

We have also seen our next example before. But now we can write it as a schema specification.

Example 60 (Generalized Selection) Given types T_1, T_2, and T_3, we specify

$$\pi_2^3$$

$$
\boxed{
\begin{array}{l}
x : T_1 \otimes T_2 \otimes T_3 \\
y : T_2 \\
\\
\hline
y = \pi_1(\pi_2(x))
\end{array}
}
$$

More interesting and less general examples require the development of a little more infrastructure, but this will have to wait until we study the various type constructors in more detail. However, the present examples should be enough to grasp the general idea.

This completes our initial discussion of the simple case of total functions. We conclude with the only result of the chapter. However, it is a conceptually important one.

6.4 The Elimination of Application

In parallel to the relation case, we show that the addition of new function symbols is conservative. Since function symbols can be iterated via composition, we can form terms such as $F(G(H(x, y), z))$. Subsequently, the proof is a little trickier.

Theorem 61 (Conservative Extension for Functional Application) *Let* **T** *be any* **TDT**. *Suppose that* Γ, Θ *do not contain apply. Then*

$$\Gamma \vdash_{\mathbf{T}^{\text{apply}}} \Theta \; \textit{implies} \; \Gamma \vdash_{\mathbf{T}} \Theta$$

Hence, anything expressible in the old language, that is provable in the new theory, is already provable in the old one. It is a corollary to the following compilation lemma that demonstrates how to eliminate all instances of functional application.

Lemma 62 (Compilation) *There is a translation* $*$ *from* $\mathbf{T}^{\text{apply}}$ *to* **T** *such that*

1. if $\Gamma \vdash_{\mathbf{T}^{\text{apply}}} \Theta$, then $\Gamma^* \vdash_{\mathbf{T}} \Theta^*$,
2. if $\Gamma \vdash_{\mathbf{T}} \Theta$, then, $\Gamma \vdash_{\mathbf{T}} \Theta^*$ iff $\Gamma \vdash_{\mathbf{T}} \Theta$,
3. if ϕ *prop* is Σ, in $\mathbf{T}^{\text{apply}}$ then ϕ^* *is* Σ *in* **T**,

where Γ^* is the translated context and Θ^* is the translated judgment.

Proof Suppose that F has been introduced as a new function symbol via the following rules.

$$\frac{i : I}{F(i) : O} \qquad \frac{i : I}{R(i, F(i))}$$

Initially, we define * on the rules of formation to remove just one instance of F. In our raw syntax, we employ DeMorgan's algorithm to push all the negations through to atomic cases. This leaves F occurring only in atomic propositions and their negations. Here we replace F, but if F does not occur, we change nothing.

$$\alpha[F(t)/y]^* = \exists v : O \cdot R(t, v) \wedge \alpha[v/y]$$
$$(\neg\alpha[F(t)/y])^* = \exists v : O \cdot R(t, v) \wedge \neg\alpha[v/y]$$

The propositional connectives $\wedge$ and $\vee$ and the quantifiers are then translated compositionally. We interpret the other judgments that involve F as follows.

$$\Gamma \vdash \Theta[F(t)/x]$$

translates to the judgment

$$\Gamma, x : O \vdash \Theta[x]$$

where if they do not involve F, they are not changed. An easy induction establishes that for any ϕ

$$\forall x : I \cdot \forall y : O \cdot R(x, y) \rightarrow (\phi[y] \leftrightarrow \phi[F[x]]^*) \tag{$\clubsuit$}$$

The base case is easy to see:

$$x : I, y : O \vdash R(x, y) \rightarrow (\alpha[y] \leftrightarrow \exists v : O \cdot R(x, v) \wedge \alpha[v])$$

The rest is also straightforward: e.g.,

$$(\eta \wedge \delta)[y] \leftrightarrow (\exists v : O \cdot R(x, v) \wedge \eta[v]) \wedge (\exists v' : O \cdot R(u, v') \wedge \delta[v'])$$

The result now follows because R is functional; i.e., $v = v'$. We now turn to the explicit proof of the various parts of the lemma. The first part contains most of the work. For it, for the removal of our single occurrence of F, we illustrate with some exemplary cases. For simplicity, in the following, the only occurrence of F is the one indicated. First consider the following introduction rule for an existing function G.

$$\frac{a : A \qquad b : B}{G(a, b) : O(A, B)}$$

Then consider the F instance

$$\frac{a : A \qquad b[F(t)/y] : B}{G(a, b[F(t)/y]) : O(A, B)}$$

The premise unpacks under the translation to

$$a : A \qquad y : O \vdash b[y] : B$$

This yields the translation of the conclusion; i.e.,

$$y : O \vdash G(a, b[y]) : O(A, B)$$

The rest of the type-inference rules of $\mathbf{T}^{\text{apply}}$ are equally easy to verify. For the logical rules, the existential quantifier rules are the only problematic ones. We illustrate with the following case.

$$\frac{\phi[s[F(t)/y]/x] \qquad s[F(t)/y] : T \qquad x : T \vdash \phi \; prop}{\exists x : T \cdot \phi}$$

The translations of the premises yield the following.

$$y : O \vdash \phi[s[y]/x]$$
$$y : O \vdash s[y] : T$$
$$x : T \vdash \phi \; prop$$

We also know by grammatical considerations that $t : I$. By $\clubsuit$ it is sufficient to show that

$$\exists y : O \cdot R(t, y) \wedge \phi[s[y]]$$

By the assumption of functionality, $\exists y : O \cdot R(t, y)$ and y is unique. Hence, by the translated premises of the rule, $s[y] : T$. By the quantifier introduction rule, we are done. This leaves us to check the new rules. $\mathbf{F}_1$ is immediate. For $\mathbf{F}_2$, we must establish

$$u : I \vdash R(u, F(u))^*$$

Using $\clubsuit$ and functionality, the result is also clear.

$$(u : I \vdash R(u, F(u))^*$$
$$\text{iff}$$
$$u : I \vdash \exists y : O \cdot R(u, y)$$

This provides the soundness of the translation for the removal of one occurrence of F. By iterating this procedure, we eventually remove them all. Here note that any removal of an application via the translation reduces that number; i.e., no new applications emerge as a result of the translation. We then only need to observe that, where there is the only occurrence to remove, the proof of $\Gamma^* \vdash_{\mathbf{T}^{\text{apply}}} \Theta^*$ can be carried out in $\mathbf{T}$. Parts 2 and 3 are routine to check: Negation aside, because of the compositional nature of the translation of the connectives and quantifiers, Σ propositions translate to Σ propositions. ∎

This completes our preliminary account of function specification. There is much more to be said. Topics that immediately spring to mind involve recursive functions and the treatment of *higher-order* functions. These will be taken up later.

References

1. Barwise, J. Admissible Sets and Structures. Springer-Verlag. Berlin. 1975.
2. Dawes, J. The VDM-SL Reference Guide. Pitman, London, 1991.
3. Jones, C.B.. Systematic Software Development Using VDM. Prentice-Hall, Inc., Englewood Cliffs, NJ, 1986.
4. Turner, R. The foundations of specification. J. Log. Comput., 15: 623–662, Oct. 2005.

Chapter 7
Preconditions

Our notions of totality and functionality are determined by the class of types in the theory. More specifically, they are dependent upon the domain of the relation: The bigger the domain, the harder it is for the relation to be total and functional. If our notion of domain could be restricted in some way, then the class of functions would be increased. One way of achieving this is to enrich the notion of specification with the concept of *precondition* [2, 3, 4]. Preconditions leave some possibilities open and in particular do not force us to declare the result of the function on the whole input type. This will provide us with a larger class of total functions and enable a more sensitive approach to specification.

To illustrate the problem with the current approach, consider the following schema specifications for the predecessor function on the natural numbers.

Example 63 (Predecessor)

$$
\begin{array}{|l}
\hline
\quad Pred_1 \\\\
\hline
\quad x : N, y : N \\\\
\hline
\quad x \neq 0 \wedge y^+ = x \\\\
\hline
\end{array}
\qquad
\begin{array}{|l}
\hline
\quad Pred_2 \\\\
\hline
\quad x : N, y : N \\\\
\hline
\quad x \neq 0 \rightarrow y^+ = x \\\\
\hline
\end{array}
$$

The first restricts the relation by restricting it to nonzero numbers. As such, it is functional but not total. The second does not exclude nonzero numbers and so is total. However, because zero does not uniquely determine an output, it is not functional. So neither specification is both total and functional. To obtain a specification that is, we need a more intrinsic way of incorporating the $x \neq 0$ condition into the body of the specification.

7.1 Specifications with Preconditions

We illustrate with binary relations. The central idea is contained in the following generalized notion of specification in which the preconditions are made explicit.

R. Turner, *Computable Models*, DOI 10.1007/978-1-84882-052-4_7,
© Springer-Verlag London Limited 2009

Definition 64 (Preconditions) *Suppose that* **T** *is any* **TDT***. Further suppose that*

$$x : I, \pi[x], y : O \vdash_{\mathbf{T}} \phi[x, y] \, prop \qquad\qquad \mathbf{R_0}$$

where π *and* ψ *are* Σ*. Then the specification*

$$R \triangleq [x : I, y : O \mid \pi[x]; \phi[x, y]] \qquad\qquad \textbf{(Preschema)}$$

is taken to introduce a new relation R that is governed by the following axioms.

$$x : I, \pi(x), y : O \vdash R(x, y) \, prop \qquad\qquad \mathbf{R_1}$$

$$\forall x : I \cdot \forall y : O \cdot \pi(x) \to (\phi[x, y] \to R(x, y)) \qquad\qquad \mathbf{R_2}$$

$$\forall x : I \cdot \forall y : O \cdot \pi(x) \to (R(x, y) \to \phi[x, y]) \qquad\qquad \mathbf{R_3}$$

Here π *is called the **precondition** of the specification and we shall now refer to* ϕ
*as the **postcondition**. Let* $\mathbf{T^R}$ *be the theory obtained from* **T** *by the addition of a new
relation symbol (R) that is governed by these axioms.*

Note that every standard specification can be considered as one with preconditions; i.e.,

$$R \triangleq [x : I, y : O \mid \phi[x, y]]$$

can be represented as

$$R' \triangleq [x : I, y : O \mid x =_I x; \phi[x, y]]$$

The two relations are logically equivalent, and so it makes sense to take this as a
generalization of the original. Observe that

$$R \triangleq [x : I, y : O \mid \pi(x) \wedge \phi[x, y]]$$
$$R \triangleq [x : I, y : O \mid \pi(x) \to \phi[x, y]]$$

both satisfy conditions $\mathbf{R_1}$, $\mathbf{R_2}$, $\mathbf{R_3}$ of **preschema.** And so the addition of relations
with preconditions is conservative. So what have we gained? We shall see that pre-
conditions lead to a natural way of revising our notions of totality and functionality.
To illustrate this, we return to the task of specifying the predecessor function. Consider the following version with preconditions.

Example 65 (Predeccessor)

$$Pred$$

$x : N, y : N$
$x \neq 0; y^+ = x$

We claim that this is total and functional. But not in the present sense of these terms, since they do not apply to specifications written with preconditions. Indeed, the introduction of preconditions, requires us to revisit our notions of *domain, totality,* and *functionality*. Somehow we have to take the precondition into account.

7.2 Totality and Functionality

We first defined our notion of domain so that the precondition bites. More specifically, we introduce a notion of domain that itself employs preconditions.

Definition 66 (Domain) *Let R be a specification with preconditions.*

$$R \triangleq [x : I \mid \pi(x); \eta[x, y]]$$

*Then we define the **domain** of R as*

$$DomR \triangleq [x : I \mid \pi(x); \exists y : O \cdot R(x, y)]$$

The domain is defined as before but now we use the precondition itself. This notion of domain replaces the old one, which is recoverable by treating relations without preconditions as relations with a tautology as precondition. So we can unambiguously use the same abbreviation for the domain of a relation. Explicitly, the new notion of domain satisfies the following.

$$\forall x : I \cdot DomR(x) \leftrightarrow (\pi(x) \rightarrow \exists y : O \cdot R(x, y))$$

And this leads to the following parallel notion of totality.

Definition 67 (Totality) *Let R be a specification with preconditions.*

$$R \triangleq [x : I \mid \pi(x); \eta[x, y]]$$

*R is **total** iff*

$$\forall x : I \cdot \pi(x) \rightarrow \exists y : O \cdot R(x, y)$$

Put differently, R is total iff

$$Dom R \triangleq [x : I \mid \pi(x)]$$

This is identical in form to the original notion of totality but with the new notion of domain. Furthermore, with this notion of totality, any relation may be turned into a total one.

Definition 68 (Totalization) *Let*

$$R \triangleq [x : I, y : O \mid \psi[x, y]]$$

*The **totalization** of R is defined as follows.*

$$\widehat{R} \triangleq [x : I, y : O \mid Dom R(x); R(x, y)]$$

This is total in the precondition sense; i.e.,

$$\forall x : I \cdot Dom R(x) \to \exists y : O \cdot R(x, y)$$

And this is in line with the traditional literature on Z schemata, which takes the domain to be the precondition of a schema. But R and $\widehat{R}$ are not logically equivalent. They are only so on the domain itself; i.e.,

$$\forall x : I \cdot Dom R(x) \to \forall y : O \cdot R(x, y) \leftrightarrow R'(x, y)$$

However, as we shall see later, the totalization provides an example of *retraction;* i.e., R' is a retraction of R.

The notion of functionality undergoes a parallel transformation. Being functional relative to such preconditions is less stringent.

Definition 69 (Functionality) *Suppose that*

$$R \triangleq [x : I, y : O \mid \pi(x); \psi[x, y]]$$

*If the following holds, we shall say that R is **functional**.*

$$\forall x : I \cdot \pi(x) \to \forall y : O \cdot \forall z : O \cdot \psi[x, y] \wedge \psi[x, z] \to y = z$$

Accordingly, it is total and functional just in case

$$\forall x : I \cdot \pi(x) \to \exists! y : O \cdot \psi[x, y]$$

As before, we shall use the abbreviations that make reference to the precondition π,

$$\textbf{Tot}(F, I, \pi, O), \ \textbf{Fun}(F, I, \pi, O), \ \textbf{TF}(F, I, \pi, O)$$

to indicate totality, functionality, and being a total function in this revised sense.

7.3 Functional Application

Preconditions enable functionality and totality to be more easily satisfied. Consequently, they give us freedom to conservatively introduce a wider class of functional relations.

Definition 70 (Functional Application) *Suppose that* **T** *is any* **TDT**. *Let* $\textbf{T}_\pi^{\text{apply}}$ *be* **T** *with a new function symbol apply, governed by the following rules. For each relation*

$$\frac{a : I \qquad \pi(a) \qquad b : O}{F(a, b) \ prop}$$

where **TF**(F, I, π, O), *we have*

$$\frac{a : I \qquad \pi(a)}{apply(F, a) : O} \qquad \textbf{F}_1$$

$$\frac{a : I \qquad \pi(a)}{F(a, apply(F, a))} \qquad \textbf{F}_2$$

The first informs us that **F**, with input in I that satisfies precondition π, returns a value in O, while $\textbf{F}_2$ guarantees that under π the input/output satisfy the original relation. Again, we shall use the abbreviated form for functional application; i.e., $F(a)$.

We can now see why the following is a better specification of predecessor in the sense that every number that satisfies the precondition has a predecessor.

Example 71 (Predecessor)

$$Pred \triangleq \left[x : N, y : N \mid x > 0; x = y^+ \right]$$

This gives rise to a new function symbol that satisfies

$$\frac{a : N \qquad a > 0}{Pred(a) : N} \qquad \textbf{F}_1$$

$$\frac{a : N \qquad a > 0}{Pred(x)^+ = x} \qquad \textbf{F}_2$$

We shall see more examples as we proceed, but to better illustrate matters we need more types in place. For the present, looking forward a little, the following example preempts our discussion of finite sets. It provides a specification of map

application. First, we define *Maps* as single-valued sets of pairs. In what follows
$Set(T)$ is the type whose members are finite sets of elements of type T.

Example 72 (Maps)

```
┌─ Map ──────────────────────────────────┐
│                                          │
│   z : Set(A ⊗ B)                         │
│  ────────────────────────────────────   │
│                                          │
│   ∀x ∈ z · ∀y ∈ z · x₁ = y₁ → x₂ = y₂    │
│                                          │
└──────────────────────────────────────────┘
```

$$z : Set(A \otimes B)$$
$$\forall x \in z \cdot \forall y \in z \cdot x_1 = y_1 \rightarrow x_2 = y_2$$

We have surreptitiously sneaked in bounded set quantifiers. Maps are single-
valued sets of pairs from the product type $A \otimes B$. We may then define the *domain*
of maps. This is analogous to domain for schema relations.

Example 73 (Map Domain)

```
┌─ Dom ──────────────────────────────────┐
│                                          │
│   u : Set(A ⊗ B), v : Set(A)             │
│  ────────────────────────────────────   │
│                                          │
│       ∀x ∈ v · ∃y ∈ u · x = y₁           │
│                  ∧                       │
│           ∀y ∈ u · y₁ ∈ v                │
│                                          │
└──────────────────────────────────────────┘
```

$$u : Set(A \otimes B), v : Set(A)$$
$$\forall x \in v \cdot \exists y \in u \cdot x = y_1$$
$$\wedge$$
$$\forall y \in u \cdot y_1 \in v$$

Finally, using preconditions, we may specify an application operator for maps.
The following is a specification of map application with the precondition that the
argument to the map is in its domain.

Example 74 (Map Application)

```
┌─ Mapapp ───────────────────────────────┐
│                                          │
│   u : Set(A ⊗ B), x : A, y : B           │
│  ────────────────────────────────────   │
│                                          │
│       Dom(u)(x); (x, y) ∈ u              │
│                                          │
└──────────────────────────────────────────┘
```

$$u : Set(A \otimes B), x : A, y : B$$
$$Dom(u)(x); (x, y) \in u$$

We shall discuss these examples in some detail in our chapter on finite sets. For
the present, we need only see map application as an example of preconditions.

7.4 Application Elimination

Almost finally, we observe that the addition of functional application with preconditions yields a conservative extension.

Suppose that Γ, Θ do not contain app. Then

$$\Gamma \vdash_{T_\pi^{apply}} \Theta \; implies \; \Gamma \vdash_T \Theta$$

This is a corollary to the following compilation lemma that shows how to remove all instances of functional application.

Lemma 75 (Compilation) *There is a translation * from T^{app} to T such that:*

1. if $\Gamma \vdash_{T_\pi^{apply}} \Theta$, then $\Gamma^* \vdash_T \Theta^*$,
2. if $\Gamma \vdash_T \Theta$, then $\Gamma \vdash_T \Theta^*$iff $\Gamma \vdash_T \Theta$,
3. if $\phi \; prop$ is Σ in $\Gamma \vdash_{T_\pi^{apply}}$,then ϕ^* *is* Σ *in* **T**,
   where Γ^* is the translated context and Θ^* is the translated judgment

Proof We proceed as the case without preconditions. In our raw syntax, we employ DeMorgan's algorithm to push all the negations through to atomic cases. In the atomic terms and their negations, we replace F as follows.

$$\alpha[F(t)/y]^* = \pi[t] \rightarrow \exists v : O \cdot R(t, v) \wedge \alpha[v/y]$$
$$(\neg\alpha[F(t)/y])^* = \pi[t] \rightarrow \exists v : O \cdot R(t, v) \wedge \neg\alpha[v/y]$$

The argument then proceeds exactly as before; i.e., the preconditions make very little difference to the argument.∎

7.5 Partial Functions

We may use this treatment of functions with preconditions to provide an account of partial application [1]. More exactly, we use the old notion of domain to furnish the precondition.

Proposition 76 *Let* **T** *be any* **TDT**. *Suppose that* **Fun**(R, I, O), *where*

$$R \triangleq [x : I, y : O \mid \psi[x, y]]$$

Then the totalization of R,

$$\widehat{R} \triangleq [x : I, y : O \mid DomR(x); R(x, y)]$$

is functional; i.e., **Fun**$(\widehat{R}, I, DomR, O)$.

This leads to the following.

Definition 77 *Suppose that* **T** *is any* **TDT**. *Let* **T**^{papppply} *be* **T** *with a new function symbol apply, governed by the following rules. For each relation R such that* **Fun**(R, I, O), *we have*

$$\frac{a : I \qquad Dom\,R(a)}{apply(R, a) : O} \qquad \mathbf{F}_1$$

$$\frac{a : I \qquad Dom\,R(a)}{R(a, apply(F, a))} \qquad \mathbf{F}_2$$

This is a special case of the above general account where the domain of the relation forms the precondition. In this way we can add application for partial functions. This will play a central role in many of our computable models and especially when we come to study programming language semantics.

This completes our account of the basic machinery of the book. We have introduced the logical framework (**TPL**), provided an account of theories of data types (**TDT**), generalized the notion of definability to arbitrary **TDT**, and introduced our notions of specification. We now turn to the development of some specific theories of data types.

References

1. Jones, C.B.. Systematic Software Development Using VDM. Prentice Hall, Inc., Englewood Cliffs, NJ, 1986.
2. Morgan. C.C. Programming from Specifications. Prentice Hall, Inc., Englewood Cliffs, second edition, 1994.
3. Potter, B., Sinclair, J., and Till, D. An introduction to formal specification and Z. Prentice Hall, Inc., Englewood Cliffs, 1991.
4. Woodcock, J. and Davies, J. Using Z: Specification, Refinement and Proof. Prentice Hall, Englewood Cliffs, NJ, 1996.

Chapter 8
Natural Numbers

Almost every programming and specification language contains a natural number type. Of course, what is associated with the language is little more than a system of type-inference rules. Nor is there a single theory of numerical data that may be associated with the natural numbers. There are many such. For one thing, the theory depends on which operations are taken as primitive and which axioms are taken to govern them. We might, for example, just select successor, addition, and multiplication as our only primitives. Or we might decide to build in all the primitive recursive functions. A second, and mathematically more significant, aspect concerns the induction principles that are adopted and, more generally, which language and encompassing theory of types provides the host for the expression of the theory. Prima facie, all such choices determine different theories of numerical data.[1]

Here we shall develop a fairly minimal theory. Its embedding in richer type theories will generate more expressive, though not necessarily mathematically stronger, ones. Indeed, the theories developed here will also be used as yardstick theories to measure the more expressive ones. More exactly, to ensure that we have a **TDT**, we must establish that it has a recursive model [1, 6], and this will be given in terms of the present theories.

Indeed, versions of the present theories have been investigated in some detail in formal number theory [5, 2]. Consequently, they will serve as a mathematical paradigm that will guide our investigation of more complex **TDT**. In addition, we shall employ them to illustrate, in miniature, a bit more about the process, and nature of specification.

8.1 A Theory of Numbers

We shall build upon the arithmetic theories outlined in earlier chapters. We begin with a minimal theory that is still mathematically useful. The language has a single type **N**, the type of natural numbers, a basic constant zero (0), a unary function

---

[1] Some are conservative extensions of each other, and some are not.

R. Turner, *Computable Models*, DOI 10.1007/978-1-84882-052-4_8,
© Springer-Verlag London Limited 2009

symbol successor ($^+$), and a single binary relation symbol, i.e., the *less-than* ordering ($<$). It is represented as follows.

$$\mathbf{Nat} = \mathbf{Th}(\mathbf{N}, \mathbf{0}, {}^+, <)$$

The first group of axioms are those listed in Chapter 3. They are essentially the rules of Peano arithmetic. The second two are the closure conditions for the type: 0 is a number, and every number has a successor. The last two insist that 0 is not the successor of any number, and that successor is injective. The third completes the Peano axioms; it is the standard numerical induction scheme restricted to the propositions of **Nat**.

$$\mathbf{N_0} \quad N \; type$$

$$\mathbf{N_1} \quad 0 : N \qquad\qquad \mathbf{N_2} \quad \frac{a : N}{a^+ : N}$$

$$\mathbf{N_3} \quad \frac{\phi[0] \quad x : N, \phi[x] \vdash \phi[x^+]}{x : N \vdash \phi[x]}$$

$$\mathbf{N_4} \quad \frac{a : N}{a^+ \neq 0} \qquad\qquad \mathbf{N_5} \quad \frac{a^+ =_N b^+}{a =_N b}$$

But these rules are not sufficient for doing arithmetic and, in particular, carrying out the reasoning required to write and argue about specifications over the natural numbers. Generally, some form of recursive relation or function is also required as a basic notion. Up to a point, it matters little which one we choose. We have chosen the ordering relation, but we could easily have started with addition. The rules for the relation are given as follows. Again, they are the standard axioms adapted to fit the present typed framework. $\mathbf{N_6}$ is the formation rule. $\mathbf{N_9}$ insists that no number is the predecessor of zero, and $\mathbf{N_7}, \mathbf{N_8}, \mathbf{N_{10}}$ together demand that a number is less than the successor of a number if and only if it is less than or equal to it.

$$\mathbf{N_6} \quad \frac{a : N \quad b : N}{a < b \; prop}$$

$$\mathbf{N_7} \quad \frac{a : N}{a < a^+} \qquad\qquad \mathbf{N_8} \quad \frac{a < b}{a < b^+}$$

$$\mathbf{N_9} \quad \frac{a < 0}{\Omega} \qquad\qquad \mathbf{N_{10}} \quad \frac{a < b^+}{a < b \vee a = b}$$

Our final group governs a new pair of quantifiers: the bounded numerical ones. These are given by the following rules, where the $\mathbf{N_{11}}$ and $\mathbf{N_{14}}$ are the formation rules for the two quantifiers and the rest are the standard introduction and elimination rules.

$$N_{11} \quad \frac{x : N \vdash \phi \; prop \qquad s : N}{\exists x < s \cdot \phi \; prop}$$

$$N_{12} \quad \frac{\phi[t/x] \qquad t < s \qquad x : N \vdash \phi \; prop}{\exists x < s \cdot \phi}$$

$$N_{13} \quad \frac{\exists x < s \cdot \phi \qquad x < s, \phi \vdash \eta}{\eta}$$

$$N_{14} \quad \frac{x : N \vdash \phi \; prop \qquad s : N}{\forall x < s \cdot \phi \; prop} \qquad\qquad N_{15} \quad \frac{x < s \vdash \phi}{\forall x < s \cdot \phi}$$

$$N_{16} \quad \frac{\forall x < s \cdot \phi \qquad t < s}{\phi[t/x]}$$

The Σ propositions include the atomic ones, including those generated by the basic function symbols and relations of **Nat**. They are then closed under conjunction, disjunction, existential quantification together with the bounded quantifiers; i.e., we take the bounded quantifiers to preserve Σ propositions.

Finally, we take the equality relation and the ordering relations to be decidable. Consequently, we add internal negations for these. i.e., we add the axiom pairs **Dec**($=$) and **Dec**($<$); i.e.,

$$N_{17} \quad \frac{n : N \quad m : N}{n \neq m \; prop} \qquad N_{18} \quad \frac{n : N \quad m : N}{n \neq m \leftrightarrow \neg(n = m)}$$

$$N_{19} \quad \frac{n : N \quad m : N}{n \not< m \; prop} \qquad N_{20} \quad \frac{n : N \quad m : N}{n \not< m \leftrightarrow \neg(n < m)}$$

And since they provide their own internal negations, bounded quantifiers preserve decidable propositions.

Proposition 78 *If $\Gamma, x : N \vdash \phi \; prop$ is decidable, then so are the following.*

$$\Gamma, y : N \vdash \forall x < y \cdot \phi \; prop$$
$$\Gamma, y : N \vdash \exists x < y \cdot \phi \; prop$$

Proof If $\overline{\phi}$ is the internal negation of ϕ, then $\neg \exists x < y \cdot \overline{\phi}$ is the internal negation of $\forall x < y \cdot \phi$. etc. ∎

A subtheory of some significance is that determined by restricting the induction principle to Σ propositions.

Definition 79 *Primitive Recursive* **Nat** *is* **Th(N, 0,$^+$, $<$)** *but where the induction scheme is restricted to Σ propositions. We shall refer to this theory as* **Nat$_\Sigma$**. [2]

---

[2] This is known to be conservative over the quantifier-free version [4].

This completes the statement of the basic theory and its variations. It is essentially pure arithmetic: Since there is only one type, the typing is redundant; i.e., the variables always range over numbers, equality always forms a proposition, and the type information in the quantifiers, and indeed most of the grammatical rules, is redundant. Consequently, most of the very flexible framework of **TPL** is wasted. However, although this theory will play a central metamathematical role later, the type **N** will also be embedded in richer and more elaborate theories of data. This will change the theory since the default option will extend the induction principle to the language of the new theory.

8.2 Numerical Specification

In this section we shall begin to explore these theories and introduce some new notions via specification. All of what follows is quite standard; what is novel is the setting and the approach, i.e., the emphasis we shall place upon specification, and eventually the role of **TPL**. Potentially, this is different to standard developments, where explicit algorithms often form the content of proofs. Here we shall only produce the specifications. But to start with, we catalogue a few of the basic properties of the system.

Proposition 80 $\forall y : N \cdot y = 0 \vee \exists u : N \cdot y = u^+$.

Proof This follows by numerical induction with the Σ induction proposition: $\phi[y]$ $y = 0 \vee \exists u : N \cdot y = u^+$. The base case is clear. Moreover, given closure for numbers, i.e., if $y = u^+$, then $y^+ = u^{++} : N$, so is the induction step. ∎

Proposition 81 *The strict ordering relation satisfies the following*

1. $\forall y : N \cdot \forall x < y \cdot x^+ < y^+$
2. $\forall y : N \cdot \forall x : N \cdot x^+ < y^+ \rightarrow x < y$
3. $\forall y : N \cdot y^+ \not< y$
4. $\forall z : N \cdot \forall y < z \cdot \forall x < y \cdot x < z$

Proof Part 1 is by induction with the proposition

$$\phi[y] = \forall x < y \cdot x^+ < y^+$$

The base step where y is zero is immediate by the axioms. For the induction step, assume that $x < y^+$. The axioms yield $x < y \vee x = y$. The second conjunct yields $x^+ = y^+$ and the axiom yields $x^+ < y^{++}$. For the first conjunct, induction gives $x^+ < y^+$. The result then follows immediately from the axioms. For part 2, let $x : N$. Then use induction with the proposition

$$\phi[y] = x < y$$

The base case is clear: if $x^+ < 1$, then by $\mathbf{N}_{10}$, $x^+ < 0 \vee x^+ = 0$, which is impossible by $\mathbf{N}_9$, and $\mathbf{N}_4$, respectively. For the induction step, assume $x^+ < y^{++}$.

Use the axioms to yield $x^+ < y^+ \vee x^+ = y^+$. The first alternative together with N_7 and the induction hypothesis yields the result. The second alternative yields the result by the axioms. For part 3, use the induction proposition

$$\phi[y] = y^+ \not< y$$

The base step is clear by axioms and the induction step follows from part 1. For part 4, let $x : N$, $y : N$. We employ the induction proposition,

$$\phi[z] = \forall y < z \cdot \forall x < y \cdot x < z$$

If $z = 0$, then the result is clear. Assume that $x < y \wedge y < z^+$. By the axioms, $y < z \vee y = z$. In the latter case we are finished. In the former, induction yields the result.■

We next introduce another basic numerical specification, the *weak* ordering relation.

Example 82 (Weak Numerical Ordering)

$$\leq \triangleq [x : N, y : N \mid x < y \vee x = y]$$

We may now introduce the maximum and minimum relations. We have already seen these, but now we can investigate them properly.

Example 83 (Maximum)

$$
\boxed{
\begin{array}{l}
\mathbf{\mathit{Max}} \\
\hline
x? : N, y? : N, z! : N \\
\hline
\\
x \leq z \wedge y \leq z \\
\wedge \\
z = x \vee z = y
\end{array}
}
$$

Example 84 (Minimum)

$$\boxed{\begin{array}{l} Min \underline{\hspace{5cm}} \\[4pt] \hline \\[-6pt] x? : N, y? : N, z! : N \\[10pt] \hline \\[-4pt] z \leq x \wedge z \leq y \\ \wedge \\ z = x \vee z = y \end{array}}$$

Proposition 85 *Maximum* and *minimum* are total functions.

Proof They are clearly functional; we show totality. Since $x \leq y \vee y \leq x$, we can without loss of generality assume the former. We then choose z to be y.∎

We now explore some properties of the weak relation. The following are some of the most obvious ones.

Proposition 86 *The weak ordering relation satisfies the following*

1. $\forall y : N \cdot \forall x \leq y \cdot x^+ \leq y^+$
2. $\forall x : N \cdot x \leq x$
3. $\forall x : N \cdot \forall y : N \cdot (x \leq y \wedge y \leq x) \rightarrow x = y$
4. $\forall x : N \cdot \forall y : N \cdot \forall z : N \cdot (x \leq y \wedge y \leq z) \rightarrow x \leq z$
5. $\forall x : N \cdot \forall y : N \cdot x \leq y \vee y \leq x$

Proof The first follows from the definition of the weak ordering and part 1 of the previous proposition. Part 2 is clear by definition. For part 3, assume $x : N, y : N$. We use induction with the proposition:

$$\phi[y] = x \leq y \wedge y \leq x \rightarrow x = y$$

If $y = 0$, then the result is clear. Assume that $x \leq y^+$. By the axioms,

$$x \leq y \vee x = y^+$$

The second disjunct yields the result. If the first disjunct holds, then we have $x \leq y \wedge y^+ \leq x$. If $y^+ = x$, $y^+ \leq y$, which is impossible by definition and the fact that $y^+ \not\leq y$. For part 4, let $x : N, y : N$. We employ the induction proposition

$$\phi[z] = x \leq y \wedge y \leq z \rightarrow x \leq z$$

If $z = 0$, then the result is clear. Assume that $x \leq y \wedge y \leq z^+$. By the axioms, and the definition,

$$y \leq z \vee y = z^+$$

In the case $y \leq z$, by induction we have $x \leq z$. By the axioms, $x < z^+$. If $y = z^+$, then $x \leq y \wedge y = z^+$; i.e. $x \leq z^+$. This completes the argument for transitivity. For part 5, let $x : N$. We employ induction with the following proposition

$$\phi[y] = x \leq y \vee y \leq x$$

The base case is immediate. Assume $x \leq y \vee y \leq x$. Assume $x \leq y$. Then by the axioms, $x \leq y^+$. If $y \leq x$, then by part 1, $y^+ \leq x^+$; i.e.

$$x^+ = y^+ \vee y^+ \leq x$$

If the first disjunct holds, then $x = y$ and so $x \leq y^+$, as required. If the second does, by the axioms, $y^+ < x \vee y^+ = x$, which yields $y^+ \leq x$.■

We have already encountered the following specifications, but we repeat them in order to more formally establish their properties.

Example 87 (Predecessor)

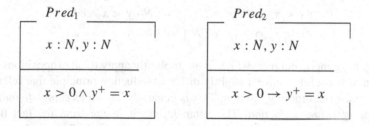

The first is a partial function but not a total one; the second is total but not functional. More explicitly,

1. $Pred_1$ is functional.
2. $Pred_2$ is total.
3. $\forall x : N \cdot \forall y : N \cdot x > 0 \rightarrow (pred_1(x, y) \leftrightarrow pred_2(x, y))$.

For part 1, let $x > 0$ and $y^+ = x$ and $z^+ = x$. Then the result is immediate. Similarly for part 2, if $x > 0$, then it follows that $\exists y : N \cdot y^+ = x$. And so it is total. The others are equally straightforward.■

But these are not total and functional. However, they are relative to the precondition version of these notions.

Example 88 (Functional Predecessor)

$$Pred$$

$$x : N, y : N$$

$$x > 0; y^+ = x$$

Relative to its preconditions, this is total and functional.

Proposition 89 TF($Pred, N, x > 0, N$).

Proof Let $x > 0$. It is immediate that $\exists! y : N \cdot y^+ = x$.∎

Finally, observe that we could have specified the bounded quantifiers.

Example 90 (Bounded Existential Quantifier) Suppose that

$$c, x : N \vdash \phi \; prop$$

Then we define

$$\exists y < x \cdot \phi \triangleq [c, x : N \mid \exists y : N \cdot y < x \wedge \phi]$$
$$\forall y < x \cdot \phi \triangleq [c, x : N \mid \forall y : N \cdot y < x \rightarrow \phi]$$

These are generic definitions; i.e., they implicitly apply to all propositions.

Often, it is useful to have a slightly different induction principle that relates directly to the strict ordering relation. This is generally known as *complete induction* or *course of values induction*. The latter derives its name from the fact that all previous values are taken into account, i.e. not just the immediate predecessor. In practice, this often proves more convenient.

Theorem 91 (Complete Induction) *For any ϕ, the following rule is derivable.*

$$\frac{x : N, \forall y < x \cdot \phi[y] \vdash \phi[x]}{x : N \vdash \phi[x]}$$

Proof Assume the premise. Let $x : N$. We use induction with the proposition

$$\forall y < x \cdot \phi[y]$$

If x is 0, then, since 0 has no predecessors, $\forall y < x \cdot \phi[y]$. Suppose that $\forall y < x \cdot \phi[y]$. Assume that $y < x^+$. Then, by the axioms, $y < x$ or $y = x$. If the former, then by induction, $\phi[y]$. If the latter, then by the main assumption, $\phi[y]$. Hence, $\forall y < x^+ \cdot \phi[y]$.∎

8.3 Recursive Specifications

Nat supports recursive specifications. And while many other theories will follow suit, arithmetic does so in a very simple and pure form. Indeed, the following will guide us in formulating recursive specifications for more elaborate theories.

Definition 92 *A recursive specification has the form*

$$R \triangleq [x : N \mid \phi[R, x]] \qquad \qquad \textbf{Rec}$$

where R occurs as a unary relation symbol in ϕ. This is taken to introduce a new relation symbol R that satisfies

$$x : N \vdash R(x) \; prop \qquad \qquad \textbf{R}_1$$

and is governed by the following versions of **R**$_2$ *and* **R**$_3$.

$$x : N, \phi[R, x] \vdash R(x) \qquad \qquad \textbf{R}_2$$

$$\frac{\forall x : N \cdot \phi[\psi, x] \rightarrow \psi[x]}{\forall x : N \cdot R[x] \rightarrow \psi[x]} \qquad \qquad \textbf{R}_3$$

for any ψ such that

$$x : N \vdash \psi[x] \; prop$$

where in the above $\phi[\psi, x]$ is obtained by replacing every occurrence of $R(x)$ by $\psi[x]$.

Examples of such specifications are easy to come by. Indeed, we cannot make much progress in the current version of arithmetic without them. The following is a recursive specification of addition.

Example 93 (Addition)

Add

$x : N, y : N, z : N$

$y = 0 \rightarrow x = z$
$\wedge$
$y \neq 0 \rightarrow \exists w : N \cdot Add(x, Pred(y), w) \wedge z = w^+$

Given this, we can specify multiplication.

Example 94 (Multiplication)

Mult

$$x : N, y : N, z : N$$

$$y = 0 \to z = 0$$
$$\wedge$$
$$y \neq 0 \to \exists w : N \cdot Mult(x, Pred(y), w) \wedge z = Add(w, x)$$

Proposition 95 *Add and Mult are functional.*

Proof Use numerical induction. Let $x : N$. For addition, to show totality, we use the induction proposition.

$$\phi[y] \triangleq \exists z : N \cdot Add(x, y, z)$$

Multiplication employs the induction hypothesis

$$\phi[y] \triangleq \exists z : N \cdot Mult(x, y, z) \blacksquare$$

Where we have established functionality, we may add application. For example, consider the relational specification of addition. Here, writing $+$ for the functional version of Add, we obtain the following version of the predicate.

$$y = 0 \to x + y = x$$
$$y \neq 0 \to \exists w : N \cdot Add(x, pred(y)), w) \wedge x + y = w^+$$

If we then use the fact that $Add(x, pred(y), x + pred(y))$, the above reduces to the standard recursion equations for addition.

$$x + 0 = x$$
$$x + y^+ = (x + y)^+$$

In this way we can obtain all the primitive recursive functions. Indeed, this can be done in **Nat$_\Sigma$**. In **Nat** exactly the Turing computable functions can be Σ-specified. We shall look at this in more detail in a later chapter devoted to recursive functions and their specifications. For now we examine some more specific examples.

The following are some fairly common relations that are facilitated by the presence of addition and multiplication. These will be used to illustrate later notions.

Example 96 (Subtraction)

$$
\begin{array}{|l|}
\hline
\quad - \\
\hline
x : N, y : N, z : N \\
\hline
x = y + z \\
\hline
\end{array}
$$

The next is a simple specification of the relation of one number being a divisor of another. Some of the next few examples will play a role when we later address issues of expressive power induced by our notion of specification [3].

Example 97 (Divides)

$$
\begin{array}{|l|}
\hline
\quad Divides \\
\hline
z : N, x : N \\
\hline
\exists u : N \cdot Mult(u, z) = x \\
\hline
\end{array}
$$

The next is a specification of common divisor.

Example 98 (Common Divisor)

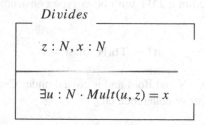

This should be enough to illustrate recursion and its applications. We shall see many more as we proceed. But before we leave recursive specifications, we must say a little about their conservative nature. Fortunately, the result for arithmetic is well known.

The addition of recursive relations to **Nat** = **Th**(**N**, **0**,$^+$, $<$) is conservative, where the conservative extension of such relational additions is immediately justified by the following result [2].

Theorem 99 (Recursion in Nat) *For each proposition ϕ, there is a proposition θ such that*

1. $\phi[\theta, x] \vdash \theta[x]$,
2. the following rule is derivable.

$$\frac{\phi[\psi, x] \to \psi[x]}{\theta[x] \to \psi[x]}$$

The result for the conservative extension for recursive schema follows immediately: Given ϕ, employ the guaranteed θ and then use the specification

$$R = [x : N \mid \theta[x]]$$

8.4 Enriched Arithmetic

In the rest of the book, the natural number type will rarely occur in isolation. More often it will be embedded in a **TDT** with other type constructors. For example, the theory

$$\textbf{Nat}^+ = \textbf{Th}(\textbf{N}, \textbf{Bool}, \otimes)$$

consists of the basic types **N** and **Bool** and is closed under Cartesian products. Typically, we shall need to prove coherence etc.

Theorem 100 *(Coherence) For the theory* **Nat**$^+$,

1. if $\Gamma \vdash \phi$, then $\Gamma \vdash \phi\ prop$,
2. if $\Gamma \vdash t : T$, then $\Gamma \vdash T\ type$,
3. if $\Gamma, x : T, \Delta \vdash \Theta$, then $\Gamma \vdash T\ type$,
4. if $\Gamma, \phi, \Delta \vdash \Theta$, then $\Gamma \vdash \phi\ prop$.

Proof The new cases involving the type **N** are all easy to check. For example, consider

$$\frac{\Gamma, x < s \vdash \phi}{\Gamma \vdash \forall x < s \cdot \phi}$$

and part 1. By induction, $\Gamma \vdash x < s\ prop$ and $\Gamma \vdash \phi\ prop$. It follows from the weakening rule that $\Gamma, x : N \vdash \phi\ prop$. By the premise and type checking applied to this new theory, $\Gamma \vdash s : N$. So we are done by the formation rule for the quantifier.∎

Within this theory we may specify the rational numbers and their associated relations and functions.

Definition 101 (Rationals) *The rational numbers are specified as*

$$Q \triangleq N \otimes N$$

We may then specify rational equality and an ordering relation.

$$=_Q \triangleq [x : Q, y : Q \mid x_1 \times y_2 = x_2 \times y_1]$$
$$<_Q \triangleq [x : Q, y : Q \mid x_1 \times y_2 < x_2 \times y_1]$$

We may also introduce rational addition in the standard way. We leave the specification of rational subtraction to the reader.

Example 102 (Rational Addition)

$+_Q$

$$f : Q, g : Q, h : Q$$

$$h_1 = (f_1 \times g_2) + (f_2 \times g_1)$$
$$h_2 = (f_2 \times g_2)$$

Finally, a notion that we shall employ later is the absolute value of the difference between two rationals (normally written as $|x - y|$) as follows.

Example 103 (Absolute Value)

$$Absolute_Q \triangleq [x : Q, y : Q, z : Q \mid x - y > 0 \rightarrow z = x - y, z = y - x]$$

This is functional and so we may write $|x - y|_Q$ for the absolute value of the difference between the inputs x and y. We shall see a more interesting example of such an embedded theory in the next chapter.

8.5 Arithmetic Interpretation

We may now provide a more precise characterization of what we intend by the term *arithmetic interpretation* . First we need a preliminary idea; i.e., we add *classes* to **Num** in the standard way:

$$\{x \cdot \phi\}$$

with the following definition for membership.

$$z \in \{x \cdot \phi\} \triangleq \phi[z] \tag{Class}$$

Since such classes can be compiled away using (Class), this is a conservative extension of **Num**. We may then be somewhat more exact about our notion of *arithmetic interpretation*.

Definition 104 *A* **TDT T** *will be said to have an* **Arithmetic Interpretation** *if there is a sound interpretation* * *from* **T** *to* **Nat** *such that*

1. *every basic relation symbol R of* **T** *is interpreted as a* Σ *relation* R^* *of* **Nat**,
2. *every type T is interpreted as a* Σ *class* T^* *of* **Nat**,
3. *every function symbol F that is functional on the types A, B of* **T** *is interpreted as a* Σ *relation of* **Nat** *such that* F^* *is a function from the class* A^* *to* B^*.

We shall use this idea to provide recursive models for our theories. We now have our yardstick theory and some of its central tools in place. While this completes our preliminary discussion of the natural numbers, throughout the book, we shall study other aspects of it, including some very particular specifications. For the present, we leave the natural numbers and turn to a central type constructor for specification, namely finite sets.

References

1. Feferman, S. Constructive theories of functions and classes. In: M. Boffa, D. van Dalen, and K. McAloon (Eds.), Logic Colloquium '78, pp. 159–225, North-Holland, Amsterdam, 1979.
2. Havel, P. Metamathematics of First Order Arithmetic. Springer-Verlag, Berlin, 1991.
3. Hayes, I.J., and Jones. C.B. Specifications are not (necessarily) harmful. Software Eng. J., 4(6), 330–339, 1990.
4. Parsons, C. On n-quantifier induction. J. Symb. Log. 37: 466–82, 1972.
5. Smorynski, C. Logical Number Theory I: An Introduction. Springer-Verlag. Amsterdam, 1991.
6. Turner, R. Weak theories of operations and types. J. Log. Comput. 6(1): 5–31, 1996.

Chapter 9
Typed Set Theory

A set, finite or otherwise, is an extensional object whose identity is determined only by its elements. Consequently, operations on them are not sensitive to the way they are presented. Sets offer a level of abstraction that facilitates the specification of programs and systems that allows implementation details to be hidden. In particular, unlike lists, the order in which the elements is given is irrelevant. Whatever the merit and clarity of such considerations, they have given some notion of set a central place in most approaches to specification.

A relatively standard notion of set forms the core of the Z specification language. This is inspired by standard set theory (e.g., [4, 5, 7]). More modest notions of set are based upon hereditarily finite sets [1] or bounded set theory [6]. Inspired by the latter, we shall study the type constructor for finite sets. This forms one of the central type constructors of **VDMSL** [2].

More specifically, we shall follow the approach to the foundations of specification taken in [8]. That paper develops a theory of data types based upon numbers, finite sets, and products (**CST** for core specification theory). And this will form the basis of the present approach and, indeed, the topic of the present chapter.

9.1 CST

The underlying set theory is an inductive theory of sets in the sense that the type will be given in terms of a closure condition and an induction principle. As with **Nat**, this theory will provide a rich source of examples to illustrate the specification process and lead to our first example of a computable model (next chapter).

The minimal theory we shall study (**CST**) is given as follows.

$$\textbf{CST} \triangleq \textbf{Th}(\textbf{N}, \textbf{CP}, \textbf{Set})$$

In words, the theory is generated from type **N** via Cartesian products and the type constructor **Set**: Given a type T, **Set**(T) generates the type of finite sets of type T. The latter has a basic constant $\emptyset_T$ for the empty set of type T and the operator $\circledast_T$ for element insertion: given an element of type T and a set of type T, it returns a

R. Turner, *Computable Models*, DOI 10.1007/978-1-84882-052-4_9,
© Springer-Verlag London Limited 2009

new set with the element added. The only basic relation is set membership ($\in_T$). We shall also include set quantifiers $\exists x \in_T s \cdot \phi$ and $\forall x \in_T s \cdot \phi$. Where the context makes matters clear, we shall drop all the type subscripts.

The rules for the theory are given as follows. We assume the rules for Cartesian products and numbers. This leaves us to deal with the rules for the new type constructor. The first group of rules includes its formation, introduction, and elimination rules.

$$S_0 \quad \frac{T \; type}{Set(T) \; type}$$

$$S_1 \quad \frac{T \; type}{\emptyset_T : Set(T)} \qquad S_2 \quad \frac{a : T \qquad b : Set(T)}{a \circledast_T b : Set(T)}$$

$$S_3 \quad \frac{\phi[\emptyset] \qquad \forall x : T \cdot \forall y : Set(T) \cdot \phi[y] \rightarrow \phi[x \circledast_T y]}{\forall x : Set(T) \cdot \phi[x]}$$

The next two are the rules for element addition. The first insists that sets contain no duplicates and the second that the order of occurrence of elements is irrelevant. These give sets their extensional character.

$$S_4 \quad \frac{a : T \qquad b : Set(T)}{a \circledast (a \circledast b) = a \circledast b} \qquad S_5 \quad \frac{a : T \qquad b : T \qquad c : Set(T)}{a \circledast (b \circledast c) = b \circledast (a \circledast c)}$$

The next group provides the rules for membership. The first is the formation rule. S_9 insists that the empty set has no elements, while the rest collectively demand that element insertion adds a single new element of the appropriate type.

$$S_6 \quad \frac{a : T \qquad b : Set(T)}{a \in_T b \; prop}$$

$$S_7 \quad \frac{a : T \qquad b : Set(T)}{a \in a \circledast b}$$

$$S_8 \quad \frac{a \in c \qquad b : T \qquad c : Set(T)}{a \in b \circledast c}$$

$$S_9 \quad \frac{a \in \emptyset_T}{\Omega} \qquad S_{10} \quad \frac{a \in b \circledast c}{a = b \vee a \in c}$$

The rules for the set quantifiers parallel the numerical ones. Aside for the formation rules themselves, we shall drop the subscripts.

$$S_{11} \quad \frac{\Gamma, x : T \vdash \phi \; prop \qquad \Gamma \vdash s : Set(T)}{\Gamma \vdash \exists x \in_T s \cdot \phi \; prop}$$

$$S_{12} \quad \frac{\phi[t/x] \qquad t \in s}{\exists x \in s \cdot \phi}$$

$$S_{13} \quad \frac{\Gamma \vdash \exists x \in s \cdot \phi \qquad \Gamma, x \in s, \phi \vdash \eta}{\Gamma \vdash \eta}$$

$$S_{14} \quad \frac{\Gamma, x : T \vdash \phi \ prop \qquad \Gamma \vdash s : Set(T)}{\Gamma \vdash \forall x \in_T s \cdot \phi \ prop}$$

$$S_{15} \quad \frac{\Gamma, x \in s \vdash \phi}{\Gamma \vdash \forall x \in s \cdot \phi} \qquad S_{16} \quad \frac{\forall x \in s \cdot \phi \qquad t \in s}{\phi[t/x]}$$

Equality and set membership are taken to be decidable. Again, these rules are now standard; i.e., we add the rules **Dec(=)**, **Dec(∈)**; i.e.,

$$S_{17} \quad \frac{a : Set(T) \qquad b : Set(T)}{a \neq b \ prop} \qquad S_{18} \quad \frac{a : Set(T) \qquad b : Set(T)}{a \neq b \leftrightarrow \neg(a = b)}$$

$$S_{19} \quad \frac{a : T \qquad b : Set(T)}{a \notin b \ prop} \qquad S_{20} \quad \frac{a : Set(T) \qquad b : Set(T)}{a \notin b \leftrightarrow \neg(a \in b)}$$

To complete the description of the theory, we introduce its class of Σ propositions.

Definition 105 *Suppose that*

$$c \vdash_{CST} \phi \ prop$$

Then ϕ is Σ if it is an atomic proposition that is generated by the basic function symbols and relations of **CST** *or it is obtained by closure under conjunction, disjunction, typed existential quantification, together with the set quantifiers.*

This concludes the rules of the theory **CST**. The following is easy to establish: The negations are supplied by the alternative set quantifier.

Proposition 106 *The set quantifiers preserve decidability.*

We again observe that the type-checking and coherence theorems remain intact. There is little that is novel in the new cases; they parallel those for numbers and so we leave the details as an exercise. In addition to those for **TPL** and products, we have the following additional type-checking properties.

Theorem 107 (Type Checking) *In* **CST** *we have*

1. $\Gamma \vdash a \in_T b \ prop$ iff $\Gamma \vdash a : T$ and $\Gamma \vdash b : Set(T)$,
2. $\Gamma \vdash a \circledast_T b : Set(T)$ iff $\Gamma \vdash a : T$ and $\Gamma \vdash b : Set(T)$,
3. $\Gamma \vdash Qx \in_T s \cdot \phi \ prop$ iff $\Gamma \vdash s : Set(T)$ and $\Gamma, x : T \vdash \phi \ prop$.

This completes our statement of the theory. In terms of the number of rules, it is quite a large theory. But it is well motivated and the rules are easy to grasp.

9.2 Elementary Properties

To begin with, we document a few elementary properties. They are all well known and some of them parallel those for the natural numbers.

Proposition 108 *For each type T, we have*

$$\forall y : Set(T) \cdot y = \emptyset_T \vee \exists u : T \cdot \exists v : Set(T) \cdot y =_T u \circledast v$$

Proof We use set induction with the following induction proposition.

$$\phi[y] \triangleq y = \emptyset_T \vee \exists u : T \cdot \exists v : Set(T) \cdot y = u \circledast v$$

The base case where $y = \emptyset_T$ follows immediately. The induction step is also immediate from the induction assumption: If $y = u \circledast v$, where $u : T$ and $v : Set(T)$, then the result is immediate. ∎

Proposition 109 *The following are provable. For each type A,*

1. $\forall y : Set(A) \cdot \forall x : A \cdot x \circledast y \neq \emptyset$,
2. $\forall y : Set(A) \cdot \forall x \in y \cdot x \circledast y = y$,
3. $\forall z : Set(A) \cdot \forall x \in z \cdot \exists y : Set(A) \cdot x \notin y \wedge z = x \circledast y$.

Proof For part 1, since $x \in x \circledast y$, from $\mathbf{S_9}$, it follows that $x \circledast y \neq \emptyset$. Part 2 follows by induction with the following induction proposition.

$$\phi[y] = \forall x \in y \cdot x \circledast y = y$$

The base case follows from $\mathbf{S_9}$: nothing is in the empty set. For the induction step, assume that $u : A$, $v : Set(A)$, and $y = u \circledast v$. By $\mathbf{S_5}$, $x \circledast (u \circledast v) = u \circledast (x \circledast v)$. Also, by $\mathbf{S_7}$ and the assumption that $x \in y$, we have $x = u$ or $x \in v$. If the former, we are done by $\mathbf{S_4}$. If $x \in v$, then by induction, $x \circledast v = v$ and so $u \circledast (x \circledast v) = u \circledast v = y$. For part 3, we also employ induction with the induction formula set to

$$\phi[z] = \forall x \in z \cdot \exists y : Set(A) \cdot x \notin y \wedge z = x \circledast y$$

As with the last case, the base case is immediate from $\mathbf{S_9}$. For the induction step, assume $u : A$, $v : Set(A)$ and $z = u \circledast v$. If $u \in v$, we are finished by induction. If

$u \notin v$, let $x : A$ and $x \in u \circledast v$. If $x = u$, then, put the required $y = v$; if $x \in v$, then by induction we may assume

$$\exists w : Set(A) \cdot x \notin w \wedge v = x \circledast w$$

We then put the required y to be $u \circledast w$.∎

9.3 Subsets and Extensionality

Sets are extensional. In this section we provide the definition and establish that it is so. To express matters, we need to introduce the following notions. The first specification introduces the notion of subset.

Example 110 (Subset) Let T be a type. It follows that

$$x : Set(T), y : Set(T) \vdash \forall z \in x \cdot z \in y \; prop \qquad (1)$$

Then we may specify

$$
\begin{array}{|l|}
\hline
\quad \subseteq_T \quad \\
\hline
x : Set(T), y : Set(T) \\
\hline
\forall z \in x \cdot z \in y \\
\hline
\end{array}
$$

Note that, in $\subseteq_T$, the type symbol is part of the metanotation. The specification is generic only in the sense that it introduces a new relation symbol for each type that satisfies (1) above. For example, N, $Set(N)$, $Set(N \otimes Set(N))$, and indeed any type generated from N via $\otimes$ and **Set**. But it is not object-level polymorphism. However, we shall later introduce a more systematic form of object level polymorphism.

As before, we shall, as in the case of equality, often drop the subscript, i.e., employ a metalanguage convention to avoid it. The same applies to all the relations and functions we shall introduce.

Proposition 111 *In* **CST***, subset is decidable.*

Proof We specify the internal negation as follows.

$$
\begin{array}{|l|}
\hline
\quad \not\subseteq_T \quad \\
\hline
x : Set(T), y : Set(T) \\
\hline
\exists z \in x \cdot z \notin y \\
\hline
\end{array}
$$
∎

We can now establish the most important property of the *sets* of the theory, namely their *extensional* nature. We first require a definition.

Definition 112 (Extensional Equality) *Let T be a type. Then*

$$x : Set(T), y : Set(T) \vdash x \subseteq_T y \wedge y \subseteq_T x \; prop$$

So it is legitimate to specify

$$\equiv_T \triangleq [x : Set(T), y : Set(T) \mid x \subseteq_T y \wedge y \subseteq_T x]$$

We shall write this in infix notation as $x \equiv_T y$. Again, we have:

Proposition 113 *Extensional equality is decidable*

The following is the statement of extensionality: If two sets have the same elements, then they are equal.

Proposition 114 (Extensionality) *Let T be a type. Then*

$$x : Set(T), y : Set(T) \vdash x =_T y \leftrightarrow x \equiv_T y$$

Proof We have only to prove the direction from right to left. Let $x : Set(T)$. We employ induction on y with the following induction proposition.

$$\phi[y] = x \equiv y \rightarrow x = y$$

Assume $y = \emptyset$. If $x = \emptyset$, we are finished by the equality rules. But if $x \neq \emptyset$, then $x = u \circledast v$ for some u, v, which is impossible by $\mathbf{S}_9$. This completes the base case. So assume that y has the form $u \circledast v$. We have to show that

$$x \equiv u \circledast v \rightarrow x = u \circledast v$$

If $u \in v$, by induction, we are finished. If $u \notin v$, since $u \in x$, by the last proposition (part 3), $x = u \circledast v'$ for some set v', $u \notin v'$. Since $u \circledast v$ and $u \circledast v'$ are extensionally equal, $u \notin v$ and $u \notin v'$, it follows that v and v' are extensionally equal. By induction, $v = v'$. So $u \circledast v = u \circledast v'$.∎

9.4 New Sets from Old

Axiomatic theories are by their nature rather minimal. In particular, the type $Set(T)$ consists of the sets constructed from the empty set by adding an element of T to an existing element of $Set(T)$. Consequently, the only given way of constructing new sets in the base theory is via the insertion function. In contrast, the representation of sets in current specification languages is much richer. For example, most admit as set constructors the standard Boolean operations on sets such as union and intersection and many also support the formation of subsets. Our objective is to build up some infrastructure for the theory and at the same time illustrate the whole process of specification in **CST**.

Our first rather simple operation is the opposite of our basic operation of addition. It subtracts an element from a set.

Example 115 (Subtraction)

$$
\begin{array}{|l}
\ominus_T \\
\hline
\begin{array}{l}
u : Set(T), x : T \\
z : Set(T)
\end{array} \\
\hline
\begin{array}{l}
x \in u \rightarrow z \circledast x = u \\
\wedge \\
x \notin u \rightarrow z = u
\end{array}
\end{array}
$$

Here we adopt the convention that inputs are on the first line and outputs on the second.

One of the most useful and elementary ways of forming a finite set is by enumerating its elements.

Example 116 (Pairing) Let T be a *type*. Then we may specify

$$
\begin{array}{|l}
Pair_T \\
\hline
\begin{array}{l}
x : T, y : T \\
z : T
\end{array} \\
\hline
z = x \circledast y \circledast \emptyset
\end{array}
$$

This is an explicit functional specification that is functional relative to the first two arguments. We shall write $Pair_T(x, y)$ as $\{x, y\}$, where we drop any reference to the type. We shall also write $\{x\}$ for $Singleton_T(x)$; i.e.,

Example 117 (Singleton)

$$
Singleton_T \triangleq [x : T, y : Set(T) \mid y = x \circledast \emptyset]
$$

More generally, pairing can be generalized to allow the enumeration of any finite number of elements $\{x_1, x_2, ..., x_n\}$ from the same type.

This is one of the basic set constructors of standard set theory. Another is simple *union*. In **VDM** this is taken to be a basic operator.

Example 118 (Simple Union) Let T be a *type*. Then

$$x : Set(T), y : Set(T), z : Set(T) \vdash \forall u \in z \cdot u \in x \vee u \in y \; prop$$
$$x : Set(T), z : set(T) \vdash \forall u \in x \cdot u \in z \; prop$$
$$y : Set(T), z : set(T) \vdash \forall u \in y \cdot u \in z \; prop$$

Hence, it is legitimate to specify

$$\cup_T$$

$$x : Set(T), y : Set(T)$$
$$z : Set(T)$$

$$\forall u \in z \cdot u \in x \vee u \in y$$
$$\forall u \in x \cdot u \in z$$
$$\forall u \in y \cdot u \in z$$

Proposition 119 *Simple union is total and functional.*

Proof Functionality follows from extensionality: There cannot be two z's. For totality we prove by set induction with the proposition

$$\phi[x] = \exists z : Set(T) \cdot (\forall u \in z \cdot u \in x \vee u \in y) \wedge (\forall u \in x \cdot u \in z) \wedge (\forall u \in y \cdot u \in z)$$

The base step and the induction step are both straightforward to verify.∎

So we may legitimately view union as a new function symbol. We shall write this in the usual way as $a \cup b$. This is a new set constructor that satisfies the following.

$$\frac{a : Set(T) \qquad b : Set(T)}{a \cup_T b : Set(T)} \qquad \frac{a : Set(T) \qquad b : Set(T)}{\forall x : T \cdot x \in a \cup_T b \leftrightarrow x \in a \vee x \in b}$$

Indeed, we could take this as a new primitive operation on sets governed by these rules. Observe that membership is still preserved in its decidable state in the sense that the following is provable.

$$\frac{a : Set(T) \qquad b : Set(T)}{\forall x : T \cdot \neg(x \in a \cup_T b) \leftrightarrow x \notin a \wedge x \notin b}$$

So given that membership for the components is decidable, so is membership for their union. This will apply to all the constructs we consider.

We proceed with our catalogue of set constructors; i.e., we immediately follow the lead of standard set theory and generalize matters.

Definition 120 (Generalized Union) *Let T be a type. Then we can legitimately specify*

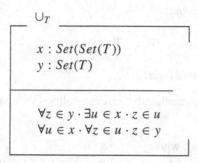

$$\cup_T$$

$$x : Set(Set(T))$$
$$y : Set(T)$$

$$\forall z \in y \cdot \exists u \in x \cdot z \in u$$
$$\forall u \in x \cdot \forall z \in u \cdot z \in y$$

Proposition 121 *Generalized union is total and functional.*

Proof Functionality follows from extensionality. For totality, we prove by set induction:

$$\phi[x] = \forall z \in y \cdot \exists u \in x \cdot z \in u \wedge \forall u \in x \cdot \forall z \in u \cdot z \in y$$

If x is the empty set, then we put $y = x$. Suppose that x has the form $x' \circledast y'$, where $x' : Set(A)$ and $y' : Set(Set(A))$. Assume inductively $\phi[y']$. Let w' be the guaranteed set. Then the required set for x is given, via simple union, as $x' \cup w'$. By extensionality, and the predicate itself, functionality follows. ■

We now come to a way of forming sets that allows the formation of *sets* by forming the subset of a given set that satisfies some property i.e. sets given via a scheme of *separation*. Notice that this operation is generic with respect to the included proposition; i.e., we uniformly introduce a new function symbol for each proposition.

Example 122 (Separation) Suppose that

$$\Gamma, x : T \vdash \psi \; prop$$

And suppose that ψ is decidable. We then specify

$$Sep_T^{\psi}$$

$$\Gamma, u? : Set(T), v! : Set(T)$$

$$\forall z \in v \cdot z \in u \wedge \psi[z]$$
$$\wedge$$
$$\forall z \in u \cdot \psi[z] \rightarrow z \in v$$

Observe that the decidability of ψ renders the predicate of the schema Σ. More-over, we have

Proposition 123 *Suppose that*

$$\Gamma, x : T \vdash \psi \; prop$$

Then Sep_ψ is functional and total.

Proof Functionality is immediate by extensionality. For totality, we need to show that

$$\Gamma, u : Set(T) \vdash \sigma[u], \text{ where}$$
$$\sigma[u] = \exists v : Set(T) \cdot (\forall x \in v \cdot x \in u \land \psi[x]) \land \forall x \in u \cdot \psi[x] \to x \in v$$

where $u \notin FV(\psi)$. We use induction with $\sigma[u]$ as the induction proposition. If u is the empty set, we take v to be u. If u has the form $w \circledast y$, by induction, we may assume $\psi[y]$. Let z be the guaranteed set for y. We take the required set to be

$$\left\{ \begin{array}{l} w \circledast z \text{ if } \psi[w] \\ z \qquad \text{if } \neg\psi[w] \end{array} \right\}$$

It is easy to see that this set satisfies the requirement. This completes the induction.∎

As a result, we can consistently add a new set constructor, actually one for each proposition, that we shall write in standard notation as follows.

$$\{x \in u \cdot \psi[x]\}$$

This satisfies

$$\frac{\Gamma, x : T \vdash \psi \; prop}{\Gamma, u : Set(T) \vdash \{x \in u \cdot \psi[x]\} : Set(T)}$$

We may now employ separation in specifications. In particular, using separation, we can introduce the *intersection* operation on sets as a direct function specification.

Example 124 (Intersection)

$$\cap_T$$

$u? : Set(T), v? : Set(T), z! : Set(T)$
$z = \{x \in u \cup v \cdot x \in u \land x \in v\}$

This is clearly functional and total. Furthermore, with generalized union and separation in place, we can introduce *generalized intersection* by direct function specification. Again, we shall use the same name.

Example 125 (Generalized Intersection)

$$
\begin{array}{|l|}
\hline
\bigcap_T \\
\hline
x? : Set(Set(T)),\ y! : Set(T) \\
\hline
y = \{z \in \bigcup x \cdot \forall u \in x \cdot z \in u\} \\
\hline
\end{array}
$$

We have now covered most of the constructors of standard set theory, but one or two are still missing. The next is a central operator of that theory. It guarantees the existence of a set that contains all the subsets of a given set.

Example 126 (Power Set)

$$
\begin{array}{|l|}
\hline
Pow_T \\
\hline
v : Set(T),\ w : Set(Set(T)) \\
\hline
\emptyset \in w \wedge (\forall z \in v \cdot \forall u \in w \cdot z \circledast u \in w) \\
\wedge \\
\forall z \in w \cdot z \subseteq v \\
\hline
\end{array}
$$

This moves us up a type level. We show that Pow is a total function. To facilitate this, we first specify a subsidiary function. This takes a set of sets (v) and an element (u) and outputs a set of sets (z) whose members are the elements of v with u inserted.

Proposition 127 *The following is a total function.*

$$
\begin{array}{|l|}
\hline
In_T \\
\hline
u? : T,\ v? : Set(Set(T)),\ z! : Set(Set(T)) \\
\hline
\forall x \in v \cdot u \circledast x \in z \\
\wedge \\
\forall y \in z \cdot \exists x \in v \cdot y = u \circledast x \\
\hline
\end{array}
$$

Proof Fix $u : A$. We first prove, by induction on v,

$$\sigma[v] \triangleq \exists z : Set(Set(A)) \cdot \forall x \in v \cdot u \circledast x \in z$$

In the case where v is empty, we put $z = \{\{u\}\}$. So assume that v has the form $y \circledast w$. By induction,

$$\exists z' : Set(Set(A)) \cdot \forall x \in w \cdot u \circledast x \in z'$$

The required set for $y \circledast w$ is then $(u \circledast y) \circledast z'$. Hence,

$$\exists z : Set(Set(A)) \cdot \forall x \in v \cdot u \circledast x \in z$$

Now, given this set, the set required for the result is given by separation as

$$\{y \in z \cdot \exists x \in v \cdot y = u \circledast x\}$$

Functionality follows from the extensional nature of sets.∎

We can now return to the proof that the power-set constructor defines a total function.

Proposition 128 *Pow is total and functional.*

Proof Functionality is immediate given extensionality for sets. Totality is the non-trivial part. We prove the result by induction, where the induction proposition is the following.

$$\phi[x] = \exists y : Set(Set(A)) \cdot \forall w : Set(T) \cdot w \in y \leftrightarrow w \subseteq x$$

If $x = \emptyset_A$, then the required set is $\emptyset_{Set(A)}$. If $x = u \circledast v$, then there are two cases. If $v = \emptyset$, then the required set is $\{\emptyset, \{u\}\}$. Otherwise, let v' be guaranteed by induction, i.e., the power set of v. Now put the power set of $u \circledast v$ to be $In(u, v') \cup v'$.∎

By analogy with the type operator, we shall write this set constructor as:

$$Set(u)$$

It satisfies

$$\forall x : Set(A) \cdot \forall w : Set(A) \cdot w \in Set(x) \leftrightarrow w \subseteq x$$

This completes our catalogue of simple set constructors. We now turn to some that employ more of the structure of **CST**.

9.5 Set-Theoretic Relations

Since we have already used the term *relation* for specifications, some confusion may arise over the use of the term for finite set-theoretic relations, so to avoid possible ambiguity, where necessary, we shall be explicit and use the term *set-theoretic relation*.

Definition 129 (Binary Relations) *The type of **set-theoretic binary relations** on the types A and B is defined as:*

$$Set(A \otimes B)$$

*More generally, the type of **n-place relations** on the types $A_1, ..., A_n$ is defined as*

$$Set(A_1 \otimes ... \otimes A_n)$$

The type constructor *Set* has a set-theoretic analogue, namely the power-set constructor on sets. The same is true of Cartesian products. The following provides our specification of the product operation on sets.

Definition 130 (Cartesian Product for Sets)

Fun $\otimes$

$$x? : Set(A), y? : Set(A), z! : Set(A \otimes B)$$

$$(\forall u \in x \cdot \forall v \in y \cdot (u, v) \in z)$$
$$\wedge$$
$$(\forall w \in z \cdot \exists u \in x \cdot \exists v \in y \cdot w = (u, v))$$

To show that this is a total function, we need the following, which is a collection principle for finite sets.

Proposition 131 (Collection) *Suppose that*

$$y : A, z : B \vdash \psi[y, z] \text{ prop}$$

Then

$$\forall x : Set(A) \cdot (\forall y \in x \cdot \exists z : B \cdot \psi[y, z]) \rightarrow \exists w : Set(B) \cdot \forall y \in x \cdot \exists z \in w \cdot \psi[y, z]$$

Proof We use set induction with the hypothesis

$$\phi[x] = (\forall y \in x \cdot \exists z : B \cdot \psi[y, z]) \rightarrow \exists w : Set(B) \cdot \forall y \in x \cdot \exists z \in w \cdot \psi[y, z]$$

If x is the empty set, then the result is immediate since the antecedent is vacuously true. Assume $x = u \circledast v$. Assume $(\forall y \in x \cdot \exists z : B \cdot \psi[y, z])$ and $\phi[v]$ and let

$$w' : Set(B) \wedge \forall y \in x \cdot \exists z \in w' \cdot \psi[y, z]$$

be the guaranteed set for v. We also know from the premise of $\phi[v]$ that for some $z : B, \psi[u, z]$. We then have the required set for x as $z \circledast w'$. ∎

Proposition 132 $\otimes$ *is a total function.*

Proof We have to show it is total and functional. Any two sets that satisfy the predicate as outputs, by extensionality, must be the same set. Hence, it is functional. For totality, let $x : Set(A), u \in x, y : Set(B)$. Then we know $u : A$. Moreover, if $v \in y$, then $v : B$. Hence, by the axioms for Cartesian products, we have: $\forall v \in y \cdot (u, v) : A \otimes B$. By collection,

$$\exists z : Set(A \otimes B) \cdot \forall v \in y \cdot (u, v) \in z$$

Hence, $\forall u \in x \cdot \exists z : Set(A \otimes B) \cdot \forall v \in y \cdot (u, v) \in z$. By collection again,

$$\exists z' : Set(Set(A \otimes B)) \cdot \forall u \in x \cdot \exists z \in z' \cdot \forall v \in y \cdot (u, v) \in z$$

Hence,

$$\exists z' : Set(Set(A \otimes B)) \cdot \forall u \in x \cdot \forall v \in y \cdot \exists z \in z' \cdot (u, v) \in z$$

Finally, we define the required set by separation.

$$\{z \in \cup z' \cdot \exists u \in x \cdot \exists v \in y \cdot z = (u, v)\} \blacksquare$$

Thus, we have set constructors corresponding to both of our type constructors. Note that we are using the same symbol for both sets and types, i.e. *Set* and $\otimes$. We shall now specify and explore some operations on relations that occur in the so-called Z toolkit and provide infrastructure for specification. The following we have seen before, but we have yet to say much about its properties.

Example 133 (Domain for Sets)

$$\begin{array}{|l}
\hline
\textit{Dom} \\
\hline
u : Set(A \otimes B), v : Set(A) \\
\hline
\forall x \in v \cdot \exists y \in u \cdot x = y_1 \\
\wedge \\
\forall y \in u \cdot y_1 \in v \\
\hline
\end{array}$$

Example 134 (Range for Sets)

$$Ran$$

$$u : Set(A \otimes B), v : Set(B)$$

$$\forall x \in v \cdot \exists y \in u \cdot x = y_2$$
$$\wedge$$
$$\forall y \in u \cdot y_2 \in v$$

Proposition 135 *Dom and Ran are total and functional.*

Proof Functionality is clear by extensionality. For totality, we illustrate with the domain. We show that

$$\forall u : Set(A \otimes B) \cdot \exists v : Set(A) \cdot \forall x \in v \cdot \exists y \in u \cdot x = y_1 \wedge \forall y \in u \cdot y_1 \in v$$

We use induction with the following induction proposition.

$$\phi[u] \triangleq \exists v : Set(A) \cdot \forall x \in v \cdot \exists y \in u \cdot x = y_1 \wedge \forall y \in u \cdot y_1 \in v$$

If u is empty, the result is clear. Suppose $u = x' \circledast y'$. Assume the result for y' where y'' is the guaranteed element of $Set(A)$. The required element for u is then $x_1' \circledast y''$.∎

We introduce the following new function symbols by direct specification. They also form part of the Z toolkit, and are all given by direct functional specifications.

We can focus upon part of the domain or part of the range of a set-theoretic relation by considering a subset. This is captured in the following specification.

Example 136 (Domain and Range Restriction) Let A,B, be types.
   We may then specify

$$\lhd \triangleq [u : Set(A \otimes B), v : Set(A), w : Set(A \otimes B) \mid w = \{x \in u \cdot x_1 \in v\}]$$
$$\rhd \triangleq [u : Set(A \otimes B), v : Set(B), w : Set(A \otimes B) \mid w = \{x \in u \cdot x_2 \in v\}]$$

We then have

Proposition 137 *The above specifications are total and functional.*

Finally, we introduce the following notion that forms a crucial part of the **VDM** toolkit. This we have also seen.

Example 138 (Maps)

$$Map \triangleq [z : Set(A \otimes B) \mid \forall x \in z \cdot \forall y \in z \cdot x_1 = y_1 \rightarrow x_2 = y_2]$$

Using preconditions, we may specify an application operator for maps. The following is a specification of map application with the precondition that the argument to the map is in its domain. The alert reader will recall that we introduced this earlier as an example of a specification with preconditions. We are now in a position to be more wholesome. We leave the reader to show that it is functional.

Example 139 (Map Application)

$$
\begin{array}{|l}
\hline
\quad Mapapp \underline{\hspace{4cm}} \\
\hline
\quad u : Set(A \otimes B), v : A, w : B \\
\hline
\\
\quad Dom(u)(v); (v, w) \in u \\
\hline
\end{array}
$$

This almost completes our chapter on the data type of sets. We shall later revisit it in order to consider recursive operations on sets. But to finish this initial skirmish, we need to consider its arithmetic interpretation.

9.6 Arithmetic Interpretation

We indicate how to model the whole of **CST** in **Num**. The reader who is prepared to take the recursive model for granted can skip this section without losing contact with the main conceptual development of the book. This applies to all of the recursive models in the book.[1]

There are several stages.

Stage 1 We add *classes* to **Num** as previously indicated.

$$\{x \cdot \phi\}$$

We interpret types of **CST** as classes. Relative to an interpretation of the basic functions and relations, because it provides an interpretation of types as classes, and so an interpretation of type quantification, it implicitly provides an interpretation of the whole **TPL**.

For **CST**, we need to be more specific and show how to interpret its types.

---

[1] These sections require some familiarity with formal number theory.

Stage 2 The pair operation on numbers can be defined as

$$(x, y) \triangleq \frac{(x + y)^2 + 3x + y}{2}$$

The pairing operation $()$ is a bijective primitive recursive function on numbers. Consequently, there are $\mathbf{Num}_\Sigma$ representable functions π_1, π_2 that support this bijective pairing. The type constructor for Cartesian products is then represented via classes.

$$A \otimes B \triangleq \{z \cdot \exists x \cdot \exists y \cdot x : A \wedge y : B \wedge z = (x, y)\}$$

Stage 3 We interpret sets as numbers by defining membership and inclusion on numbers. There are many ways of achieving this, but we follow [3]. We first state a few results of formal arithmetic from [3].

Lemma 140 *For each x, y, there are unique $u \le y$, $v \le 1$, $w \le 2^x$ such that*

$$y = u \times 2^{x+1} + v \times 2^x + w$$

We may then specify set membership.

Example 141 (Set Membership)

$$
\frac{\in}{
\boxed{
\begin{array}{l}
x : N, y : N \\[2mm]
\hline \\[-1mm]
\exists u \le y \cdot \exists w < 2^x \cdot y = u \times 2^{x+1} + 2^x + w
\end{array}
}
}
$$

This provides our representation of membership between numbers. Note that under this, zero represents the empty set. The following provides the existence of the *insertion* operation; more generally, the union operation. Again, a proof can be found in [3].

Proposition 142

$$\forall x \cdot \forall y \cdot \exists! z \cdot \forall u \cdot u \in z \leftrightarrow u = x \vee u \in y$$

Hence, in arithmetic we may conservatively add a new functional operator $\circledast$ that, together with $\in$, satisfies our rules for sets. Finally, we use the recursion operator on numbers to define the type of sets as a recursive predicate on numbers.

Example 143 (Set)

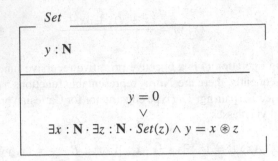

All the rules of **CST** are sound under this interpretation. Hence, we have

Theorem 144 CST *has a recursive model.*

References

1. Barwise, J. Admissible Sets and Structures. Springer-Verlag, Berlin. 1975.
2. Dawes, J. The VDM-SL Reference Guide. Pitman, London, 1991.
3. Havel, P. Metamathematics of First Order Arithmetic. Springer-Verlag, Berlin, 1991.
4. Krivine, J.L. Introduction to Axiomatic Set Theory. Springer-Verlag, New York, 1971.
5. Potter, M.D. Sets: An Introduction. Clarendon Press, Oxford, 1990.
6. Sazonov, V.Y. On bounded set theory. Invited talk at the 10th international Congress on Logic, Methodogogy and Philosophy of Science, Florence, August 1995. In: Volume 1: Logic and Scientific Method, pp. 85–103. Kluwer Academic Publishers, Dordrecht, 1997.
7. Turner, R. Type inference for set theory. Theor. Comput. Sci. 266(1–2): 951–974. 2001.
8. Turner, R. The foundations of specification. J. Log. Comput., 15: 623–662, Oct. 2005.

Chapter 10
Systems Modeling

We now have enough formal machinery to tackle the specification of a *system* with several interrelated parts. The main function of the present case study is to provide a mathematically simple example of a computable model. The kind of structure that will emerge from this case study consists of a suite of interconnected specifications [2, 1]. However, the model will not constitute a very exciting example of a computable model. It is typical of the kind of system that emerges from software systems. There is very little of real foundational or mathematical interest. That is not the main forté of software systems. Indeed, we shall have to wait some time to see more sophisticated examples, i.e., ones that possess more theoretical interest.

However, although a toy system, it will be sufficient to illustrate a range of issues about the nature of the specification process and of computable model construction. For example, it will point to the need for more infrastructure for specifications: how to build complex ones from simple ones. In addition, we shall demonstrate how the theory enables us to formally address questions such as the *consistency* and *completeness* of the model.

10.1 The Requirements

We begin with a rather simple description that provides the top-level requirements of a system and will be employed as a guide to the construction of the formal model. Although this is a well-worn example, it is sufficient to illustrate some general points about computable modeling.

1. A *library* comprises a *stock* of *copies* of *books* and a community of *registered readers*.
2. There may be several *copies* of the same *book*.
3. At any time a certain number of *copies* are *issued* to *registered readers*; the remainder are *shelved*.
4. The system must record which *copies* are *issued* to which *readers*.
5. Copies can be *borrowed* and *returned* by *registered readers*.
6. New copies can be added to the *stock*, i.e., *catalogued*.
7. New readers can be *registered*.

R. Turner, *Computable Models*, DOI 10.1007/978-1-84882-052-4_10,
© Springer-Verlag London Limited 2009

Observe that in these requirements we have italicized various items. The representation of these will form the backbone of the model. However, among them there is a distinction to be drawn. There are two different kinds of italicized items: *types* and *operations*. The former are the types of information held about the system's state. The following pieces of information are present.

Shelved	Issued	Copies
Registered	Books	Reader

Operations act upon the system and may change its state. In the present study we have the following operations.

Borrow	Return	Register	Catalogue

We may now begin the process of model building. We shall work in the theory **CST** extended with some atomic types. Corresponding to the above distinction are two stages to the process. The first involves constructing a model of the *state,* and the second involves modeling the *operations*.

10.2 The State

First observe that some of the data items are given structure in the requirements definition and some are not. For example, although in reality books have a title, an author, a publication date, etc., since nothing in the requirements definition requires or refers to this information, we abstract away from it and call the type of such items *Book*. This can be treated as an atomic type since it has no structure. There may be several *copies* with the same title, author etc., (RD2); the type *Copy* is the type of actual books. Finally, the type *Reader* represents the type of all possible readers of the library system. Such atomic data types are given no further structure in the requirements definition.[1]

With these singled out, we can proceed to develop a model of the database, the underlying *state* of the system. This must be a model of all possible configurations of the system: It must capture the general structure of the state not its content at any given time. A little reflection on the requirements definition suggests that there are several components of the state. These can be informally described as follows:

1. the type of copies currently Shelved (RD3,5),
2. the type Issued records the information about which copies are issued to which readers (RD4),
3. the type of readers currently Registered (RD1),
4. the type of the Stock (RD6).

---

[1] All the atomic types could be modeled as numbers, but for pedagogical reasons , we take them as new atomic types.

At any point, the current state of the system must record which copies are currently shelved, i.e., the current set of copies. This will vary as the database is updated. Consequently, this component of the state is modeled as follows:

$$Shelved \triangleq Set(Copy)$$

Next consider the registered readers. At any point, some readers will be registered and some will not. Since we need to model the general structure of the state, and not its content at a particular time, this component takes a similar shape to the first.

$$Reg \triangleq Set(Reader)$$

The stock component must link copies and authors, so it consists of set-theoretic relations.

$$Stock \triangleq Set(Copy \otimes Book)$$

This brings us to the final component, namely that linking readers and the copies on loan.

$$Issued \triangleq Set(Copy \otimes Reader)$$

We now have all four type components in place. We now need to reflect on any global constraints that need to be imposed upon the database of the system. To achieve this, we can distinguish between two different components of the whole database: that containing the information about the actual stock and that containing the information about the readers and the copies they have on loan. We deal with the stock information first. We ought to insist that no copy can be both issued and shelved (implicit in RD3). Moreover, a copy should only be issued to registered readers (RD3, RD1) and every copy should either be issued or on the shelves (RD3). This leads to the following specification of this part of the state, where we use names for the variables.

Definition 145 (Library Items)

$Libraryitems$

$shelved : Shelved$
$issued : Issued$
$stock : Stock$

$Map(stock)$
$Map(issued)$
$Dom(issued) \cap shelved = \Phi$
$Dom(issued) \cup shelved = Dom(stock)$

The stock component must link each copy to its author, title, etc., and no copy is to be associated with more than one book. Hence, the stock has to be a map. Similarly, no copy should be issued to more than one reader and so the issued component has to be a map.

For the component of the state that records which readers have which copies on loan, we should note that items should not be loaned to readers who are not registered. This leads to the following specification.

Definition 146 (Library Reader)

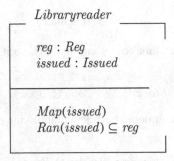

$$Libraryreader$$

$$reg : Reg$$
$$issued : Issued$$

$$Map(issued)$$
$$Ran(issued) \subseteq reg$$

The full state might be introduced as the conjunction of these two.

Definition 147 (State)

$$Library \triangleq Libraryitems \cup Libraryreader$$

which yields, after some logical simplification, the following schema.

$$Library$$

$$shelved : Shelved$$
$$issued : Issued$$
$$stock : Stock$$
$$reg : Reg$$

$$Map(stock)$$
$$Map(issued)$$
$$Dom(issued) \cap shelved = \Phi$$
$$Dom(issued) \cup shelved = Dom(stock)$$
$$Map(issued)$$
$$Ran(issued) \subseteq reg$$

10.3 Operations

First consider the operation of *Registering* a new reader. This simply adds a new reader to the state. This operation only changes the *Reg* component; no other component is affected, and so we only need to refer to it.

Definition 148 (Register)

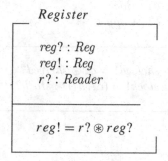

$$
\begin{array}{l}
Register \\
\hline
reg? : Reg \\
reg! : Reg \\
r? : Reader \\
\hline
reg! = r? \circledast reg?
\end{array}
$$

The operations of *returning* and *borrowing* copies can be represented as follows. Here both the shelved and issued components come into play.

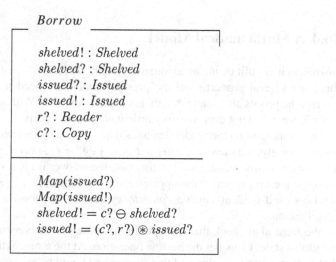

$$
\begin{array}{l}
Borrow \\
\hline
shelved! : Shelved \\
shelved? : Shelved \\
issued? : Issued \\
issued! : Issued \\
r? : Reader \\
c? : Copy \\
\hline
Map(issued?) \\
Map(issued!) \\
shelved! = c? \ominus shelved? \\
issued! = (c?, r?) \circledast issued?
\end{array}
$$

Finally, the operation *Catalogue* affects the shelved and stock components.

Definition 149 (Catalogue)

$$
\begin{array}{|l}
\hline
\textit{Catalogue} \\
\hline
\begin{array}{l}
\textit{shelved!} : \textit{Shelved} \\
\textit{shelved?} : \textit{Shelved} \\
\textit{stock?} : \textit{Stock} \\
\textit{stock!} : \textit{Stock} \\
\textit{b?} : \textit{Book} \\
\textit{c?} : \textit{Copy}
\end{array} \\
\hline
\begin{array}{l}
\textit{shelved!} = \textit{c?} \circledast \textit{shelved?} \\
\textit{stock!} = (\textit{c?}, \textit{b?}) \circledast \textit{stock?}
\end{array} \\
\hline
\end{array}
$$

A great deal is unsatisfactory about this specification. Nevertheless, its simplicity is a virtue in that we can employ it to illustrate a range of important general issues about system specification.

10.4 A Mathematical Model

Insofar as it is built inside an axiomatic system, this a mathematical model. Indeed, there are several properties of the present model that need to be established. Of course, the proofs are simple, but that is beside the point. Without the mathematical setting, we could not even sensibly articulate these properties.

One constraint on the model demands that the state is not vacuous. To put matters more precisely, are there $x \in Shelved$, $y \in Reg$, $w \in Issued$, $z \in Stock$ such that all the constraints are satisfied? In this case the answer is clear since we can choose all to be the empty set of the appropriate type. However, in general, things might not be so self-evident. Such a *consistency* check must form a part of any system specification.

We must also check that the operations preserve the constraints imposed upon the global state. Consider the borrow operation. At the moment there is no guarantee that it does; there is no demand that the reader should be registered. We can remedy this as follows. Now notice that we have included the registration component of the state.

Definition 150 (Borrow)

Borrow

shelved! : Shelved
shelved? : Shelved
issued? : Issued
issued! : Issued
reg? : Reg
reg! : Reg
r? : Reader
c? : Copy

$r? \in Reg?;$
$shelved! = c? \ominus shelved?$
$issued! = (c?, r?) \circledast issued?$
$reg! = reg?$

This is a very clumsy operation and cries out for some more infrastructure, which we shall return to later.

We might also wish to check whether our operations are total and functional. Suppose that having specified an *operation*, we want to check that all possible configurations of the state are covered, i.e., that the operation is *total*. First consider again the following reformulation of the original register operation.

Example 151 (Register)

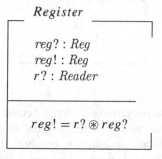

Register

reg? : Reg
reg! : Reg
r? : Reader

$reg! = r? \circledast reg?$

This is total. But there are two possible scenarios that are blurred in it. In one the incoming reader is already registered, and in the other she is not. Even though no

harm is done by the crude form, i.e. the state constraints are preserved, it is still un-
acceptable since we would not wish to perform an update when the reader is already
registered. We can get over this by specifying the two situations separately. The first
specification below covers the case where the reader is not already registered and
the second where she is. In the first we update the registered component, while in
the second we leave it as it is.

Definition 152 (Register$^+$)

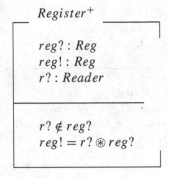

Definition 153 (Register$^-$)

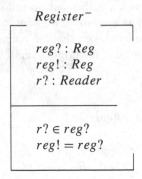

However, neither of these operations is *total*, whereas the original was. We could
define a more sophisticated version of the original that covered both cases, but,
having got this far, it would be convenient to combine them in some way. For this
we may use schema union (they have the same type), which provides the union of
the two pieces of information.

$$Fullregister \triangleq Register^+ \cup Register^-$$

This results in the schema.

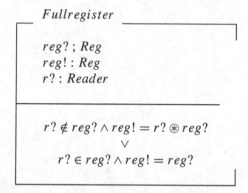

$$Fullregister$$

$$reg? ; Reg$$
$$reg! : Reg$$
$$r? : Reader$$

$$r? \notin reg? \land reg! = r? \circledast reg?$$
$$\lor$$
$$r? \in reg? \land reg! = reg?$$

We shall examine an algebra of schemata later. For the present, we note that this is a step in the direction of modularity: New specifications can be built from old ones.

Although a very trivial model both mathematically, and in terms of its size as a software specification, and while technically every specification is a computable model, this is the first example that consists of a suite of interrelated specifications. There are many other design and mathematical issues thrown up by this example, but we shall deal with them later.

References

1. Potter, B., Sinclair, J., and Till, D. An introduction to formal specification and Z. Prentice Hall, Inc., Englewood Cliffs, 1991.
2. Woodcock, J. and Davies, J. Using Z: Specification, Refinement and Proof, Prentice Hall, Englewood Cliffs, NJ, 1996.

Chapter 11
A Type of Types

Current specification languages support some form of generic/polymorphic specification. For example, **VDM** supports a form of generic function specification for explicitly defined functions. In particular, it allows type variables to occur in function definitions. And Z has its notion of generic schema. In this chapter we consider how our theories might be enriched with some such notions.

In our present treatment of types, we must rely on the metanotation of type terms to indicate genericity in type definitions. For example, where

$$x_1 : T_1, ..., x_n : T_n \vdash T \ type$$

then the following is a specification of subset.

$$\begin{array}{|l} \hline \quad \subseteq_T \\ \hline x_1 : T_1, ..., x_n : T_n \\ x : Set(T), y : Set(T) \\ \hline \forall z \in x \cdot z \in y \\ \hline \end{array}$$

This provides a form of generic specification where the above specifies a whole family of subset relations that is parameterized by T. However, T is not an objectlevel type variable, so officially we need to spell out the fact that

$$x_1 : T_1, ..., x_n : T_n \vdash T \ type$$

and include $x_1 : T_1, ..., x_n : T_n$ as part of the declaration context of the schema. This is necessary because there are no objectlevel variables that range over types. And this is so because there is no *type of types*. Consequently, we cannot bind or quantify over them. This is a substantial limitation on the expressive power of our theories. In this chapter we remedy this. Our aim is a treatment that is more

R. Turner, *Computable Models*, DOI 10.1007/978-1-84882-052-4_11,
© Springer-Verlag London Limited 2009

mathematically honest and uniform, a treatment where type declarations are on a par with others and one that brings us to the the brink of a uniform form of polymorphic specification [5].

11.1 The Type type

We add a type of types to our theories. This enables types to become first class objects in the sense that we can quantify over them and reason about their properties in the object language.

Definition 154 *Let* **T** *be any* **TDT**. *A **universe of types** for* **T** *is a type (called **type**) governed by the following rules.*

$$U_1 \quad \textbf{\textit{type}} \; type \qquad U_2 \quad \frac{T \; type}{T : \textbf{\textit{type}}} \qquad U_3 \quad \frac{T : \textbf{\textit{type}}}{T \; type}$$

$$U_4 \quad \frac{A : \textbf{\textit{type}} \qquad B : \textbf{\textit{type}}}{A \neq_{type} B \; prop} \qquad U_5 \quad \frac{A : \textbf{\textit{type}} \qquad B : \textbf{\textit{type}}}{\neg(A =_{type} B) \leftrightarrow A \neq_{type} B}$$

According to the first three rules, the elements of **type** are exactly the types of the hosting theory **T** plus **type** itself. The last two rules govern equality for types and insist that it is decidable; i.e., via U_4 and U_5, we have added type inequality ($\neq_{\text{type}}$), where type inequality is taken to generate a Σ proposition. This is justified as follows. As objects, types are intensional; i.e., they are not to be identified in terms of their sets of elements. More precisely, equality for types is a primitive notion that is not taken to be identical with extensional membership; i.e., being the same type is not identified with having the same elements. So we are free to take the equality of the type to be decidable.

A second aspect of the type **type,** one that is made possible by the intensional nature of types, concerns its reflexive nature; i.e., **type** is a member of itself. Such inclusions usually result in inconsistency and lead to a layering of types; i.e., a first layer of types and then a second layer where the universe of the first layer lives, and so on. But we are not forced to layer our types in the sense of a predicative theory; we may treat types in an impredicative way. This often leads to inconsistency [1, 6, 7, 2]. However, since types are intensional objects, the impredicativity is that inherent in standard computability theory.[1] Indeed, there is a recursive model of the theory where the types are modeled as the codes of recursively enumerable sets and **type** is their recursive enumeration (cf. [3]). We shall return to this later.

An alternative approach to a type of types is to allow the rules of type formation to generate an inductive type. For example, we might adopt the inductive type whose elements are the types of **Th(N,DP,Set)**. This type would be determined by the following rules.

---

[1] In the arithmetic interpretation they will be modeled as codes of recursively enumerable sets and the universe will be the code of their enumeration.

N : **type**

x : **type**, y : **type** $\vdash x \otimes y$: **type**

x : **type** $\vdash Set(x)$: **type**

$$\frac{\phi[\mathbf{N}] \quad \forall x : \textbf{type} \cdot \forall y : \textbf{type} \cdot \phi[x] \wedge \phi[y] \rightarrow \phi[x \otimes y] \quad \forall y : \textbf{type} \cdot \phi[Set(x)]}{\forall x : \textbf{type} \cdot \phi[x]}$$

However, if the type **type** is taken not to be in this inductive listing of types, a layering of the types would result, i.e., a second layer where the type of the first layer lives etc. We shall not explore this option further. We merely indicate its possibility for further possible exploration. Indeed, we shall return to the topic of induction and recursion later in the book.

11.2 Dependent Types

In any theory with the type **type**, type terms may contain variables. For example, the following is now a valid sequent.

$$u : \textbf{type}, v : \textbf{type}, x : u, y : v \vdash (x, y) : u \otimes v$$

Indeed, we devised **TPL** to allow room for this possibility. Because of this dependency, we have already seen that we may introduce a standard generalization of Cartesian products (i.e., *dependent Cartesian products*, **DP**), that exploits it. This type constructor is determined by the following rules that generalize those for simple products. In them, $x \notin FV(T)$. Simple products are a special case where $x \notin FV(S)$.

$$\mathbf{D_0} \quad \frac{x : T \vdash S \, type}{\Sigma x : T \cdot S \, type}$$

$$\mathbf{D_1} \quad \frac{x : T \vdash S \, type \qquad a : T \qquad b : S[a/x]}{(a, b) : \Sigma x : T \cdot S}$$

$$\mathbf{D_2} \quad \frac{p : \Sigma x : T \cdot S}{\pi_1(p) : T} \qquad \mathbf{D_3} \quad \frac{p : \Sigma x : T \cdot S}{\pi_2(p) : S[\pi_1(p)]}$$

$$\mathbf{D_4} \quad \frac{p : \Sigma x : T \cdot S}{p = (\pi_1(p), \pi_2(p))]}$$

The notion of one type being dependent on another may be illustrated by the following example derivation.

Example 155 (Type Dependency) The following is valid.

$$u : \textbf{type}, v : \textbf{type} \vdash u \otimes v : \textbf{type}$$

Given this, by D_0, we have

$$u : \textbf{type} \vdash \Sigma v : \textbf{type} \cdot u \otimes v : \textbf{type}$$

And finally, again by D_0, we have

$$\Sigma u : \textbf{type} \cdot \Sigma v : \textbf{type} \cdot u \otimes v : \textbf{type}$$

The following provides an example of how a context can contain dependencies that enable later type assignments to depend for their legitimacy on earlier ones.

Example 156 (Dependency in Contexts)

$$u : \textbf{type}, x : u, y : u \vdash x =_u y \ prop$$

The type **type** supports such dependency and so we shall include them as part of any theory that contains the type **type**.

The type-checking proposition continues to hold. As does the coherence theorem. But now we have the following modification.

Theorem 157 $c \vdash \Sigma x : T \cdot S \ type \ iff \ c, x : T \vdash S \ type.$

This completes the statement of the theory; for any theory

$$\textbf{Th}(O_1, ..., O_k)$$

the universe extension will take the shape

$$\textbf{Th}(O_1, ..., O_k, \textbf{type}, \textbf{DP})$$

We shall now demonstrate the utility of such extensions.

11.3 Dependent Specifications

While specifications in such theories still take the following general form:

$$R \triangleq [x_1 : A_1, ..., x_n : A_n \mid \phi], \qquad\qquad \textbf{Spec}$$

they may also display a form of dependency in the declaration. The following example illustrates this; the second and third declarations depend for their legitimacy on the first.

Example 158 (Dependent Relations)

$$\subseteq$$

$$
\boxed{
\begin{array}{l}
u : \textbf{type}, \, x : Set(u), \, y : Set(u) \\[1.5em]
\hline \\[-0.5em]
\forall z \in x \cdot z \in y
\end{array}
}
$$

Because of this, we can no longer use simple products to reduce general specifications to unary ones. To rewrite them as unary schemata, we must employ dependent products. More explicitly, a specification of the form **Spec** is now rewritten as a unary schema, as follows.

$$R \triangleq \left[x : \Sigma x_1 : A_1 \cdot \dots \cdot \Sigma x_{n-1} : A_{n-1} \cdot A_n \mid \phi[x_1, \dots, x_n] \right]$$

For example, subset would now take the following shape.

Example 159 (Subset)

$$\subseteq$$

$$
\boxed{
\begin{array}{l}
x : \Sigma u : \textbf{type} \cdot Set(u) \otimes Set(u) \\[1.5em]
\hline \\[-0.5em]
\forall z \in x_2 \cdot z \in x_3
\end{array}
}
$$

Hence, for theoretical purposes, specifications can still be taken to have the previous simple form; i.e.,

$$R \triangleq [x : T \mid \phi] \qquad\qquad \textbf{Spec}$$

11.4 Polymorphic Specifications

We motivated the inclusion of a universe of types by reference to the need to be wholesome and honest about the treatment of generic specifications; i.e., the simultaneous specifications of whole families of relations. We may now more formally indicate how this is to be achieved. We illustrate with the simplest case. By definition,

$$R \triangleq [u : \textbf{type}, x : T[u] \mid \phi[u, x]]$$

introduces a relation that satisfies the following.

$$\frac{A : \textbf{type} \qquad\qquad a : T[A]}{R(A, a) \leftrightarrow \phi[A, a]}$$

This provides a form of explicit polymorphism for specifications. We illustrate matters with a sequence of examples where, to begin with, we employ some theory-neutral ones.

We may specify the *polymorphic equality* relation via the following schema.

Example 160 (Polymorphic Equality)

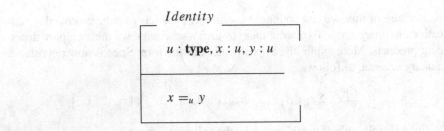

The following provides a polymorphic version of relational composition.

Example 161 (Composition) Let R, S be any given relations such that

$$u : \textbf{type}, v : \textbf{type}, x : u, y : v \vdash R(u, v, x, y) \ prop$$
$$v : \textbf{type}, w : \textbf{type}, y : v, z : w \vdash S(v, w, y, z) \ prop$$

Then we may specify their **composition** via the following schema.

```
 ┌─ Comp ──────────────────────────────────────────────────┐
 │  u : type, w : type, x : u, z : w                         │
 │ ─────────────────────────────────────────────────────    │
 │  ∃v : type · ∃y : v · R(u, v, x, y) ∧ S(v, w, y, z)       │
 └──────────────────────────────────────────────────────────┘
```

We can make matters a little more palatable by introducing **type** variables X, Y, U, V, W to range over elements of **type**. This is achieved by the following conventions.

$$\exists X \cdot \phi[X] \triangleq \exists u : \textbf{type} \cdot \phi[u/X]$$
$$[x : T[X] \mid \phi[X]] \triangleq [u : \textbf{type}, x : T[u] \mid \phi[u/X]]$$

We shall often, though not always, employ this form. For example, using it, composition takes the following, more succinct form.

Example 162 (Composition) Let R, S be any given relations such that

$$u : \textbf{type}, v : \textbf{type}, x : u, y : v \vdash R(u, v, x, y) \; prop$$
$$v : \textbf{type}, w : \textbf{type}, y : v, z : w \vdash S(v, w, y, z) \; prop$$

Then we may specify their **composition** via the following schema.

$Comp_{X,Z}$

$$x : X, z : Z$$

$$\exists Y \cdot \exists y : Y \cdot R(X, Y, x, y) \wedge S(Y, Z, y, z)$$

Our next example yields polymorphic versions of the domain and range of a given relation. Let R be any binary relation such that

$$u : \textbf{type}, v : \textbf{type}, x : u, y : v \vdash R(u, v, x, y) \; prop$$

Then we may specify the **domain** and **range** of R as follows.

Example 163 (Polymorphic Domain)

$Dom R_U$

$$x : U$$

$$\exists V \cdot \exists y : V \cdot R(U, V, x, y)$$

Example 164 (Polymorphic Range)

$Ran R_V$

$$y : V$$

$$\exists U \cdot \exists x : U \cdot R(U, V, x, y)$$

These are now more wholesome versions of our original generic style of specification. Types are now part of the theory and the looseness of the metatheoretic style has been justified. For example, unpacked so that the full type information is displayed, the first takes the following shape.

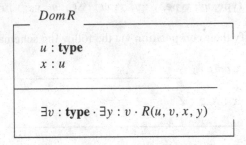

This completes our general examples, i.e., those that are not theory-dependent. We now turn to some that require some host theory.

11.5 Polymorphic Set Theory

We motivated the inclusion of polymorphism by reference to the need to make our typed set theory more wholesome in its genericity. We can now make good on this promise. We have seen a good number of set-theoretic specifications that are informally generic. Here we revisit some of them with our type of types to hand. *Polymorphic* **CST** is given as the following theory.

$$\mathbf{PCST} \triangleq \mathbf{Th(N, DP, Set, type)}$$

Here we may define explicit versions of all the set-theoretic operators. We begin with the one with which we began this chapter.

Example 165 (Polymorphic Subset)

$$
\begin{array}{|l|}
\hline
\subseteq \\
\hline
u : \textbf{type}, \, x : Set(u), \, y : Set(u) \\
\hline
\forall z \in x \cdot z \in y \\
\hline
\end{array}
$$

Using our conventions, this can be written more succinctly as follows.

Example 166 (Polymorphic Subset)

$$\boxed{\begin{array}{l} \underline{\subseteq_U} \\[4pt] x : Set(U), y : Set(U) \\ \hline \\ \forall z \in x \cdot z \in y \end{array}}$$

In this form, it is not a million miles away from the original, except that U is now an object-level variable ranging over **type**.

The following example also has some theoretical significance. It introduces a notion of extensional equivalence for sets.

Example 167 (Extensional Equivalence)

$$\equiv_U \triangleq [x : Set(U), y : Set(U) \mid x \subseteq_U y \wedge y \subseteq_U x]$$

Our next few examples illustrate the specification of new polymorphic set constructors.

Example 168 (Polymorphic Pairing)

$$Pair_U \triangleq [x? : U, y? : U, z! : Set(U) \mid z = x \circledast_U y \circledast_U \emptyset_U]$$

Similarly, we may introduce a polymorphic version of generalized union. This is identical to the original, but it is more mathematically complete.

Example 169 (Generalized Union)

$$\boxed{\begin{array}{l} \underline{\cup_U} \\[4pt] x : Set(Set(U)), y : Set(U) \\ \hline \\ \forall z \in y \cdot \exists w \in x \cdot z \in w \\ \wedge \\ \forall w \in x \cdot \forall z \in w \cdot z \in y \end{array}}$$

Like its original, this generic version is also functional. But it is functional in both of its arguments. More exactly, we have

$$\forall u : \textbf{type} \cdot \forall x : Set(Set(u)) \cdot \exists! y : Set(u) \cdot \cup_u(x, y)$$

Similarly, we can specify a polymorphic version of power set.

Example 170 (PowerSet)

$$
\boxed{\begin{array}{l}
\underline{Pow_U} \\[4pt]
v : Set(U),\, w : Set(Set(U)) \\[8pt]
\hline \\[-6pt]
\emptyset \in w \wedge (\forall z \in v \cdot \forall u \in w \cdot z \circledast u \in w) \\
\wedge \\
\forall z \in w \cdot z \subseteq v
\end{array}}
$$

This generic version is also functional in both of its arguments. More exactly, we have the following.

$$\forall u : \textbf{type} \cdot \textbf{TF}(Pow_u, Set(u), Set(Set(u)))$$

Finally, we specify a polymorphic version of separation. This is slightly different in that it still employs a metavariable over propositions.

Example 171 (Polymorphic Separation) Suppose that

$$c, u : \textbf{type}, x : u \vdash \psi \; prop$$

We then specify

$$
\boxed{\begin{array}{l}
\underline{Sep^{\psi}} \\[4pt]
c, u : type, x : Set(u),\, y : Set(u) \\[8pt]
\hline \\[-6pt]
\forall z \in y \cdot z \in x \wedge \psi[z] \\
\wedge \\
\forall z \in x \cdot \psi[z] \rightarrow z \in y
\end{array}}
$$

All these are syntactically close to the originals. But they are now to be interpreted as object-level specifications where each is a single specification, not a whole family that is located in the metalanguage.

11.6 Specifications and Types

The conservative extension result for relations generalizes directly to the present framework. But we have to do a little work in the case of functional application. Let

$$\mathbf{T} = \mathbf{Th}(O_1, ..., O_k, \mathbf{type}, \mathbf{DP})$$

Theorem 172 (Conservative Extension) *Suppose that* Γ, Θ *do not contain app. Then*

$$\Gamma \vdash_{\mathbf{T^{app}}} \Theta \ implies \ \Gamma \vdash_{\mathbf{T}} \Theta$$

As before, this is a corollary to the following compilation lemma that demonstrates how to remove all instances of functional application.

Lemma 173 (Compilation) *There is a translation* $*$ *from* $\mathbf{T^{app}}$ *to* $\mathbf{T}$ *such that:*

1. if $\Gamma \vdash_{\mathbf{T^{app}}} \Theta$, then $\Gamma^* \vdash_{\mathbf{T}} \Theta^*$,
2. if $\Gamma \vdash_{\mathbf{T^{app}}} \Theta$, then, where Θ does not contain R, $\Gamma \vdash_{\mathbf{T}} \Theta^* \leftrightarrow \Theta$,
3. if ϕ *prop* is Σ in $\mathbf{T^{app}}$, then ϕ^* *is* Σ *in* $\mathbf{T}$,
   where Γ^* is the translated context and Θ^* is the translated judgment.

Proof We proceed as in the original proof. Suppose that F has been introduced as a new function symbol via the following rules.

$$\frac{i : I}{F(i) : O} \qquad \frac{i : I}{R(i, F(i))}$$

We define $*$ on the rules of formation to remove just one instance of F. But there is a new complication that arises from the fact that type terms can contain function symbols. Suppose that

$$\frac{i : \mathbf{type}}{F(i) : \mathbf{type}}$$

The are two different cases: one where the type term starts with a variable binder (e.g., Σ) and one where it does not. While the latter is a special case of the former, for pedagogical reasons we treat both cases. For the latter, we translate as follows. We illustrate matters with the binary case.

$$\forall z : O(A, B[F(i)/v]) \cdot \phi[z]$$
$$\implies$$
$$\exists v : \mathbf{type} \cdot F(i, v) \wedge \forall z : O(A, B[v]) \cdot \phi[z]$$
$$\exists z : O(A, B[F(i)/v]) \cdot \phi[z]$$
$$\implies$$
$$\exists v : \mathbf{type} \cdot F(i, v) \wedge \exists z : O(A, B[v]) \cdot \phi[z]$$

Where a variable binder is involved, we have to allow that the argument to the function may contain the corresponding bound variable.

$$\forall z : \Sigma x : A \cdot B[x, F(i[x])] \cdot \phi[z] \Rightarrow$$
$$\forall x : A \cdot \exists v : \textbf{type} \cdot F(i[x], v) \land \forall y : B[x, v] \cdot \phi[(x, y)]$$

$$\exists z : \Sigma x : A \cdot B[x, F(i[x])] \cdot \phi[z] \Rightarrow$$
$$\exists x : A \cdot \exists v : \textbf{type} \cdot F(i[x], v) \land \exists y : B[x, v] \cdot \phi[(x, y)]$$

In both cases the rules are routine to verify.■

11.7 Arithmetic Interpretation

Finally, we show how any such theory is to be interpreted in **Nat**. We shall assume some knowledge of formal number theory and, in particular, Gödel numbering. But we shall supply references to the literature. The reader who is prepared to take the recursive model for granted can skip this section without losing contact with the main conceptual and technical development of the book. Once more, we split matters into several steps.

Stage 1: Types as arithmetic classes

The types of the base theory are represented as Σ classes, i.e., the theory without the type **type**. For example, we know how to do this for the base theory that includes numbers and is closed under products and sets.

Stage 2: Gödel numbering

Given a representation of the types of any base theory as Σ classes, we take matters one stage further and Gödel code the propositions (wff) and the Σ classes. In what follows $\lceil \phi[x_1, ..., x_n] \rceil$ will denote the code of the propositions $\phi[x_1, ..., x_n]$ and $\lceil \{x \cdot \phi[x, x_1, ..., x_n]\} \rceil$ will denote the code of the class $\{x \cdot \phi[x, x_1, ..., x_n]\}$. There are endless ways of achieving this, but we only require one with the standard properties of providing an isomorphism between the codes and the classes.

Stage 3: Class membership

We represent class membership in such codes as a Σ relation of **Nat** [4, 8]. Our major tool is the following.

Theorem 174 (Nat$_\Sigma$) *Let* $n > 0$ *be given. There is a Σ-definable relation* $Sat_n(x, x_1, ..., x_n)$ *such that for each Σ wff ϕ of* **Nat** *with exactly the free variables* $x_1, ..., x_n$ $(n > 0)$.

$$Sat_n(\lceil \phi \rceil, x_1, .., x_n) \leftrightarrow \phi[x_1, .., x_n]$$

where $\lceil \phi \rceil$ *is the code of* ϕ.

We then define membership on the codes of Σ classes as follows.

$$x \in y \triangleq \mathrm{Sat}_{n+1}(\lceil \phi \rceil, x, x_1, ..., x_n)$$

where $y = \lceil \{x \cdot \phi[x, x_1, ..., x_n]\} \rceil$.

Stage 4: The type **type**

To complete the interpretation of the theory, we have to interpret the type **type**: The type **type** is interpreted as the code of the recursively enumerable class of all the codes of recursively enumerable classes with membership in **type** interpreted as $\in$. Hence,

Theorem 175 *If* **Th**($O_1, ..., O_k$) *is a conservative extension of* **Nat**, *then so is* **Th**($O_1, ..., O_k, type$, **DP**).

This gives us justification to include a type **type** in any such theory. And most of the time we shall do so. Here not only have we provided a relative consistency proof for any such theory, but we have also shown that any such theory has a recursive model.

References

1. Barendregt, H.P. Lambda calculus with types. In S. Abramsky, D.M. Gabbay, and T.S.E. Maibaum, (Eds), Handbook of Logic in Computer Science, pp. 118–310, Oxford University Press, Oxford, 1992.
2. Couquand, T. An analysis of Girard's paradox. Proc. IEEE Symp. Log. Comp. Sci. 227–236, 1986.
3. Feferman, S. Constructive theories of functions and classes. In: M. Boffa, D. van Dalen, and K. McAloon (Eds.), Logic Colloquium '78, pp. 159–225, North-Holland, Amsterdam, 1979.
4. Havel, P. Metamathematics of First Order Arithmetic. Springer-Verlag, New York, 1991.
5. Reynolds, J.C. Introduction to polymorphic lambda-calculus. In: G. Huet (Ed.), Logical Foundations of Functional Programming, pp. 77–86. Addison-Wesley, Reading, MA, 1990.
6. Russell, B.A.W. Mathematical logic as based on the theory of types Ameri. J. of Math. 30: 222–262.
7. Russell, B.A.W. Letter to Frege. In: J. van Heijenoort, (ed.). From Frege to Gödel, pp 124-1250. Harvard University Press, Cambridge, MA, 1967.
8. Smorynski, C. Logical Number Theory I: An Introduction. Springer-Verlag, New York, 1991.

Chapter 12
Schemata

We have now introduced theories of data types generated by type constructors such as numbers, Cartesian products, and finite sets. In addition, we considered the polymorphic impact of a universal type. In the process we introduced our notion of specification and explored its use as a means of constructing simple computable models. However, all the theories introduced so far are limited in that they do not support any form of *higher-order* specification, i.e., contexts where specifications themselves may be declared in specifications and their properties and relations articulated in the predicate part of a specification. To put matters differently, presently, schemata [3], [6] are not objects of the theory; they do not have types. But this seems necessary for our framework to provide a general foundation for specification, and certainly for the construction of more theoretically oriented computable models. In particular, any set-theoretic modeling that employs higher-order functions will require more sophisticated notions than those explicitly available in **CST**.

In this chapter we consider the addition of a type constructor whose members are the schemata themselves. In terms of its type structure, this will move us closer to the expressive power of Russell's simple type theory [2], where our schemata replace the properties of the latter. But it will differ from this theory in that our schemata are restricted to Σ ones, whereas the properties of simple type theory are not. Indeed, generally our theories are closer to the intensional theories of Feferman [1] and [4], [5]. Moreover, our theory still has a recursive model.

12.1 A Theory of Relations

Our proposed theory of schemata is a theory of relations; i.e., the notation

$$R \triangleq [x_1 : T_1, ..., x_n : T_n \mid \phi] \qquad \text{(Schema)}$$

introduces a new relation symbol into the language. But now, rather than taking it as a definition, we axiomatically characterize such relations and their types by the following rules. In what follows, ϕ is Σ.

R. Turner, *Computable Models*, DOI 10.1007/978-1-84882-052-4_12,
© Springer-Verlag London Limited 2009

$$\mathbf{Sc_0} \quad \frac{T\ type}{\mathbf{S}(T)\ type}$$

$$\mathbf{Sc_1} \quad \frac{x : T \vdash \phi\ prop}{[x : T \mid \phi] : \mathbf{S}(T)}$$

$$\mathbf{Sc_2} \quad \frac{s : \mathbf{S}(T) \qquad\qquad t : T}{s(t)\ prop}$$

$$\mathbf{Sc_3} \quad \frac{x : T \vdash \phi\ prop \qquad t : T \qquad \phi[t/x]}{[x : T \mid \phi](t)}$$

$$\mathbf{Sc_4} \quad \frac{x : T \vdash \phi\ prop \qquad t : T \qquad [x : T \mid \phi](t)}{\phi[t/x]}$$

$$\mathbf{Sc_5} \quad \frac{x : T \vdash \phi\ prop}{[x : T \mid \phi] =_{\mathbf{S}(T)} [y : T \mid \phi[y/x]]}$$

Here **S** is the new type constructor; i.e., $\mathbf{S}(T)$ is the *type of schema of type T*. To distinguish them from the schema specifications themselves, we shall call these objects *schema relations* (or just *schemata*). $\mathbf{Sc_0}$ is the formation rule: $\mathbf{S}(T)$ is a type if T is. $\mathbf{Sc_1}$ informs us that (where ϕ is Σ) a schema relation $[x : T \mid \phi]$ has type $\mathbf{S}(T)$. The variable x in the declaration is bound and, by $\mathbf{S_5}$, we may rename bound variables. $\mathbf{Sc_2}$ enables the use of schemata to form Σ propositions via application; i.e., the application of schema relations to their arguments yields Σ propositions. $\mathbf{Sc_3}$ and $\mathbf{Sc_4}$ together inform us that, under application, schemata behave as expected, i.e., as given by the original axiomatic conditions for the introduction of schema specifications.

In addition, as with types, we take schemata to be intensional notions that have decidable equality, where, as usual, $\neq$ names the inequality relation.

$$\mathbf{Sc_6} \quad \frac{s : \mathbf{S}(T) \qquad s' : \mathbf{S}(T)}{s \neq_{\mathbf{S}(T)} s'\ prop} \qquad\qquad \mathbf{Sc_7} \quad \frac{s : \mathbf{S}(T) \qquad s' : \mathbf{S}(T)}{\neg(s =_{\mathbf{S}(T)} s') \leftrightarrow s \neq_{\mathbf{S}(T)} s'}$$

So, along with types, relations may function as data items.

Next observe that, in any theory containing the type constructor **S**, the schema

$$[x : T \mid \phi]$$

is now an *object* of that theory; i.e., it has a type.

$$[x : T \mid \phi] : \mathbf{S}(T)$$

It is in this sense that schemata obtain their status as objects of the theory. Consequently,

$$R \triangleq [x : T \mid \phi[x]]$$

may be taken as a standard definition; i.e., it can be understood as naming the schema $[x : T \mid \phi[x]]$ as R. The rules $\mathbf{R_1} - \mathbf{R_3}$ are now consequences of the axioms for $\mathbf{S_3}$ and $\mathbf{S_4}$. In contrast, in pure **TPL** the schema specification

$$R \triangleq [x : T \mid \phi[x]]$$

is a piece of metanotation that heralds the introduction of a new relation symbol that satisfies $\mathbf{R_1} - \mathbf{R_3}$.

Although the actual theory only posits unary schemata, within this theory, using products, we can easily represent the more complex ones; i.e., as before, we rewrite the schema

$$[x_1 : A_1, ..., x_n : A_n \mid \phi]$$

as

$$\left[x : \Sigma x_1 : A_1 \cdot ... \cdot \Sigma x_{n-1} : A_{n-1} \cdot A_n \mid \phi[x_1, ..., x_n] \right]$$

The following example is the empty schema of type T.

Example 176 (Empty Schema)

$$\mathbf{E} \triangleq \left[x : T \mid \Omega \right]$$

This can now be taken as a definition of a new object of the theory named *Empty*. The new object is a scheme relation whose type is given as follows.

$$\mathbf{E} : \mathbf{S}(T)$$

Given the presence of the type **type**, the following specification introduces a universal schemata for each type, i.e., it holds for each element of the given type.

Example 177 (Universal Schemata)

$$Univ \triangleq [u : \mathbf{type}, x : u \mid x =_u x]$$

Finally, notice that the following schema specification involves quantification over a collection that includes the schema s itself.

$$s \triangleq [x : N \mid \exists z : \mathbf{S}(N) \cdot \psi[x, z]]$$

On the face of it, this is an *impredicative* specification, but such impredicativity is only significant when it is combined with extensionality; i.e., an object introduced by quantification over an extensional collection that includes the object under definition. And this we do not have; our relations and types are not extensional. Once more, the impredicativity here is similar to that found in the recursively enumerable sets and their codes; i.e., there is a recursive enumeration of the codes of such sets.

12.2 A Minimal Theory

Our minimal theory of schemata is obtained from the theory

$$\textbf{Th(N, CP, type)}$$

by the addition of schemata as objects; i.e., we start with the theory that is generated from the natural numbers and the type of types by dependent products, and add schema formation.

$$\textbf{SC} = \textbf{Th(N, DP, type, S)}$$

All the properties of **Th(N, CP, type)** remain intact. In particular, the coherence theorem still holds and there are obvious extensions to the type-checking result. We leave the reader to extend the induction to the new cases. Of particular importance is part 2. This informs us that every schema can be split into a declaration part and a predicate part.

Proposition 178 *(Type Checking)*

1. $\Gamma \vdash s(t)$ *prop* iff $\Gamma \vdash t : T$ and $\Gamma \vdash s : S(T)$, *for some* T,
2. $\Gamma \vdash f : S(T)$ iff there exists f^+ and f^- such that $\Gamma \vdash f^+$ *type* and $\Gamma, x : f^+ \vdash f^-(x)$ *prop and* $f = [x : f^+ \mid f^-(x)]$
3. $\Gamma \vdash S(T)$ *type* iff $\Gamma \vdash T$ *type*

Proof By induction on the derivations. Consider part 1. Apart from an application of the structural rules, the only way a conclusion of the form $f : S(T)$ is possible is via an application of Sc_1. The result is then immediate. For the structural rules, consider the following instance.

$$\frac{\Gamma, \Delta \vdash f : S(T) \qquad \Gamma \vdash T \ type}{\Gamma, x : T, \Delta \vdash f : S(T)}$$

By the induction hypothesis,

$$\Gamma, \Delta \vdash f^+ \ type \qquad \Gamma, \Delta, x : f^+ \vdash f^-(x) \ prop$$

Now use the structural rule itself to obtain

$$\frac{\Gamma, \Delta \vdash f^+ \; type \qquad \Gamma \vdash T \; type}{\Gamma, x : T, \Delta \vdash f^+ \; type} \qquad \frac{\Gamma, \Delta, x : f^+ \vdash f^-(x) \; prop \qquad \Gamma \vdash T \; type}{\Gamma, x : T, \Delta, x : f^+ \vdash f^-(x) \; prop}$$

as required. Moreover, all the other structural rules follow suit. ∎

The use of schemata enables a more compact and wholesome expression of the theoretical properties of schemata. We begin with a very standard idea, the obvious notion of subschemata.

Definition 179 (Subschema) *Let* $f : \mathbf{S}(T)$ *and* $g : \mathbf{S}(T)$. *Then we define*

$$f \subseteq g \triangleq \forall x : T \cdot f(x) \rightarrow g(x)$$

This leads to the following notion of equivalence.

Definition 180 (Schema Equivalence) *Let* $f : \mathbf{S}(T)$ *and* $g : \mathbf{S}(T)$. *Then we define*

$$f \equiv g \triangleq f \subseteq g \land g \subseteq f$$

This is an equivalence relation. But it is not identical with equality: Our relations are intensional and we do have the following *rule of extensionality*.

$$\frac{f : \mathbf{S}(T) \qquad g : \mathbf{S}(T) \qquad f \equiv g}{f =_{\mathbf{S}(T)} g}$$

It is in this precise sense that schemata are not extensional objects.

Next observe that our definitions of *totality* and *functionality* can be recast in a more abstract way as properties of actual objects in the theory.

Definition 181 *Suppose that*

$$R : \mathbf{S}(I \otimes O)$$

We shall say that R *is* **total** *if*

$$\forall x : I \cdot \exists y : O \cdot R(x, y)$$

and **functional** *if*

$$\forall x : I \cdot \forall y : O \cdot \forall z : O \cdot R(x, y) \land R(x, z) \rightarrow y = z$$

Finally, we say that R *is a* **function** *if it is both total and functional.*

The next definition introduces the standard notions of *reflexive, symmetric,* and *transitive* relations.

Definition 182 *Suppose that*

$$R : \mathbf{S}(T \otimes T)$$

*We shall say that R is **reflexive** if*

$$\forall x : T \cdot R(x, x)$$

*and **symmetric** if*

$$\forall x : T \cdot \forall y : T \cdot R(x, y) \rightarrow R(y, x)$$

*We say that R is **transitive** if*

$$\forall x : T \cdot \forall y : T \cdot \forall z : T \cdot R(x, y) \wedge R(y, z) \rightarrow R(x, z)$$

*If it is all three, we call R an **equivalence relation**.*

These observations are only possible given the fact that schemata are now objects of the theory, i.e., have a type and are subject to quantification.

12.3 Operations on Schemata

We now illustrate the process of specification in **SC** by introducing a range of examples, most of which we have seen as specifications, but now all are carried out in the object theory.

Our first two examples yield schema union and intersection. These form some of the basic set-like operations on schemata.

Example 183 (Schema Union)

$$\begin{array}{|l}
\cup_U \\\hline
f? : \mathbf{S}(U), g? : \mathbf{S}(U), h! : \mathbf{S}(U) \\\hline
h = [x : U \mid fx \vee gx]
\end{array}$$

Within **SC**, this specification, viewed as schema object, now has the following type.

$$\cup_U : \mathbf{S}(\Sigma u : \mathbf{type} \cdot \mathbf{S}(u) \otimes \mathbf{S}(u) \otimes \mathbf{S}(u))$$

Moreover, it satisfies the following rules.

$$\frac{U : \textbf{type} \qquad a : \textbf{S}(U) \qquad b : \textbf{S}(U)}{a \cup b : \textbf{S}(T)}$$

$$\frac{U : \textbf{type} \qquad a : \textbf{S}(U) \qquad b : \textbf{S}(U)}{\forall x : \textbf{S}(U) \cdot (a \cup b)(x) \leftrightarrow a(x) \vee b(a)}$$

We will not always be so explicit. The following is a special case of simple union and one that will shortly prove useful.

Example 184 (Element Addition)

$$\circledast_U$$

$$\begin{array}{|l}
\hline
x : U, y : \textbf{S}(U), z : \textbf{S}(U) \\
\hline
z = \{x\} \cup y \\
\hline
\end{array}$$

Our next example is the dual of union; i.e., schema intersection.

Example 185 (Schema Intersection)

$$\cap_U$$

$$\begin{array}{|l}
\hline
f? : \textbf{S}(U), g? : \textbf{S}(U), h! : \textbf{S}(U) \\
\hline
h = [x : T \mid fx \wedge gx] \\
\hline
\end{array}$$

This specification, viewed as schema object, has the following type.

$$\cap_U : \textbf{S}(\Sigma u : \textbf{type} \cdot \textbf{S}(u) \otimes \textbf{S}(u) \otimes \textbf{S}(u))$$

We can now mimic some of the material from our original case study. For example, we may specify our two original register operations as schemata.

Definition 186 (Register)

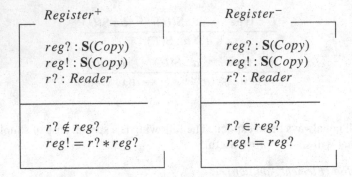

We may then use schema union to join them and so generate a total operation.

$$Register^* \triangleq Register^+ \cup Register^-$$

Our next operator is also part of the basic operations of set theory. It is the standard generalization of simple union.

Example 187 (Generalized Union)

$$\cup_U$$

$$f? : \mathbf{S}(\mathbf{S}(U)), g! : \mathbf{S}(U)$$

$$g = [x : T \mid \exists z : \mathbf{S}(U) \cdot f(z) \wedge z(x)]$$

This has the following type

$$\cup_U : \mathbf{S}(\Sigma u : \mathbf{type} \cdot \mathbf{S}(\mathbf{S}(u)) \otimes \mathbf{S}(u))$$

and satisfies the following rules.

$$\frac{U : \mathbf{type} \qquad s : \mathbf{S}(\mathbf{S}(U))}{\cup s : \mathbf{S}(U)} \qquad \frac{U : \mathbf{type} \qquad s : \mathbf{S}(\mathbf{S}(U)) \quad (\cup s)(a)}{\exists x : \mathbf{S}(U) \cdot s(x) \wedge x(a)}$$

$$\frac{U : \mathbf{type} \qquad s : \mathbf{S}(\mathbf{S}(U)) \qquad \exists x : \mathbf{S}(U) \cdot s(x) \wedge x(a)}{(\cup s)(a)}$$

These operations point toward some form of calculus or algebra of schema that enables the specification of more complex ones from simple ones. Thus far the operations mimic the set-theoretic operations. But we can go further. Indeed, Z contains many operations that operate on (its notion of) schema. While our notion is semantically quite different, it is syntactically quite similar. And so we can develop versions of these operations. Specifically, we explore how many of the operations of the Z schema calculus may be articulated in the present theory of schema relations.

In our initial chapter on specification, we defined the domain and range of given relations. We can now provide these in the object theory as abstract operations on schemata.

Example 188 (Domain)

$$
\begin{array}{|l}
\hline
\quad Dom \underline{\hspace{5cm}} \\
\hline
u : \textbf{type}, v : \textbf{type} \\
f? : S(u \otimes v) \\
g! : S(u) \\
\hline
g = [x : u \mid \exists y : v \cdot f(x, y)] \\
\hline
\end{array}
$$

It is easy to see that *Dom* and *Ran* have the following types:

$$S(\Sigma u : \textbf{type} \cdot \Sigma v : \textbf{type} \cdot S(u \otimes v) \otimes S(u))$$
$$S(\Sigma u : \textbf{type} \cdot \Sigma v : \textbf{type} \cdot S(u \otimes v) \otimes S(v))$$

where *Ran* is specified as follows.

Example 189 (Range)

$$
\begin{array}{|l}
\hline
\quad Ran \underline{\hspace{5cm}} \\
\hline
u : \textbf{type}, v : \textbf{type} \\
f? : S(u \otimes v) \\
g! : S(v) \\
\hline
g = [y : v \mid \exists x : u \cdot f(x, y)] \\
\hline
\end{array}
$$

A generalized version of these, where existential quantification can occur anywhere in a complex product, is given as follows.

Example 190 (Hiding)

$Hide_i$

$f? : \mathbf{S}(U_1 \otimes ... \otimes U_n)$
$g! : \mathbf{S}(U_1 \otimes ... \otimes U_{i-1} \otimes U_{i+1} \otimes ... \otimes U_n)$

$g = [x : U_1 \otimes ... \otimes U_{i-1} \otimes U_{i+1} \otimes ... \otimes U_n \mid \exists x_i : U_i \cdot f(x_1, ..., x_n)]$

Its type is given as follows.

$$Hide_i : \mathbf{S}(\Sigma(u : \mathbf{type}^n \cdot \mathbf{S}(u_1 \otimes ... \otimes u_n) \otimes \mathbf{S}(u_1 \otimes ... \otimes u_{i-1} \otimes u_{i+1} \otimes ... \otimes u_n)))$$

The next specification introduces the abstract polymorphic version of relational composition, and the following one introduces relational inverse.

Example 191 (Polymorphic Composition)

∘

$u : \mathbf{type}, v : \mathbf{type}, w : \mathbf{type}$
$f? : \mathbf{S}(u \otimes v), g? : \mathbf{S}(v \otimes w), h! : \mathbf{S}(u \otimes w)$

$h = [x : u \otimes w \mid \exists y : v \cdot f(x_1, y) \wedge g(y, x_2)]$

This results in the addition of a relation that has the following type.

$$\mathbf{S}(\Sigma u : \mathbf{type} \otimes \mathbf{type} \otimes \mathbf{type} \cdot \mathbf{S}(u_1 \otimes u_2) \otimes \mathbf{S}(u_2 \otimes u_3) \otimes \mathbf{S}(u_1 \otimes u_3))$$

Example 192 (Relational Inverse)

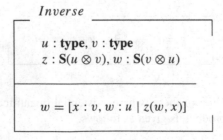

We can restrict the domain and range of schema relations. These operations, and many of the above and below, form part of the Z-toolkit.

Example 193 (Domain Restriction)

$\lhd$

$u : \textbf{type}, v : \textbf{type}$
$y : \textbf{S}(u), z : \textbf{S}(u \otimes v), w : \textbf{S}(u \otimes v)$

$w = [x : u, w : v \mid z(x, w) \land y(x)]$

Example 194 (Range Restriction)

$\rhd$

$u : \textbf{type}, v : \textbf{type}$
$y : \textbf{S}(v), z : \textbf{S}(u \otimes v), w : \textbf{S}(u \otimes v)$

$w = [x : u, w : v \mid z(x, w) \land y(w)]$

Respectively, these have the following types.

$$\textbf{S}(\Sigma u : \textbf{type} \cdot \Sigma v : \textbf{type} \cdot \textbf{S}(u) \otimes \textbf{S}(u \otimes v) \otimes \textbf{S}(u \otimes v))$$
$$\textbf{S}(\Sigma u : \textbf{type} \cdot \Sigma v : \textbf{type} \cdot \textbf{S}(v) \otimes \textbf{S}(u \otimes v) \otimes \textbf{S}(u \otimes v))$$

The next provides the specification of schema product—with the following type.

$$\textbf{S}(\Sigma u : \textbf{type} \cdot \Sigma v : \textbf{type} \cdot \textbf{S}(u) \otimes \textbf{S}(v) \otimes \textbf{S}(u \otimes v))$$

Example 195 (Schema Product)

$\otimes$

$u : \textbf{type}, v : \textbf{type}$
$f? : \textbf{S}(u), g? : \textbf{S}(v), h! : \textbf{S}(u \otimes v)$

$h = [x : u \otimes v \mid f(x_1) \land g(x_2)]$

Next, consider the following version of product. This parallels the natural product of relational database theory where equality is enforced on the common domain.

Example 196 (Natural Product)

$\otimes$

u : **type**, v : **type**, w : **type**
$f?$: $S(u \otimes v)$, $g?$: $S(v \otimes w)$, $h!$: $S(u \otimes v \otimes w)$

$h = [x : u \otimes v \otimes w \mid f(x_1, x_2) \wedge g(x_2, x_3)]$

These examples illustrate how schemata are used as data items that themselves have types. They also establish the expressive power of the notion of schemata in being able to express much of the schema calculus of Z in a mathematically wholesome way.

And almost finally, a rather pleasant application of polymorphic schemata yields a representation or specification of the combinators of combinatorial logic in their polymorphic guise. The following are the two basic combinators of that system.

Example 197 (The Combinator K)

K

u : **type**, v : **type**
$x : u$, f : $S(v \otimes u)$

$f = [y : v, w : u \mid w = x]$

This has the following type. It is functional and returns a function.

$$\mathbf{K} : S(\Sigma u : \textbf{type} \cdot \Sigma v : \textbf{type} \cdot u \otimes S(v \otimes u))$$

The last is a relational version of the **S** combinator of combinatorial logic. It is also functional.

Example 198 (The Combinator S)

S_{Rel}

$u : \textbf{type}, v : \textbf{type}, w : \textbf{type}$
$f : S(u \otimes S(v \otimes w))$
$g : S(u \otimes v)$
$h : S(u \otimes w)$

$$h$$
$$=$$
$$[x : u, z : w \mid \exists y : v \cdot \exists y' : S(v \otimes w) \cdot f(x, y') \wedge g(x, y) \wedge w(y, z)]$$

This has the type

$$\Sigma u : \textbf{type} \cdot \Sigma v : \textbf{type} \cdot \Sigma w : \textbf{type} \cdot S(u \otimes S(v \otimes w)) \otimes S(u \otimes v) \otimes S(u \otimes w)$$

To conclude, we revisit our separation example for sets. We may now, for the version restricted to schemata, include the propositional part as a schema.

Example 199 (Separation) We specify

Sep

$u : \textbf{type}, f : S[u], x? : Set(u), y! : Set(u)$

$$\forall z \in y \cdot z \in x \wedge f(z)$$
$$\wedge$$
$$\forall z \in x \cdot f(z) \rightarrow z \in y$$

12.4 Arithmetic Interpretation

We now complete our simple treatment of schemata by laying out their recursive interpretation, i.e., provide the recursive interpretation of **SC** in **Nat**. We shall assume that the theory

$$\textbf{Th}(\textbf{N}, \textbf{DP}, \textbf{type})$$

has been interpreted as in the last chapter. Here we concentrate on the interpretation of schemata and their types.

Stage 1: Schemata as classes

The schemata are interpreted as classes. More explicitly, the schema $[x : T \mid \phi]$ is interpreted as the class

$$\{x \cdot x : T \wedge \phi\}$$

Stage 2: Gödel numbering

Given a representation of the schemata of any base theory as Σ classes, we Gödel code the propositions and the Σ classes. Again, there are endless ways of achieving this, but we only require one with the standard properties of providing an isomorphism between the codes and the classes.

Stage 3: Schemata predication

As with the type **type**, we represent class membership as a Σ relation, i.e., as $\mathbf{Sat}_n(x, x_1, .., x_n)$ where for each Σ proposition ϕ of **Nat** with exactly the free variables $x_1, ..., x_n$ $(n > 0)$.

$$\mathbf{Sat}_n(\ulcorner \phi \urcorner, x_1, ..., x_n) \leftrightarrow \phi[x_1, .., x_n]$$

where $\ulcorner \phi \urcorner$ is the code of ϕ.
We then represent schema predication as follows.

$$[x : T \mid \phi[x, x_1, ..., x_n]] \, (x) \triangleq \mathbf{Sat}_{n+1}(\ulcorner \phi \urcorner, x, x_1, ..., x_n)$$

Stage 4: Schemata types

To complete the interpretation of the theory, we have to interpret the schema types: $\mathbf{S}(T)$ is interpreted as (the code of) the recursively enumerable class of all the codes of classes of the form $[x : T \mid \phi[x, x_1, ..., x_n]]$.

Theorem 200 Th(N, DP, type, S) *is a conservative extension of* **Nat**.

References

1. Feferman, S. Constructive theories of functions and classes. In: M. Boffa, D. van Dalen, and K. McAloon (Eds.), Logic Colloquium '78, pp. 159–225, North-Holland, Amsterdam, 1979.
2. Russell, B.A.W. Mathematical logic as based on the theory of types Ameri. J. of Math. 30: 222–262.

3. Spivey, J.M. Understanding Z. Cambridge University Press, Cambridge, 1988.
4. Turner, R. Lazy theories of operations and types. J. Log. Comput. 3(1): 77–102, 1993.
5. Turner, R. Weak theories of operations and types. J. Log. Comput. 6(1): 5–31, 1996.
6. Woodcock, J. and Davies, J. Using Z: Specification, Refinement and Proof, Prentice Hall, Englewood Cliffs, NJ, 1996.

Chapter 13
Separation Types

Some specification languages admit *subtypes* and some do not. For example, **VDM** [2], [1] allows *invariant* definitions in type declarations; they act somewhat like a propositional restriction on types. But, strictly speaking, they are not types. Rather, they are part of the specification, not the type. Z [6], [8] allows separation on sets, which include types, but the result is a set and not a type. Moreover, while schema are treated as types in Z, the role of predicates seems minimal. One major specification framework that does explicitly allow genuine subtypes is **PVS** [5]; it allows subtypes formed by abstraction on a proposition. This is similar to the role of separation in set theory [4]. Our approach is closer to that of the latter; i.e., via a scheme of separation, we add subtypes to our theories. It is also similar to the treatment of subtypes in constructive type theory [7], but ours is a restricted version in that we only admit Σ types.

The addition of subtypes greatly enhances the expressive power of our notion of specification. For instance, by extending the notion of type, we are able to represent the domain and range of relations as types. This has several knock-on effects. Initially, it will facilitate a very simple treatment of specifications with preconditions; in its turn, this will yield an elegant treatment of partial functions as total ones.

13.1 Theories with Separation

Let

$$\mathbf{Th}(O_1, ..., O_k)$$

be any **TDT**. In this section we shall work in the corresponding theories

$$\mathbf{Th}(O_1, ..., O_k, \mathbf{Sep}, \mathbf{DP})$$

where $\mathbf{Sep}(T)$ is the class of subtypes of the type T and **DP** is the type of dependent products. We have already dealt with the rules for the latter and we shall shortly

R. Turner, *Computable Models*, DOI 10.1007/978-1-84882-052-4_13,
© Springer-Verlag London Limited 2009

indicate how subtypes generate the context for these. But first we need to put in place the rules for separation types. In what follows, ϕ is Σ.

$$\textbf{Sep}_0 \quad \frac{x : T \vdash \phi \; prop}{\{x : T \mid \phi\} \; type}$$

$$\textbf{Sep}_1 \quad \frac{x : T \vdash \phi \; prop \qquad a : T \quad \phi[a/x]}{a : \{x : T \mid \phi\}}$$

$$\textbf{Sep}_2 \quad \frac{a : \{x : T \mid \phi\}}{a : T}$$

$$\textbf{Sep}_3 \quad \frac{a : \{x : T \mid \phi\}}{\phi[a/x]}$$

$\textbf{Sep}_0$ is the formation rule for subtypes, $\textbf{Sep}_1$ is the introduction rule, and $\textbf{Sep}_2$ and $\textbf{Sep}_3$ are the elimination rules. In all these rules, $x \notin FV(T)$. A few observations are in order. First, notice that type formation now depends upon proposition formation ($\textbf{Sep}_0$). The following illustrates this.

$$\frac{x : T \vdash x =_T x \; prop}{\{x : T \cdot x =_T x\} \; type}$$

In its wake, type membership now depends upon the truth of propositions ($\textbf{Sep}_1$).

$$\frac{x : T \vdash x =_T x \; prop \qquad a : T \qquad a =_T a}{a : \{x : T \cdot x =_T x\}}$$

Indeed, type terms can contain free variables ($\textbf{Sep}_0$). The following is an instance.

$$\frac{x : T, y : T \vdash x =_T y \; prop}{y : T \vdash \{x : T \cdot x =_T y\} \; type}$$

Hence, types can depend upon other terms, and this supports and facilitates *dependent Cartesian products*.

This concludes the description of $\textbf{Th}(O_1, ..., O_k, \textbf{Sep}, \textbf{DP})$. The type-checking result is preserved; i.e., if $\textbf{Th}(O_1, ..., O_k)$ satisfies it, so does the theory $\textbf{Th}(O_1, ..., O_k, \textbf{Sep}, \textbf{DP})$. But we must add a new clause.

Proposition 201 *(Type Checking)* In $\textbf{Th}(O_1, ..., O_k, \textbf{Sep}, \textbf{DP})$ *we have:*

$$\Gamma, x : T \vdash \phi \; prop \; iff \; \Gamma \vdash \{x : T \mid \phi\} \; type$$

However, we no longer have the independence of the logic and the type system: via $\textbf{Sep}_1$, type membership may now depend upon the truth of propositions. But, as we shall see, the addition of separation is conservative.

13.2 Subtypes in Specification

We shall first illustrate the use of separation in the specification process with some simple observations. More interesting examples will be introduced later.

Example 202 (Dom and Ran) In $\mathbf{Th}(O_1, ..., O_k, \mathbf{Sep}, \mathbf{DP})$, specify

$$R \triangleq [x : I, y : O \mid \psi]$$

We may then define the *domain* and range of R as types as follows.

$$Dom\,R \triangleq \{x : I \mid \exists y : O \cdot \psi\}$$
$$Ran\,R \triangleq \{y : O \mid \exists x : I \cdot \psi\}$$

where now the definiens are types.

Example 203 (Even and Odd) In the theory $\mathbf{Th}(\mathbf{N}, \mathbf{DP}, \mathbf{Set}, \mathbf{Sep})$, the even and odd numbers can be defined as types as follows.

$$Even \triangleq \{x : N \cdot \exists y : N \cdot x = 2 * y\}$$
$$Odd \triangleq \{x : N \cdot \exists y : N \cdot x = 2 * y + 1\}$$

Example 204 (Maps) In the theory $\mathbf{Th}(\mathbf{N}, \mathbf{DP}, \mathbf{Set}, \mathbf{Sep})$, the **type of maps**, a subtype of the type of set-theoretic relations, is defined as

$$A \rightarrow_m B \triangleq \{z : Set(A \otimes B) \cdot \forall x \in z \cdot \forall y \in z \cdot x_1 = y_1 \rightarrow x_2 = y_2\}$$

Similarly, the type of **injective maps** may be defined as a subtype of the type of maps.

$$A \rightarrowtail_m B \triangleq \{z : A \rightarrow_m B \cdot \forall x \in z \cdot \forall y \in z \cdot x_2 = y_2 \rightarrow x_1 = y_1\}$$

Finally, some more concrete examples. Here we demonstrate how the use of separation can provide a more mathematically attractive account of schema inclusion.

Example 205 (States) In the theory $\mathbf{Th}(\mathbf{N}, \mathbf{DP}, \mathbf{Set}, \mathbf{Sep})$, consider the following specification of the state of a system that has two components: one is a set of items and the other is a set-theoretic relation. The constraint or invariant insists that the domain of the relation and the set of items do not intersect.

$$State_{B,L} \triangleq \{x : \mathbf{Set}(B) \otimes (B \rightarrow_m L) \cdot x_1 \cap Dom(x_2) = \Phi_B\}$$

Our concrete instantiation is a library database $State_{B,L}$, where B represents the class of library books or items and L the library users. Under this interpretation, $x : \mathbf{Set}(B)$ represents the books currently on the shelves and $y : B \rightarrow_m L$ provides information about which readers have specific books. The insistence for books not to be both on the shelves and on loan is imposed by the disjointedness requirement. We can then use it in the following operation, which updates the state. It represents the operation of loaning a new item to a specified reader.

Example 206 (Loan Operation)

$Loan_{B,L}$

$z : State_{B,L}, z' : State_{B,L}$
$u : B, v : L$

$z'_1 = z_1$
$z'_2 = \{x : B, y : L \cdot (x = u \land y = v) \lor \exists w : z_2 \cdot (x, y) = w\}$

13.3 Preconditions and Functions

Using the subtype constructor we may obtain the effect of preconditions in standard specifications; i.e., with subtypes we can get by with the simple notion of specification. To demonstrate this, suppose that

$$x : \{x : I \cdot \pi[x]\}, y : O \vdash \phi[x, y] \; prop$$

where π and ψ are Σ. Then consider the following standard specification using subtypes, but with no preconditions.

$$R \triangleq [x : \{x : I \cdot \pi[x]\}, y : O \mid \phi[x, y]]$$

This specification is equivalent to the specification

$$R \triangleq [x : I, y : O \mid \pi[x]; \phi[x, y]]$$

in that the axioms governing the two are logically equivalent. This provides the full impact of preconditions in the standard style of specification. Moreover, with separation types present, our original notions of totality and functionality unwind to yield the precondition versions. In particular, we can specify relations that are functions under the assumption of the precondition. Our first example is a specification of map application.

Example 207 (Map Application)

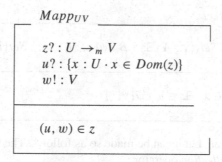

$$Mapp_{UV}$$

$$z? : U \to_m V$$
$$u? : \{x : U \cdot x \in Dom(z)\}$$
$$w! : V$$

$$(u, w) \in z$$

Proposition 208 *The above specification defines a total function.*

Proof Here, $u \in Dom(z)$ guarantees totality and $z : U \to_m V$ guarantees functionality.■

The impact upon the specification of partial functions is inherited from our treatment of pre-conditions. So where R is single-valued, i.e.,

$$x : I, y : O, z : O, R(x, y), R(x, z) \vdash y = z$$

but not total, we can turn into one that is by the specification

$$\widehat{R} \triangleq [x : \{x : A \cdot (DomR)(x)\}, y : B \mid R(x, y)]$$

This is now single-valued and total, in the original sense of those terms.

In the rest of this section we work in the theory **Th(N, Sep, Set, DP)**. Our first example is similar to the *collection* principles of standard set theory. To facilitate matters, recall the following principle of collection.

Proposition 209 *Suppose that*

$$y : A, z : B \vdash \psi[y, z] \, prop$$

Then

$$\forall x : Set(A) \cdot (\forall y \in x \cdot \exists z : B \cdot \psi[y, z]) \to \exists w : Set(B) \cdot \forall y \in x \cdot \exists z \in w \cdot \psi[y, z]$$

With this at hand, we can justify the totality of the following specification.

Example 210 (Collection) Suppose that

$$y : A, z : B \vdash \psi[y, z] \, prop$$

We specify a **Collect** operator as follows.

Collect
$$x? : Set(\{y : A \cdot \exists z : B \cdot \psi[y, z]\}), w! : Set(B)$$

$$\forall y \in x \cdot \exists z \in w \cdot \psi[y, z]$$

This is not a function, but it can be made so as follows. The following is a specification of a *strong collection* operator.

Example 211 (Strong Collection) Suppose that

$$y : A, z : B \vdash \psi[y, z] \, prop$$

We may then specify

Strongcollect
$$x? : Set(\{y : A \cdot \exists z : B \cdot \psi[y, z]\}), w! : Set(B)$$

$$\forall u \in x \cdot \exists v \in w \cdot \psi[u, v] \wedge \forall z \in w \cdot \exists y \in x \cdot \psi[y, z]$$

We can now strengthen the last result.

Corollary 212 *Strong collection is total and functional.*

Proof Given the last result, we know it is total. Moreover, given the last result and the guaranteed set w that satisfies the consequent, we put

$$w' = \{z \in w \cdot \exists y \in x \cdot \psi[y, z]\}$$

The guaranteed set is now unique and so the specification is functional.∎

These provide examples where subtypes do not only occur in simple precondition positions and enable the articulation of a richer class of specifications.

13.4 Polymorphism and Subtypes

We now consider the impact of polymorphism on subtypes. The inclusion of the type **type** allows us to treat types, including subtypes, as objects.

Let

$$\mathbf{Th}(O_1, ..., O_k)$$

be any **TDT**. Then consider the corresponding theories with separation and **type**.

$$\mathbf{Th}(O_1, ..., O_k, \mathbf{Sep}, \mathbf{DP}, \mathbf{type})$$

In the presence of the type **type**, types, including subtypes, become first-class objects. Since types may contain bound variables (via separation terms), we allow for them to be renamed.

$$\mathbf{Sep_4} \quad \frac{x : T \vdash \phi \; prop}{\{x : T \mid \phi\} =_{\text{type}} \{y : T \mid \phi[y/x]\}}$$

In the polymorphic theories we obtain more abstract versions of our various instances of subtypes. The following version of maps illustrates this.

Example 213 (Polymorphic Maps) In the theory

$$\mathbf{Th}(\mathbf{N}, \mathbf{DP}, \mathbf{Set}, \mathbf{Sep}, \mathbf{type})$$

we define the type of **polymorphic maps** as

$$\{u : \mathbf{type}, v : \mathbf{type}, z : Set(u \otimes v) \cdot \forall x \in z \cdot \forall y \in z \cdot x_1 = y_1 \rightarrow x_2 = y_2\}$$

This is an abbreviation for the type

$$\{z : \Sigma u : \mathbf{type} \cdot \Sigma v : \mathbf{type} \cdot Set(u \otimes v) \cdot \forall x \in z_3 \cdot \forall y \in z_3 \cdot x_1 = y_1 \rightarrow x_2 = y_2\}$$

13.5 The Elimination of Subtypes

Despite this greater expressive power, the addition of subtypes is conservative. This agrees with one's basic intuition that subtypes are a luxury rather than a necessity and that, in some sense, anything we can do with them we can do without them. This is the substance of the following translation that compiles away the subtypes. We shall illustrate matters with the following theories that contain all the major components. However, one should take note that the introduction of additional type constructors places one under an obligation to extend the translation.

$$T_1 = \mathbf{Th}[\mathbf{N}, \mathbf{DP}, \mathbf{type}, \mathbf{S}, \mathbf{Sep}]$$
$$T_2 = \mathbf{Th}[\mathbf{N}, \mathbf{DP}, \mathbf{type}, \mathbf{S}]$$

For each t, a proposition, term, and type of $\mathbf{T_1}$, we associate, by a simultaneous recursion, an expression t^* of $\mathbf{T_2}$. We shall deal with specifications separately.

We first deal with all the types. A type A translates to A^*, which is a pair consisting of a type A^+ and a schema A^-. This removes the predicate information from the types and places it in the predicate of the schema; i.e.,

$$A^* \triangleq (A^+, A^-)$$

where

$$(\Sigma x : A \cdot B)^+ \triangleq \Sigma x : A^+ \cdot B^+$$
$$(\Sigma x : A \cdot B)^- \triangleq [x : \Sigma x : A^+ \cdot B^+ \mid A^-(x_0) \wedge B(x_0)^-(x_1)]$$
$$\{x : A \cdot \phi\}^+ \triangleq A^+$$
$$\{x : A \cdot \phi\}^- \triangleq [x : A^+ \mid A^-(x) \wedge \phi[x]^*]$$
$$\mathbf{S}(A)^+ \triangleq \mathbf{S}(A^+)$$
$$\mathbf{S}(A)^- \triangleq [x : \mathbf{S}(A^+) \mid x = x]$$
$$\mathbf{type}^+ \triangleq \Sigma u : \mathbf{type} \cdot S[u]$$
$$\mathbf{type}^- \triangleq [x : \Sigma u : \mathbf{type} \cdot S[u] \mid x = x]$$
$$N^+ \triangleq N$$
$$N^- \triangleq [x : N \mid x = x]$$

With this in place, we may translate all the terms. Except for the schemata, the rest are straightforward.

$$0^* \triangleq 0$$
$$Succ(a)^* \triangleq Succ(a^*)$$
$$(a, b)^* \triangleq (a^*, b^*)$$
$$\pi_i(a)^* \triangleq \pi_i(a^*)$$
$$f(a)^* = f^*(a^*)$$
$$[x : A \mid \phi]^* \triangleq [x : A^+ \mid A^-(x) \wedge \phi^*[x]]$$

This leaves the translation of the propositions. In what follows R^* translates the atomic R (set membership, etc.).

$$(t =_T s)^* \triangleq (t^* =_{T^+} s^*) \wedge T^-(t^*)$$
$$R(t_1, ..., t_n)^* \triangleq R^*(t_1^*, ..., t_n^*)$$
$$(\neg \phi)^* \triangleq \neg \phi^*$$
$$(\phi \wedge \psi)^* \triangleq \phi^* \wedge \psi^*$$
$$(\phi \vee \psi)^* \triangleq \phi^* \vee \psi^*$$
$$(\phi \rightarrow \psi)^* \triangleq \phi^* \rightarrow \psi^*$$
$$(\exists x : T \cdot \phi)^* \triangleq \exists x : T^+ \cdot T^-(x) \wedge \phi^*$$
$$(\forall x : T \cdot \phi)^* \triangleq \forall x : T^+ \cdot T^-(x) \rightarrow \phi^*$$

The only interesting cases are equality and the quantifiers. Here we need to explicitly include the propositional information that resides in the types. This completes the translation. The following is by induction on the rules.

Lemma 214 *(Substitution) For each judgment* Θ *and term t of* $\mathbf{T}_1$*, we have*

$$\Theta[x/t]^* = \Theta^*[t^*/x]$$

Lemma 215 *The above translation satisfies the following.*

1. *If* $\Gamma \vdash_{\mathbf{T}_1} T$ *type, then* $\Gamma^* \vdash_{\mathbf{T}_2} T^+$ *type and* $\Gamma^* \vdash_{\mathbf{T}_2} T^- : \mathbf{S}(T^+)$.
2. *If* $\Gamma \vdash_{\mathbf{T}_1} \phi$ *prop, then* $\Gamma^* \vdash_{\mathbf{T}_2} \phi^*$ *prop and, if* ϕ *is* Σ*, so is* ϕ^*.
3. *If* $\Gamma \vdash_{\mathbf{T}_1} t : T$*, then* $\Gamma^* \vdash_{\mathbf{T}_2} t^* : T^+$ *and* $\Gamma^* \vdash_{\mathbf{T}_2} T^-(t^*)$.
4. *If* $\Gamma \vdash_{\mathbf{T}_1} \phi$*, then* $\Gamma^* \vdash_{\mathbf{T}_2} \phi^*$.
5. *If* $\Gamma \vdash_{\mathbf{T}_2} T$ *type, then* $\Gamma \vdash_{\mathbf{T}_2} t : T$ *iff* $\Gamma \vdash_{\mathbf{T}_2} t^* : T^+$.
6. *If* $\Gamma \vdash_{\mathbf{T}_2} \phi$ *prop, then* $\Gamma \vdash_{\mathbf{T}_2} \phi$ *iff* $\Gamma \vdash_{\mathbf{T}_2} \phi^*$.

Proof We prove all parts by simultaneous induction in the derivations in $\mathbf{T}_1$. Parts 1 and 2 are routine to check. Part 3 requires some work. For separation types, consider the introduction rule. The translation of the rule follows the arrow.

$$\frac{a : A \qquad \phi[a/x]}{a : \{x : A \cdot \phi\}} \Rightarrow \frac{a^* : A^+ \qquad A^-(x) \qquad \phi[a/x]^*}{a^* : \{x : A^+ \cdot A^-(x) \wedge \phi[a/x]^*\}}$$

The result is then immediate by definition of the translation. The elimination rule is similar. Next consider the rules for the universe of types. The introduction and elimination rules are parallel. To illustrate matters, we document the first.

$$\frac{A\ type}{A : \mathbf{type}} \Rightarrow \frac{A^+\ type \qquad A^- : \mathbf{S}(A^+)}{(A^+, A^-) : \Sigma u : \mathbf{type} \cdot S[u]}$$

For schema types, we proceed as follows. All the rules are covered.

$$\frac{x:A\vdash\phi\ prop}{[x:A \mid \phi]:\mathbf{S}(A)} \Rightarrow \frac{x : A^+, A^- : \mathbf{S}(A^+) \vdash \phi^*\ prop}{[x : A^+ \mid A^-(x) \wedge \phi^*] : \mathbf{S}(A^+)} \Rightarrow$$

$$\frac{x : A^+ \vdash (A^-(x) \wedge \phi^*)\ prop}{[x : A^+ \mid A^-(x) \wedge \phi^*] : \mathbf{S}(A^+)}$$

$$\frac{f:\mathbf{S}(A) \qquad a:A}{f(a)\ prop} \Rightarrow \frac{f^* : \mathbf{S}(A) \qquad a^* : A}{f^*(a^*)\ prop}$$

$$\frac{[x:A \mid \phi](a)}{\phi[a]} \Rightarrow \frac{[x : A^+ \mid A^-(x) \wedge \phi^*](a^*)}{\phi^*[a^*/x]}$$

$$\frac{[x:A \mid \phi](a)}{a:A} \Rightarrow \frac{[x : A^+ \mid A^-(x) \wedge \phi^*](a^*)}{a^* : A^+}$$

$$\frac{[x:A \mid \phi](a)}{a:A} \Rightarrow \frac{[x : A^+ \mid A^-(x) \wedge \phi^*](a^*)}{A^-(a^*)}$$

$$\frac{a:A \qquad \phi[a]}{[x:A \mid \phi](a)} \Rightarrow \frac{a^* : A^+ \qquad A^-(a^*) \qquad \phi^*[a^*/x]}{[x : A^+ \mid A^-(x) \wedge \phi^*](a^*)}$$

The rules for dependent product types are routine to check. For example,

$$\frac{a : A \qquad b : B[a/x]}{(a, b) : \Sigma x : A \cdot B} \Rightarrow$$
$$\frac{a^* : A^+ \qquad A^-(a^*) \qquad b^* : B^+ \qquad B^-(a^*, b^*)}{(a^*, b^*) : A^+ \otimes B^+}$$

$$\frac{a : A \qquad b : B[a/x]}{(a, b) : \Sigma x : A \cdot B} \Rightarrow$$
$$\frac{a^* : A^+ \qquad A^-(a^*) \qquad b^* : B^+ \qquad B^-(a^*, b^*)}{(\Sigma x : A \cdot B)^-(a^*, b^*)}$$

Apart from the quantifier rules, part 4 is relatively straightforward. We illustrate with existential quantification. The introduction rule translates to

$$\frac{x : A^+, A^-(x) \vdash \phi[x]^* \qquad t^* : A^+ \wedge A^-(t^*)}{\exists x : A^+ \cdot A^-(x) \wedge \phi[x]^*}$$

which follows. Part 5 is by induction on the rules. By part 3, we need only consider the right-to-left implication. For example,

$$\frac{z : \Sigma x : A^+ \cdot B^+}{z_0 : A^+} \qquad \frac{z : \Sigma x : A^+ \cdot B^+}{z_1 : B^+[z_0]}$$

By induction, and the introduction rule for dependent types, we obtain the required.

$$\frac{z_0 : A \qquad z_1 : B[z_0]}{z : \Sigma x : A \cdot B}$$

Part 6 is almost immediate where the quantifier case is clear from part 5.∎

Theorem 216 T_1 *is a conservative extension of* T_2.

We have said nothing about the impact of the translation upon specifications. Here the complication concerns the occurrence of subtypes in the declaration and, in particular, its impact upon totality and functionality; i.e., presumably, schemata that are total and functional should remain so. Here is where pre-conditions play a role. We translate

$$R \triangleq [x : I, y : O \mid \phi]$$

as follows.

$$R^* \triangleq [x : I, y : O \mid I^-(x); O^-(x, y) \wedge \phi]$$

This transforms total functions into total functions.

Thus, subtypes may be eliminated. Indeed, given the last result, and that of the last chapter to the effect that T_2 is a conservative extension of **Nat**, we have

Theorem 217 T_1 *is a conservative extension of* **Nat**.

References

1. Dawes, J. The VDM-SL Reference Guide. Pitman, London, 1991
2. Jones, C.B.. Systematic Software Development Using VDM. Prentice-Hall, Inc., Englewood Cliffs, NJ, 1986.
3. Martin Lof, P. An intuitionistic theory of sets, predicative part. In Logic Colloquim, 73. North-Holland, Amsterdam, 1975.
4. Potter, M. D. Sets: An Introduction. Clarendon Press, Oxford, 1990
5. http://pvs.csl.sri.com/.
6. Spivey, J.M. Understanding Z. Cambridge University Press, Cambridge, 1988.
7. Thompson, S. Type Theory and Functional Programming. Addison-Wesley. Reading, MA, 1991.
8. Woodcock, J. and Davies, J. Using Z: Specification, Refinement and Proof, Prentice Hall, Englewood Cliffs, NJ, 1996.

Chapter 14
Recursive Schemata

Recursion is one of the more important mechanisms of abstraction in computer science. Indeed, almost every high-level programming language has some form of recursion built in. In older programming languages such as those of the Algol family, it manifests itself in the form of recursive procedures. This is sometimes complemented by the inclusion of built-in inductive/recursive types of various forms; e.g., most languages have natural numbers and lists as basic. In addition, some, and in particular functional ones such as Miranda™ and Haskell, have user-defined recursive types.

Recursion is also found its way into specification languages. For example, in **VDM** [3], [1] it is used in the specification of explicitly defined recursive functions. It is also present in the **VDM** definition of recursive types. In Z a simple general form of recursive types, which includes lists and trees, and their associated structural induction schemes, is built into the core of the language [4], [6].

In an earlier chapter we exhibited examples of recursive schema specifications involving numbers. These examples clearly illustrate how the use of recursion often facilitates the expression of more elegant and seemingly natural specifications. Indeed, in the case of numbers, it is rather difficult to do without them. In this chapter we move away from these simple instances and consider recursive schemata in general. For illustrative purposes, we shall work in the theory

$$SC = Th(N, DP, type, S)$$

and its extensions. This contains almost all the apparatus we require for the articulation of the general case.

14.1 Closure and Induction

Given our goal of ensuring that our theories have a recursive model, we shall be guided by the forms of recursion supported in arithmetic [5], [2]. Consequently, recursive schema specifications take the form of a closure condition and a corresponding induction principle where these principles parallel those of arithmetic.

R. Turner, *Computable Models*, DOI 10.1007/978-1-84882-052-4_14,
© Springer-Verlag London Limited 2009

Definition 218 *In the theory* **SC**, *assume that*

$$x : T, f : S(T) \vdash \phi[f, x] \; prop \qquad\qquad \mathbf{R_0}$$

where, when f occurs in φ, it occurs as a predicate. Then a recursive schema specification has the following form:

$$R \triangleq [x : T \mid \phi[R, x]] \qquad\qquad \mathbf{Rec}$$

where φ[R, x] is obtained by replacing every occurrence of f by R. This is taken to introduce a new relation symbol that satisfies the following versions of **R₁**, **R₂**, *and* **R₃**.

$$x : T \vdash R(x) \; prop \qquad\qquad \mathbf{R_1}$$

$$\forall x : T \cdot \phi[R, x] \rightarrow R(x) \qquad\qquad \mathbf{R_2}$$

$$\frac{x : T \vdash \theta[x] \; prop \qquad \forall x : T \cdot \phi[\theta, x] \rightarrow \theta[x]}{\forall x : T \cdot R(x) \rightarrow \theta[x]} \qquad \mathbf{R_3}$$

As with the simple case, **R₂** is still a closure condition, but **R₃** is now an induction principle. We may specialize the latter where θ is restricted to Σ propositions. In this case it can be stated in terms of schemata as follows.

$$\frac{h : S(T) \qquad \forall x : T \cdot \phi[h, x] \rightarrow h(x)}{\forall x : T \cdot R(x) \rightarrow h(x)} \qquad (\mathbf{R_3^{\Sigma}})$$

Initially at least, we shall take an inclusive view of these theories whereby recursive schema are added to the stock of schema. More exactly,

Definition 219 *Let* **SCR** *be the theory given as*

$$\mathbf{SCR} \triangleq \mathbf{Th(N, DP, type, S, Rec)}$$

i.e., **SC** *with recursive schema satisfying* **R₁**, **R₂**, *and* **R₃** *added. Let* **SCR**$_\Sigma$ *be theory with recursive schema satisfying* **R₁**, **R₂**, *and* **R₃**$^\Sigma$ *added; i.e., induction is restricted to* Σ *propositions. More generally, for any theory* **T** *extending* **SC**, **TR** *will be the theory that results from the addition of recursive schemata to* **T**.

To summarize, in **TR** for any Σ proposition ϕ that satisfies **R₀**, there exists a Σ relation R that satisfies **R₁**, **R₂** and **R₃**. Observe that we take the new relations that arise from recursive schemata to be Σ. They are thus taken to form part of their corresponding schema type, i.e., where

$$R \triangleq [x : T \mid \phi[R, x]]$$

R is taken to be Σ and $R : S(T)$.

We now provide a few examples to illustrate the general idea. We begin with a common use of recursion.

Example 220 (Transitive Closure)

Tr

$u : \mathbf{type}, v : S(u \otimes u), w : S(u \otimes u)$

$$w = [x : u, y : u \mid v(x, y) \vee \exists z : u \cdot v(x, z) \wedge Tr(u, z, y)]$$

The following is straightforward to establish.

Proposition 221 *For any type T and and relation $r : S(T \otimes T)$, we obtain the following closure rules.*

$$\frac{a : T \qquad b : T \qquad r(a, b)}{Tr(a, b)}$$

$$\frac{a : T \qquad b : T \qquad c : T \qquad r(a, b) \qquad Tr(b, c)}{Tr(a, c)}$$

and the following Σ induction principle. Where

$$x : T, y : T \vdash \phi[x, y] \ prop$$

we have

$$\frac{\forall x : T \cdot \forall y : T \cdot r(x, y) \to \phi[x, y] \qquad \forall x : T \cdot \forall y : T \cdot r(x, y) \wedge \phi[y, z] \to \phi[x, z]}{\forall x : T \cdot \forall y : T \cdot \phi[x, y] \to Tr(x, y)}$$

Our next example is a little more sophisticated. It is a generalized recursion operator taken from Gödel's functionals of finite type. The recursion is driven by the natural numbers but delivers schemata of higher types.

Example 222 (Recursion Operator)

R

$u : \mathbf{type}, x : u, f : S(\mathbf{N} \otimes u \otimes u), y : \mathbf{N}, z : u$

$$y = 0 \wedge z = x$$
$$\vee$$
$$y \neq 0 \wedge \exists w : u \cdot R(u, x, f, pred(y), w) \wedge f(pred(y), w, z)$$

This is already quite a complex recursive operator. But it is easy to see what it does via the following rewriting of its closure conditions. For a given type T, we obtain, suppressing some of the background information, a relation that satisfies the following closure rules.

$$\frac{a : T}{R(a, 0, a)}$$

$$\frac{a : T \qquad f(n, b, c) \qquad R(a, n, b)}{R(a, n^+, c)}$$

It is more familiar in its functional guise. Indeed, we shall return to it later when we discuss recursive functions.

The last example involves types. It generates a predicate that, given a type, characterizes all of its Cartesian products that may be constructed from it, i.e., all possible iterations of $\otimes$.

Example 223 (Products)

$$
\begin{array}{|l|}
\hline
Prod \\
\hline
u : \textbf{type}, v : \textbf{type} \\
\hline
\\
v = u \\
\vee \\
\exists z : \textbf{type} \cdot Prod[z] \wedge v = u \otimes z \\
\\
\hline
\end{array}
$$

For any given $a : \textbf{U}$, the predicate applies to all the types

$$a, a \otimes a, a \otimes (a \otimes a), \ldots$$

14.2 Simultaneous Recursion

Simultaneous recursive specifications can be found in the specification of programming language syntax and in the specification of many common recursive function definitions. In this section we demonstrate how to represent them. To motivate matters, we specify a very common form of example found in the computer science literature [1]. The following provides a simple example that defines the syntax of a simple artificial programming language.

Example 224 (A Simple Programming Language)

$$B ::= true \mid false \mid E < E \mid \textbf{if } B \textbf{ then } B \textbf{ else } B$$
$$E ::= 0 \mid Ide \mid E^{+}$$
$$C ::= Ide := E \mid \textbf{if } B \textbf{ then } C \textbf{ else } C \mid C;C \mid \textbf{while } B \textbf{ do } C$$

Booleans are generated from *true* and *false* by the less-than relation ($<$) between expressions and a conditional. The expression language contains zero, and identifiers and is closed under successor operation. The language of commands is generated by simple assignment statements, conditionals, sequencing, and a while loop. The whole grammar presents an example of a simultaneous recursion given by the following simultaneous recursive specifications. Note that we are using some general type of terms from which to build our syntactic objects.

In all three cases, the above grammar generates the predicate of the schema. We begin with the Boolean expressions. The four alternates of the grammar correspond to the four disjunctions in the predicate.

B

$u : Term$

$u = true \lor u = false$
$\lor$
$\exists x : Term \cdot \exists y : Term \cdot E(x) \land E(y) \land u = x{<}y$
$\lor$
$\exists x : Term \cdot \exists y : Term \cdot \exists z : Term \cdot B(x) \land B(y) \land B(z) \land$
$u = \textbf{if } x \textbf{ then } y \textbf{ else } z$

This reflects the structure of the grammar and so makes reference to the expression language, which is also specified as a schema specification, i.e., the general class of expressions is given by the following schema specification.

E

$u : Term$

$u = 0 \lor u = Ide \lor \exists x : Term \cdot E(x) \land u = x^{+}$

Finally, we provide the schema for the programs of the language, i.e., the syntactic class of commands.

$$
\begin{array}{|l}
\hline
C \\
\hline
\quad u : Term \\
\hline
\quad \exists x : Term \cdot \exists y : Term \cdot Ide(x) \wedge E(y) \wedge u = x := y \\
\quad \vee \\
\quad \exists x : Term \cdot \exists y : Term \cdot \exists z : Term \cdot B(x) \wedge C(y) \wedge C(z) \\
\qquad \qquad \wedge u = \textbf{if } x \textbf{ then } y \textbf{ else } z \\
\quad \vee \\
\quad \exists x : Term \cdot \exists y : Term \cdot C(x) \wedge C(y) \wedge u = x; y \\
\quad \vee \\
\quad \exists x : Term \cdot \exists y : Term \cdot B(x) \wedge C(y) \wedge u = \textbf{while } x \textbf{ do } y \\
\hline
\end{array}
$$

We shall demonstrate that such recursions can be represented in terms of our general pattern of recursive schemata. We shall illustrate with the binary case with the following simple instance. More complex cases follow much the same pattern.

Where A and B are nonempty types, the specification

$$
R \triangleq [x : A \mid \phi[R, S, x]]   \qquad\qquad \textbf{(SimRec)}
$$
$$
S \triangleq [y : B \mid \psi[R, S, y]]
$$

is taken to introduce two relations R and S that satisfy the following formation, closure and induction principles.

$$
x : A \vdash R(x) \; prop \qquad\qquad y : B \vdash S(y) \; prop
$$

$$
\forall x : A \cdot \phi[R, S, x] \rightarrow R(x) \qquad \forall y : B \cdot \psi[R, S, y] \rightarrow S(y)
$$

$$
\dfrac{
\begin{array}{l}
x : A \vdash \alpha[x] \; prop \\
y : B \vdash \beta[y] \; prop \quad \forall x : A \cdot \phi[\alpha, \beta, x] \rightarrow \alpha[x] \\
\forall y : B \cdot \psi[\alpha, \beta, y] \rightarrow \beta[y]
\end{array}
}{
\forall x : A \cdot R(x) \rightarrow h(x)
}
$$

$$
\dfrac{
\begin{array}{l}
x : A \vdash \alpha[x] \; prop \\
y : B \vdash \beta[y] \; prop \quad \forall x : A \cdot \phi[\alpha, \beta, x] \rightarrow \alpha[x] \\
\forall y : B \cdot \psi[\alpha, \beta, y] \rightarrow \beta[y]
\end{array}
}{
\forall y : B \cdot S(y) \rightarrow k(y)
}
$$

We now demonstrate that this simultaneous recursion can be represented using our simple form.

Proposition 225 *Simultaneous recursion can be expressed as a simple recursion.*

Proof Consider the following recursive specification.

$$K \triangleq [z : A \otimes B \otimes Bool \mid \iota[K, z]]$$

where

$$\iota[K, z] \triangleq Cond(z_3, \phi[R, S, z_0], \psi[R, S, z_1])$$

and

$$R = [x : A \mid \exists y : B \cdot K(x, y, 0)]$$
$$S = [y : B \mid \exists x : A \cdot K(x, y, 1)]$$

We establish that this satisfies the closure and induction principles. For closure, assume that $x : A$ and $\phi[R, S, x]$. Given that B is nonempty, we have that, for some $b : B$, $K(x, b, true)$. Hence, $R(x)$. The other closure condition is similar. For induction, assume that

$$\forall x : A \cdot \phi[\alpha, \beta, x] \rightarrow \alpha[x] \quad \forall y : B \cdot \psi[\alpha, \beta, y] \rightarrow \beta[y] \tag{1}$$

The induction scheme for K takes the following general form.

$$\frac{\forall w : A \otimes B \otimes Bool \cdot \iota[H, z] \rightarrow H(z)}{\forall w : A \otimes B \otimes Bool \cdot K(w) \rightarrow H(w)}$$

Consider the instance where

$$H(x, y, z) = Cond(z, \alpha[x], \beta[y])$$

Then

$$\alpha[x] \leftrightarrow \exists y : B \cdot H(x, y, 0)]$$
$$\beta[y] \leftrightarrow \exists x : A \cdot H(x, y, 1)]$$

and the induction for K unpacks as

$$\frac{\forall w : A \otimes B \otimes N \cdot Cond(w_3, \phi[\alpha, \beta, w_0], \psi[\alpha, \beta, w_1])}{\forall w : A \otimes B \otimes Bool \cdot K(w) \rightarrow H(w)} \tag{2}$$

Since (1) provides the premise of (2), we can conclude

$$\forall w : A \otimes B \otimes Bool \cdot K(w) \rightarrow H(w) \tag{3}$$

which yields

$$\forall x : A \cdot R(x) \to \alpha[x] \quad \text{and} \quad \forall y : B \cdot S(y) \to \beta[y] \tag{4}$$

Which completes the proof.■

14.3 Arithmetic Interpretation

Our overall objective is to ensure that all our theories have a recursive model. In the case of recursive schemata, we set things up to ensure this; i.e., we based our notion of recursive schemata upon the recursions supported in arithmetic. But we still have to check matters. Actually, we have a little more.

Theorem 226 SCR *is a conservative extension of* **Nat** *and* **SCR$_\Sigma$** *is a conservative extension of* **Nat$_\Sigma$.**

Proof Given the interpretation of **SC** in **Nat**, we have only to check that the recursive schemata translate to recursive schemata in arithmetic. Given this translation, we put

$$\eta[R, x] \triangleq x : T \wedge \phi[R, x]$$

Using the recursive schemata of arithmetic, we obtain the following rules.

$$\eta[R, x] \vdash R(x) \qquad \frac{x : T \vdash \alpha[x] \; prop \quad \eta[\alpha, x] \vdash \alpha[x]}{R[x] \vdash h(x)}$$

which yield

$$\forall x : T \cdot \phi[R, x] \to R(x) \qquad \frac{x : T \vdash \alpha[x] \; prop \quad \forall x : T \cdot \phi[R, x] \to \alpha[x]}{\forall x : T \cdot R[x] \to \alpha[x]}$$

■

So recursive schemata are sanctioned by recursive relations in arithmetic. Moreover, we are justified in including them in the Σ fragment since recursive schemata of arithmetic are Σ.

14.4 Sets and Schemata

Our objective is to demonstrate that, within a rich enough base theory, the addition of recursive relations is conservative. There are less expressive theories that will work, but the following involves little coding. We shall work in the following theory, which is obtained by the addition of finite sets to our minimal theory of schemata.

$$\mathbf{SCSet} = \mathbf{Th(N, DP, Set, type, S)}$$

Our aim is to show that the addition of recursive schemata to **SCSet** is conservative.

To facilitate the investigation, we need to introduce some properties of schemata. We begin with the definitions of *monotonicity* and *compactness* properties for schemata.

Definition 227 (Monotone and Compact)

$$Mon(f) \triangleq \forall h : \mathbf{S(S}(T)) \cdot \forall f : \mathbf{S}(T) \cdot \forall g : \mathbf{S}(T) \cdot f \subseteq g \rightarrow h(f) \subseteq h(g)$$
$$Com(f) \triangleq \forall h : \mathbf{S(S}(T)) \cdot \forall f : \mathbf{S(S}(T)) \cdot h(\cup f) \subseteq \cup h(f)$$

Using products, the generalization to two-place operators over T, S is straightforward; i.e., they are monotone and compact with respect to $T \otimes S$. We first show that all our schemata satisfy these constraints.

Lemma 228 *Monotone and compact schema are closed under conjunction, disjunction, existential quantification, and the bounded quantifiers.*

Proof We treat monotonicity first. Assume that $f, f', g, g' : \mathbf{S}(T)$ and that $f \subseteq g$ and $f' \subseteq g'$. Then it is clear that the following hold.

$$[x : T \mid f(x) \wedge g(x)] \subseteq [x : T \mid f'(x) \wedge g'(x)]$$
$$[x : T \mid f(x) \vee g(x)] \subseteq [x : T \mid f'(x) \vee g'(x)]$$

For the existential quantifier, assume $f, g, : \mathbf{S}(T \otimes S)$ and $f \subseteq g$, i.e.,

$$x : T, y : S \vdash f(x, y) \subseteq g(x, y)$$

Then, it is again quite clear that

$$[x : T \mid \exists y : S \cdot f(x, y)] \subseteq [x : T \mid \exists y : S \cdot g(x, y)]$$

For compactness, assume that $f, g : \mathbf{S(S}(T))$. Assume $(\cup f \wedge \cup g)(x)$. By definition, we have

$$\exists v : \mathbf{S}(T) \cdot f(v, x) \wedge \exists w : \mathbf{S}(T) \cdot g(w, x)$$

By monotonicity, $f(v \cup w, x) \wedge g(v \cup w, x)$. It follows that

$$\exists v : \mathbf{S}(T) \cdot f(v, x) \wedge g(v, x)$$

For compactness, assume that $h(\cup f \cap \cup g)(x)$. Then, by montonicity of h, $h(\cup f)(x)$ and $h(\cup g)(x)$. By compactness for the two conjuncts, we have, for some n, m, $h(f_n)(x)$ and $h(g_m)(x)$. By choosing the maximum of these, k say, we have

$(h(f \cup g)_k)(x)$, as required. A parallel argument yields the disjunction case. Finally, consider the compactness case for the existential quantifier. Suppose that $f : \mathbf{S}(\mathbf{S}(T \otimes S))$. Assume that $(\exists y : S \cdot \cup f)(x)$. By definition,

$$\exists w : \mathbf{S}(T \otimes S) \cdot \exists y : S \cdot f(w, x, y)$$

Hence,

$$\exists y : S \cdot \exists w : \mathbf{S}(T \otimes S) \cdot f(w, x, y)$$

as required. ∎

Corollary 229 *Every (nonrecursive) schemata in* **SCSet** *is monotone and compact.*

With this achieved, we can proceed to the main result of the section.

Theorem 230 SCSetR *is a conservative extension of* **SCSet**.

Proof We define

$$R = \cup R_n$$

where

$$
\begin{array}{|l}
\hline
R_n \\
\hline
\quad x : T \\
\hline
\quad \exists f : N \Rightarrow_{map} \mathbf{S}(T) \cdot \forall x \in dom(f) \cdot x < n \\
\quad \wedge \forall x < n \cdot x \in dom(f) \\
\quad \wedge f(0) = \Phi \\
\quad \wedge \forall k < n \cdot f(k^+) = [x : T \mid \phi[f(k), x]] \\
\quad\quad\quad\quad \wedge \\
\quad\quad\quad f(n)(x) \\
\hline
\end{array}
$$

First claim that R satisfies induction ($\mathbf{R_3}$). We illustrate with the weaker induction principle.

$$\frac{x : T \vdash \phi[h, x] \to h(x)}{x : T \vdash R[x] \to h(x)}$$

Assume the premise, $x : T$ and $R[x]$. By definition, for some $n : \mathbf{N}$ and $f : Set(N \otimes Set(T))$, where $Map(f)$, we have

$$\phi[f(n), x]$$

Now for each $k \leq n$,

$$f(k) \subseteq h$$

Why? Because $f_0 = \Phi \subseteq h$ and if $f(i) \subseteq h$, then, by monotonicity (for the first inclusion below) and the assumption (for the second inclusion), we have

$$[x : T \mid \phi[f(i), x]] \subseteq [x : T \mid \phi[h, x]] \subseteq [x : T \mid h(x)]$$

It follows that

$$f(i^+)(x) = [x : T \mid \phi[f(i), x]](x) \subseteq [x : T \mid h(x)](x) \subseteq h(x)$$

$\mathbf{R}_3$ follows. For $\mathbf{R}_2$, suppose that $\phi[R, t]$. Hence, it follows by compactness that

$$\exists n : \mathbf{N} \cdot \exists f : Set(N, Set(T)) \cdot f(0) = \Phi \wedge$$
$$\forall k < n \cdot \forall y \in f(k^+) \cdot \phi[f(k), y] \wedge t \in f(n)$$

Hence, by definition, $R[t]$.∎

So the addition of recursive schemata is conservative. Finally, we can justify our original notation for schemata, i.e., that the introduction of a new relation symbol is taken to be equivalent to the defining proposition; i.e., the following shows that both directions of the original biconditional characterization still hold.

Theorem 231 *For each recursive specification*

$$R \triangleq [x : T \mid \phi[R, x]]$$

we have

$$\forall x : T \cdot R(x) \leftrightarrow \phi[R, x]$$

Proof By closure we have only to demonstrate the following.

$$\forall x : T \cdot R(x) \rightarrow \phi[R, x]$$

Let

$$h = [z : \mathbf{S}(T), x : T \mid \phi[z, x]]$$

By closure and the specification of h, we have

$$h[R, x] \rightarrow R(x)$$

By the monotonicity of schemata applied to h, we obtain the following.

$$h([x : T \mid \phi[R, x]], x) \rightarrow h[R, x]$$

Hence, by definition of h,

$$\phi([x : T \mid h[R, x]], x) \rightarrow [x : T \mid h[R, x]](x)$$

By induction,

$$x : T, R(x) \rightarrow [x : T \mid h[R, x]](x)$$

By definition,

$$x : T, R(x) \rightarrow \phi[R, x]$$

as required.∎

This completes our first chapter on recursion. There are two more to come. In them we shall look at two special cases: recursive types and recursive functions.

References

1. Dawes, J. The VDM-SL Reference Guide. Pitman, London, 1991
2. Havel, P. Metamathematics of First Order Arithmetic. Springer-Verlag, New York, 1991
3. Jones, C.B. Systematic Software Development Using VDM. Prentice-Hall, Inc., Englewood Cliffs, NJ, 1986.
4. Potter, B. Sinclair, J. and Till, D. An introduction to formal specification and Z. Prentice Hall, Inc. Englewood Cliffs, NJ, 1991.
5. Smorynski, C. Logical Number Theory I : An Introduction. Springer-Verlag. New York, 1991.
6. Woodcock, J. and Davies, J. Using Z: Specification, Refinement and Proof, Prentice Hall, Englewood Cliffs, NJ, 1996.

Chapter 15
Inductive Types

Most programming and specification languages have built-in recursive types. Usually, some version of the natural numbers is taken as basic and the language is enriched by a form of user-defined recursive types. In this chapter we consider such type specifications. More exactly, we consider a version of such types that are more accurately described as *inductive*. These are presented in three parts:

- a formation rule,
- closure principles,
- an induction principle.

The formation rule dictates how the type is constructed from given types, while the closure conditions determine what is in the type. Finally, the induction principle supports reasoning about the type and, in particular, guarantees that the type is *the smallest one* that satisfies the closure conditions. We have already seen several examples of such types. For instance, the natural numbers are characterized by such principles. In this case the formation rule is the simple assertion that **N** is a type, but in general it will be more complex and involve other types as parameters. For instance, lists, finite sets, and trees employ parameter types. Slightly different examples emanate from the definition of languages where several different grammatical categories are simultaneously defined. Other instances involve the specification of a category of subtypes of a given theory of types. For example, one might wish to pick out the type of finite schemata from the type of all schemata over a given type.

15.1 The General Form

Our general form of inductive type emanates from our general scheme for recursive specifications. Let

$$\mathbf{Th}(O_1, ..., O_k)$$

be any **TDT**. In this section we shall work in the corresponding theory

R. Turner, *Computable Models*, DOI 10.1007/978-1-84882-052-4_15,
© Springer-Verlag London Limited 2009

$$\mathbf{Th}(O_1, ..., O_k, \mathbf{I})$$

The new type constructor $\mathbf{I}[T, \phi]$, where T is the base type from which all the elements are selected and ϕ is the generating condition, is governed by the following rules, where ϕ is Σ.

$$\frac{x : T \vdash \phi[T, x] \; prop}{\mathbf{I}[T, \phi] \; type} \qquad \mathbf{I_1}$$

$$\frac{a : T \qquad \phi[\mathbf{I}[T, \phi], a]}{a : \mathbf{I}[T, \phi]} \qquad \mathbf{I_2}$$

$$\frac{x : T \vdash \theta[x] \; prop \qquad \forall x : T \cdot \phi[\theta, x] \to \theta[x]}{\forall x : \mathbf{I}[T, \phi] \cdot \theta[x]} \qquad \mathbf{I_3}$$

$\mathbf{I_1}$ is the formation rule, $\mathbf{I_2}$ is the closure condition, and $\mathbf{I_3}$ is the induction principle. In these rules $\phi[\mathbf{I}[T, \phi], a]$ is obtained by replacing every occurrence of T by $\mathbf{I}[T, \phi]$. Note that where T occurs in a proposition, it occurs in a subterm of the form $\exists x : T \cdot \sigma$. Consequently, $\phi[\theta, x]$ is obtained from $\phi[T, x]$ by replacing every occurrence of $\exists x : T \cdot \sigma$ by $\exists x : T \cdot \theta[x] \wedge \sigma[x]$. As before, we may restrict matters by restricting $\mathbf{I_3}$ to Σ propositions, i.e., where θ is Σ. We first illustrate matters with some concrete examples.

15.2 Some Inductive Types

Our first few examples are familiar ones. We begin with the most common kind of inductive structure, the paradigm case.

Example 232 (Numbers) Recall that the type Num was determined by the following rules.

$$\mathbf{N_0} \quad Num \; type$$

$$\mathbf{N_1} \quad 0 : Num \qquad\qquad \mathbf{N_2} \quad \frac{a : Num}{a^+ : Num}$$

Given this, we can form an inductive type $\mathbf{I}[Num, \phi]$, where

$$\phi[T, y] \triangleq y = 0 \vee \exists x : T \cdot y = x^+$$

This yields the standard induction principle of **Nat**. Substituting in the principle gives

$$x : T \vdash \theta[x] \; prop$$
$$\frac{\forall x : Num \cdot (x = 0 \vee (\exists z : Num \cdot \theta[z] \wedge x = z^+)) \rightarrow \theta[x]}{\forall x : \mathbf{I}[T, \phi] \cdot \theta[x]}$$

which simplifies to

$$\frac{x : T \vdash \theta[x] \; prop \qquad \theta[0] \qquad \forall z : Num \cdot \theta[z] \rightarrow \theta[z^+]}{\forall x : \mathbf{I}[T, \phi] \cdot \theta[x]}$$

The strength of induction satisfied depends upon the induction assumed in the general inductive type. The same is true of the following example.

Example 233 (Lists) The type Baby Lists is given by the following rules.

$$\mathbf{List_0} \quad \frac{T \; type}{List(T) \; type}$$

$$\mathbf{List_1} \quad \frac{T \; type}{[]_T : List(T)} \qquad \mathbf{List_2} \quad \frac{a : T \qquad b : Bl(T)}{a \star_T b : List(T)}$$

Given this, we can form an inductive type $\mathbf{I}[List, \phi]$, where

$$\phi[T, y] \triangleq y = [] \vee \exists u : T \cdot \exists x : List[T] \cdot y = u \star x$$

Once again we have constructed an inductive type from one that is built from the bare material of the type. Again, the standard induction principle is derivable.

$$\frac{\theta[[]_T] \quad \forall x : T \cdot \forall y : List(T) \cdot \theta[y] \rightarrow \theta[x \star_T y]}{\forall x : List(T) \cdot \theta[x]}$$

Specification languages such as **Z** have a very simple form of inductive type built in. Indeed, lists are a special case of such. These are often referred to as *structural inductive types* since they are generated by some functional operators. Essentially, these are trees [1], [2]. Since it is simple to define and contains the essence of such types, we shall illustrate with the type of binary trees.

Example 234 (Binary Trees) Given the type of baby binary trees that satisfy the following closure conditions

$$\mathbf{Bt_1} \quad \frac{A \; type}{Tree(A) \; type} \qquad \mathbf{Bt_2} \quad \frac{a : A}{Node(a) : Tree(A)}$$

$$\mathbf{Bt_3} \quad \frac{a : A \qquad b : Tree(A) \qquad c : Tree(A)}{Branch(a, b, c) : Tree(A)}$$

we can form an inductive type that satisfies

$$\frac{\forall z : A \cdot \phi[Node(z)] \qquad \forall z : A \cdot \forall x : Tree(A) \cdot \forall y : Tree(A) \cdot (\phi[x] \wedge \phi[y]) \to \phi[Branch(z, x, y)]}{\forall x : Tree(A) \cdot \phi[x]}$$

by putting $\phi[A, y]$ equal to

$$\exists u : A \cdot y = Node(u) \vee \exists v : Tree(A) \cdot \exists w : Tree(A) \cdot y = Branch(z, x, y)$$

This technique can be replayed with arbitrary terms to yield the general case of structural types.

The next example is slightly different. We present the theory **CST** as an inductive type. Here we assume that we are working in the following theory:

$$\textbf{Th(N, DP, Set, type, S)}$$

i.e., all the type constructors of **CST** are included. In that case, the following is the recursive definition of the types of **CST**.

Example 235 (CST Types) We may form an inductive type that satisfies the following closure conditions

$$\textbf{Nat} : \textbf{CST} \qquad \frac{T : \textbf{CST}}{Set(T) : \textbf{CST}} \qquad \frac{T : \textbf{CST} \qquad S : \textbf{CST}}{T \otimes S : \textbf{CST}}$$

by putting

$$\phi[T, u] \triangleq \left(\begin{array}{c} u = \textbf{N} \\ \vee \\ \exists v : \textbf{type} \cdot \exists w : \textbf{type} \cdot \textbf{CST}(v) \wedge \textbf{CST}(w) \wedge u = v \otimes w \\ \vee \\ \exists v : \textbf{type} \cdot \textbf{CST}(v) \wedge u = Set(v) \end{array} \right)$$

This yields an inductive type that characterizes the types of **CST**.

It also provides the corresponding induction principle that facilities reasoning about the types of **CST**.

$$\frac{\phi[\textbf{Nat}] \qquad \forall z : \textbf{CST} \cdot \phi[z] \to \phi[Set(z)] \qquad \forall x : \textbf{CST} \cdot \forall y : \textbf{CST} \cdot \phi[x] \wedge \phi[y] \to \phi[x \otimes y]}{\forall z : \textbf{CST} \cdot \phi[z]}$$

15.3   Conservative Extensions

We next demonstrate that such types can be obtained from recursive relations by using separation.

Theorem 236 *Recursive types can be represented in*

$$\mathbf{Th(N, DP, type, S, Rec, Sep)}$$

Proof Given the schema

$$R \triangleq [x : T \mid \phi[R, x]] \qquad\qquad\qquad \mathbf{Rec}$$

use separation to form the recursive type $I \triangleq \{x : T \cdot R(x)\}$.

Recall that the schema R provides a relation determined by the following rules.

$$x : T \vdash R(x)\ prop \qquad\qquad\qquad\qquad\qquad \mathbf{R_1}$$

$$\forall x : T \cdot \phi[R, x] \rightarrow R(x) \qquad\qquad\qquad\qquad \mathbf{R_2}$$

$$\frac{x : T \vdash \theta[x]\ prop \qquad\qquad \forall x : T \cdot \phi[\theta, x] \rightarrow \theta[x]}{\forall x : T \cdot R(x) \rightarrow \theta[x]} \qquad \mathbf{R_3}$$

Then we obtain the principles, for I.■

Since

$$\mathbf{Th(N, DP, type, S, Rec, Sep)}$$

is a conservative extension of

$$\mathbf{Th(N, DP, type, S, Rec)}$$

we have that the addition of inductive types yields a conservative extension of the latter.

15.4 Finite Schemata

Finally, we carry out a case study that further illustrates the usefulness of recursive specifications and recursive types. We show how the notion of a finite set, and much of its associated machinery, can be specified using inductive types and recursion.

We begin with the main specification; i.e., the following yields a recursive definition of the relation of being a finite collection of objects.

Example 237 (Finite Schemata)

$$
\begin{array}{|l|}
\hline
\mathbf{F}_T \\
\hline
y : \mathbf{S}(T) \\
\hline
y = \mathbf{E}_T \\
\vee \\
\exists x : T \cdot \exists z : \mathbf{S}(T) \cdot \mathbf{F}_T(z) \wedge y = x \circledast z \\
\hline
\end{array}
$$

where

$$
\mathbf{E}_T = [x : T \mid x \neq x]
$$

is the empty schema of type T.

We then use

$$
\phi[T, y] \triangleq \mathbf{F}_T(y)
$$

to introduce the corresponding inductive type $\mathbf{Set}(T)$. This satisfies the following principles of closure.

$$
\frac{T \text{ type}}{\mathbf{E}_T : \mathbf{Set}(T)} \qquad \frac{s : \mathbf{Set}(T) \qquad a : T}{a \circledast s : \mathbf{Set}(T)}
$$

The principle of induction reflects this: Any schema closed under element insertion and containing the empty schema is a property of every finite set.

$$
\frac{\phi[\mathbf{E}_T] \qquad \forall y : T \cdot \forall x : \mathbf{Set}(T) \cdot \phi[x] \rightarrow \phi[y \circledast x]}{\forall x : \mathbf{Set}(T) \cdot \phi[x]}
$$

Finite schemata resemble finite sets. Indeed, the following specification of membership strengthens this impression.

$$
\in \; \triangleq \; [x : T, y : \mathbf{Set}(T) \mid y(x)]
$$

In our account of finite sets, the set quantifiers form an essential ingredient. But these may also be defined using recursion. We introduce existential and universal quantification over finite schemata as follows.

Example 238 (Existential Set Quantifier)

$$EQS$$

$$y : \mathbf{Set}(T), f : \mathbf{S}(T)$$

$$\exists x : T \cdot \exists z : \mathbf{Set}(T) \cdot y = x \circledast z \wedge (f(x) \vee EQS(z, f))$$

$EQS(y, f)$ holds if $y = x \circledast z$, and either f holds of x or it (recursively) holds of z. The parallel specification of the universal quantifier is given as follows.

Example 239 (Universal Set Quantifier)

$$UQS$$

$$y : \mathbf{Set}(T), f : \mathbf{S}(T)$$

$$\exists x : T \cdot \exists z : \mathbf{Set}(T) \cdot y = x \circledast z \wedge f(x) \wedge UQS(z, f)$$

The universal quantifier holds if the schemata is empty or it can be expressed as $y = x \circledast z$ and f holds of x and it (recursively) holds of z.

To be somewhat more conventional (and neater), we shall write the set quantifiers as follows.

$$EQS(y, f) \text{ as } \exists x \in y \cdot f(x)$$
$$UQS(y, f) \text{ as } \forall x \in y \cdot f(x)$$

Proposition 240 (Set Quantifiers) *The set quantifiers satisfy the restricted introduction and elimination rules for the bounded set quantifiers.*

Proof We illustrate with the existential quantifier. We must show that

$$\frac{s : Set(T) \quad f : \mathbf{S}(T) \quad s(t) \quad f(t)}{\dfrac{\exists x \in s \cdot f(x)}{\dfrac{f : \mathbf{S}(T) \quad \exists x \in s \cdot f \quad x : T, s(x) \vdash \phi}{\phi}}}$$

We begin with the elimination rule. Assume the premises. We use induction of the inductive definition of *Set*. If s is empty, we are done since $s(x)$ is false. Assume that

$$s = a \circledast b$$

where $b : Set(T)$ and $a : T$. By assumption, $s(a)$ or $\exists x \in b \cdot f$. If the former, then since $x : T, s(x) \vdash \phi$, we are done. Assume that $\exists x \in b \cdot f$. We know that $x : T, b(x) \vdash \phi$. By induction, ϕ. In either case we have the result. For the introduction rule, assume the premises. Again, we use induction. s cannot be empty, so we may assume that

$$s = a \circledast b$$

where $b : Set(T)$ and $a : T$. We have $t = a$ or $t \in b$. If $t = a$ then we are finished by the specification of the existential quantifier, and if $t \in b$, we are finished by the induction hypothesis.∎

The only thing that prevents finite schemata from behaving as finite sets is its inherited notion of equality, i.e., the one it inherits from schemata in general. The following introduces an extensional equality relation on finite schemata, again by recursion on their structure.

Example 241 (Extensional Equality)

EQS_T

$y : \mathbf{Set}(T), z : \mathbf{Set}(T)$
$\forall x \in y \cdot z(x)$ $\forall x \in z \cdot y(x)$

So that equality for finite schemata is given in terms of their membership; i.e., they are the same when they apply to the same objects. We shall write this in standard infix notation; i.e.,

$$EQS_T(a, b) \triangleq a =_T b$$

These notions satisfy the following. The proof is straightforward.

1. EQS_T is an equivalence relation.
2. $\forall y : \mathbf{Set}(T) \cdot \forall z : \mathbf{Set}(T) \cdot y = z \rightarrow \forall x : T \cdot x \circledast y = x \circledast z$

We can thus mimic all the set operations that we delivered earlier. In particular, we have

Example 242 (Simple Union)

Union
$$u : \mathbf{Set}(T),\ v : \mathbf{Set}(T),\ w : \mathbf{Set}(T)$$

$$(v = \emptyset \wedge w = u)$$
$$\vee$$
$$\exists x : T \cdot \exists y : Set(T) \cdot v = x \circledast y \wedge$$
$$\exists z : Set(T) \cdot Union(u, y, z) \wedge w = x \circledast z$$

Our final example uses numbers and sets.

Example 243 (Size of a Set)

$\|$
$$u : Set(T),\ z : N$$

$$u = \emptyset \wedge z = 0$$
$$\vee$$
$$\exists x : Set(T) \cdot \exists y : T \cdot y \notin x \wedge u = y \circledast x \wedge z = |x|$$
$$\vee$$
$$\exists x : Set(T) \cdot \exists y : T \cdot y \in x \wedge u = y \circledast x \wedge z = |x| + 1$$

There are many other forms of such recursive types that have been introduced to handle reasoning about programs. Many of these schemes have recursive interpretations, but not all.

References

1. Potter, B., Sinclair, J., and Till, D. An introduction to formal specification and Z. Prentice Hall, Inc., Englewood Cliffs, 1991.
2. Woodcock, J. and Davies, J. Using Z: Specification, Refinement and Proof, Prentice Hall, Englewood Cliffs, NJ, 1996.

Chapter 16
Recursive Functions

In many applications recursive functions are the natural tool of specification. For example, in computability theory [1], [3] and formal number theory [2], they are fundamental. Indeed, without much loss of elegance, transparency, and proof-theoretic ease, it is hard to see how it could be recast in relational form.

Since recursive functions are a special form of recursive relations, we ought to be able to justify their addition as a special case of the addition of recursive relations. We can, but matters are a little involved. Establishing that a recursive relation is single-valued and/or total is somewhat more complex in the recursive case. And generally, we need to use induction. We shall study various styles of recursive definition. Our first examples deal with standard recursive and iterative styles of recursion that are derived from computability theory, including primitive recursion, and a general form of iteration. We shall then move on to consider more general examples.

16.1 General Form

Our general form of recursive function specification is derived from the following simple observation that provides a sufficient condition for functionality; i.e., if the defining predicate of the schema preserves functionality, the whole schema is functional.

Lemma 244 (Functionality) *Given*

$$F \triangleq [x : I, y : I \mid \phi[F, x, y]]$$

and

$$\iota[x, y] \triangleq (\forall z : I \cdot F(x, z) \to y = z)$$

and

$$\forall x : I \cdot \forall y : I \cdot \phi[\iota, x, y] \to \iota[x, y]$$

then F is functional.

R. Turner, *Computable Models*, DOI 10.1007/978-1-84882-052-4_16,
© Springer-Verlag London Limited 2009

Proof We use the induction scheme for F with the following proposition.

$$\iota[x, y] \triangleq \forall z : I \cdot F(x, z) \to y = z$$

The premise of the induction schema is satisfied by assumption, and so we have

$$\forall x : I \cdot \forall y : I \cdot F[x, y] \to \iota[x, y]$$

This yields $\forall x : I \cdot \forall y : I \cdot R[x, y] \wedge R[x, z] \to y = z.\blacksquare$

Now consider the following apparently single-valued relation F.

$$\forall x : I \cdot (Dom F)(x) \to (F(x) = t[F(s), x]) \tag{1}$$

where $F(s)$ occurs somewhere in t. We say "apparently", since although it is defined by explicit function definition, it involves a recursion, and this must be justified. (1) can be easily generalized to allow for many-place function symbols, and to cater for several occurrences of F. But for expositional purposes, we concentrate on this simple case where we assume that F occurs as a function symbol; i.e., it occurs somewhere in the form $F(s)$, where $x : I, v : I \vdash t[F(s)/v, x] : I$.

In order to show that the addition of such functions is conservative, we need to indicate how they are to be eliminated in favor of recursive relations. To begin with, observe that using our translational means (∗) for the removal of functional application, (1) unpacks to the following relational form.

$$\forall x : I \cdot (Dom F)(x) \to \exists y : I \cdot F(x, y) \wedge \exists z : I \cdot F(s, z) \wedge y = t[z, x] \tag{2}$$

This unwraps to the following recursive relation specification.

$$F \triangleq [x : I, y : I \mid \exists v : I \cdot F(s, v) \wedge y = t[v, x]] \tag{3}$$

Now we have to check that such a specification generates a function.

Proposition 245 *The relation F given as*

$$F \triangleq [x : I, y : I \mid \exists v : I \cdot F(s, v) \wedge y = t[v, x]]$$

satisfies the conditions of the functionality lemma.

Proof We have to show that

$$\forall x : I \cdot \forall y : I \cdot (\exists v : I \cdot \iota(s, v) \wedge y = t[v, x]) \to \iota(x, y)$$

So assume that $x : I, y : I, v : I$, and $\iota(s, v) \wedge y = t[v, x]$. Further assume that $z : I$ and $F(x, z)$. Then we know that for some $u : I$, we have $F(s, u) \wedge y = t[u, x]$. But by assumption, $\iota(s, v)$ and so $u = v$. But then we have $y = t[v, x] = y = t[u, x]$ and so $\iota(x, y)$.∎

Consequently, we have

$$\forall x : I \cdot \forall y : I \cdot Dom(F)(x) \rightarrow (F(x) = y \leftrightarrow \exists v : I \cdot F(s) = v \wedge (y = t[v, x])$$

i.e.,

$$\forall x : I \cdot Dom F(x) \rightarrow F(x) = t(F(s), x)$$

We shall abbreviate $Dom F(x) \rightarrow F(x) = t(F, x)$ as

$$F(x) \simeq t(F, x)$$

so that (1) takes the form

$$\forall x : I \cdot F(x) \simeq t(F, x)$$

Effectively, $\simeq$ denotes partial equality (i.e., where the right-hand side is defined, so is the left and equal to it).

We can generalize this setting as follows. Suppose that

$$G : S(S(I \otimes I), S(I \otimes I))$$

Further suppose that G is functional; i.e.,

$$\mathbf{Fun}(G, S(I \otimes I), S(I \otimes I))$$

(but not necessarily total) and it preserves functions; i.e.,

$$\forall f : S(I \otimes I) \cdot \mathbf{Fun}(f, I, I) \rightarrow \mathbf{Fun}(G(f), I, I)$$

Then we have

$$\forall x : I \cdot F(x) \simeq G(F)(x) \tag{4}$$

where

$$t(F, x) = G(F)(x)$$

F is the *least solution* of (1) in the sense of the guaranteed induction scheme; i.e., it is an instance of a fixed-point operator that is the least, in the sense of the induction principle, function that satisfies (1).

In the next few sections we shall illustrate the use of these ideas in a variety of different cases. We shall work within extensions of the theory **SCR**.

To begin with, we employ a somewhat forgotten formulation of recursion. Mc-Carthy introduced a way of defining recursive functions that may be taken to apply to any type.

Example 246 (Conditional Expressions) We work within any extension of the theory **SCR**. The following provides a specification of a partial recursive function over a type T.

$$F(x) \approx b_1(x) \rightarrow t_1[x, F], b_2(x) \rightarrow t_2[x, F], ..., b_n(x) \rightarrow t_n[x, F]$$

Here we put

$$t[x, F] \doteq b_1(x) \rightarrow t_1[x, F], b_2(x) \rightarrow t_2[x, F], ..., b_n(x) \rightarrow t_n[x, F]$$

This is a version of McCarthy's conditional expressions.

16.2 Numerical Recursion

We first apply the general result to the standard theory of recursive functions over the natural numbers. This yields the Church computable functions. Our first example allows the specification of multiplication from addition.

Example 247 (Multiplication) We put

$$t[x, y, F] \triangleq y = 0 \rightarrow x, x + F(x, y - 1)$$

We need to check that this generates a recursive function that satisfies

$$F(x, y) = y = 0 \rightarrow x, x + F(x, y - 1)$$

We can rewrite the recursion in standard form as a pair of recursion equations as follows.

$$F(x, 0) = x$$
$$F(x, y^+) = x + F(x, y)$$

This can be generalized to yield the schema of primitive recursion.

Example 248 (Primitive Recursion) Suppose that $h : \mathbf{S}(N^{n+2} \otimes N)$ and $g : \mathbf{S}(N^n \otimes N)$ are total functions from N^{n+2} to N and N^n to N, respectively. Then consider the term

$$t[x_1, ..., x_n, y, F] \triangleq y = 0 \rightarrow g(x_1, ..., x_n), h(x_1, ..., x_n, y, F(x_1, ..., x_n, y - 1))$$

This generates the standard representation of primitive recursion, viz.

$$F(x_1, ..., x_n, 0) = g(x_1, ..., x_n)$$
$$F(x_1, ..., x_n, y + 1) = h(x_1, ..., x_n, y, F(x_1, ..., x_n, y))$$

We can go further and bring partial functions into play by the use of the classical minimization operator of recursive function theory.

Example 249 (Minimization) Given a binary numerical total function $f : \mathsf{S}(N \otimes N)$, the minimization operator returns a unary function g that, given an input x, returns the smallest number y for which $f(x, y) = 0$. We put

$$t(x, n, F) = f(x, n) \neq 0 \rightarrow F(x, n^+), n$$

The function is normally defined as

$$g(x) = F(x, 0)$$
$$where\ F(x, n) = f(x, n) \neq 0 \rightarrow F(x, n^+), n$$

These two, together with the appropriate basic functions, generate all the Turing computable functions. We can also move up the type levels. Recall the following example.

Example 250 (Functionals of Finite Type)

$$
\begin{array}{|l|}
\hline
R \\
\hline
u : \textbf{type}, x : u, f : \mathsf{S}(N \otimes (u \otimes u)), y : \mathbf{N}, z : u \\
\hline
y = 0 \wedge z = x \\
\vee \\
y \neq 0 \wedge \exists w : u \cdot R(u, x, f, pred(y), w) \wedge f(pred(y), w) \\
\hline
\end{array}
$$

On the assumption that f is functional, it is provable by induction that R is functional and satisfies

$$R(u, x, f, 0) = x$$
$$R(u, x, f, y^+) = f(y, R(u, x, f, y))$$

This yields the standard notion of Gödel's functionals of finite type.

16.3 Recursive Functions and Inductive Types

Inductive types give rise to a notion of recursive function that follows the structure of the type. In order to illustrate matters, we employ the following type of binary trees.

$$\frac{A\ type}{Tree(A)\ type} \qquad \frac{a:A}{Node(a):Tree(A)}$$

$$\frac{a:A \quad b:Tree(A) \quad c:Tree(A)}{Branch(a,b,c):Tree(A)}$$

$$\frac{\forall z:A\cdot\phi[Node(z)] \atop \forall z:A\cdot\forall x:Tree(A)\cdot\forall y:Tree(A)\cdot(\phi[x]\wedge\phi[y])\rightarrow\phi[Branch(z,x,y)]}{\forall x:Tree(A)\cdot\phi[x]}$$

Proposition 251 *The following principles of recursion can be derived via the induction rule.*

$$\frac{z:A\vdash g(z):C \atop z:A,x:Tree(A),y:Tree(A),u:C,v:C\vdash F(z,x,y,u,v):C}{x:Tree(A)\vdash rec(x,g,F):C}$$

$$\frac{z:A\vdash g(z):C \atop z:A,x:Tree(A),y:Tree(A),u:C,v:C\vdash F(z,x,y,u,v):C}{z:A\vdash rec(Node(z),g,F)=g(z)}$$

$$z:A\vdash g(z):C$$
$$z:A,x:Tree(A),y:Tree(A),u:C,v:C\vdash F(z,x,y,u,v):C$$
$$\underline{z:A,x:Tree(A),y:Tree(A)}$$
$$rec(Node(z,x,y),g,F)=F(z,x,y,rec(x,g,F),rec(y,g,F))$$

Proof We have to justify the existence of *rec* as a function. For this we have to show that the recursive relation given as

$$R$$

$$x:I,z:C$$

$$\exists y:A\cdot x=Node(y)\wedge z=g(y)$$
$$\vee$$
$$\exists x_1:I\cdot\exists x_2:I\cdot\exists y:A\cdot w=node(y,x_1,x_2)\wedge$$
$$\exists u:C\cdot\exists v:C\cdot R(x_1,u)\wedge R(x_2,v)\wedge$$
$$F(y,x_1,x_2,u,v,x,z)$$

is functional. We use the induction scheme for R with the following proposition.

$$\phi[x,u]\triangleq\forall v:C\cdot R(x,v)\rightarrow u=v$$

The proof is then routine.■

A further simple example is afforded by the following, more interesting, notion.

Example 252 (Higher Types) We specify

$$F$$

$$x : N, z : \textbf{type}$$

$$x = 0 \land z = \textbf{N}$$
$$\lor$$
$$\exists y : \textbf{N} \cdot \exists u : \textbf{type} \cdot x = y^+ \land R(y, u) \land z = \textbf{S}(u)$$

This is functional, and leads to a recursive function that satisfies

$$F(0) = \textbf{N}$$
$$F(n^+) = \textbf{S}(F(n))$$

There are many other obvious examples, but we shall return to this topic at several places in the rest of the book and, in particular, in our treatment of programming language semantics.Cutland, N. Computability: An Introduction to Recursive Function Theory. Cambridge. 1990.

References

1. Cutland, N. Computability: An Introduction to Recursive Function Theory. Cambridge Univ. Press, Cambridge, 1990.
2. Havel, P. Metamathematics of First Order Arithmetic. Springer-Verlag, New York, 1991
3. Rogers, H. Theory of Recursive Functions and Effective Computability. McGraw Hill, New York, 1967; 1988.

Chapter 17
Schema Definitions

Schema specifications are intended to articulate the required relationship between the input and output of a program. But are there conditions that we might wish to impose upon a program that they cannot express? More generally, are there aspects of computable modeling that such specifications cannot accommodate? In this chapter we shall explore this issue. On the face of it there are several different reasons why we might wish to go beyond schema specifications.

For one thing, it is often more convenient and natural to employ, at least initially, a definition that is not Σ. For example, the simplest definition of the greatest common divisor of two numbers demands that the GCD is greater than all common divisors. And, the naive formulation of this is not Σ. However, such a characterization is the obvious one, and the one that requires the least knowledge of number theory. Indeed, in general, with the expressive power of the full language available, such non-Σ definitions are often less syntactically complex. So one argument for their employment is that they enable more obvious definitions that demand less knowledge of the underlying theory.

A second reason stems from the fact that certain properties that we wish to impose upon a specification go beyond the simple relationship between input and output. Instead, they are properties of the relation as a whole, properties of the actual schema as an object. And these properties may not be Σ properties. Indeed, we have already encountered some obvious examples of this; e.g., the demand that a relation be a total function falls into this category. Properties of schemata such as *monotonicity* and *compactness* provide other examples. In other words, we shall need to express properties of specifications that are not Σ, and the natural way of packaging such type and predicate information is via the following idea.

17.1 Schema Definitions

To incorporate these considerations, we extend our schema notation to allow for the expression of a more general class of definitions. We immediately include preconditions and permit definitions of the form

R. Turner, *Computable Models*, DOI 10.1007/978-1-84882-052-4_17,
© Springer-Verlag London Limited 2009

$$R \triangleq [x : I, y : O \mid \pi[x]; \phi[x, y]]$$

where π, ϕ may not be Σ propositions. To distinguish matters, we shall call these more general definitions *schema definitions* rather than schema specifications. The latter are a special case.

Definition 253 (Schema Definitions) *Suppose that* **T** *is any* **TDT**. *Further suppose that*

$$x : I, \pi[x], y : O \vdash_{\mathbf{T}} \phi[x, y] \; prop \qquad\qquad \mathbf{R_0}$$

Then the schema definition

$$R \triangleq [x : I, y : O \mid \pi(x); \phi[x, y]] \qquad\qquad \textbf{(Preschema)}$$

is taken to introduce a new relation (R), not necessarily Σ, *that is governed by the following axioms.*

$$x : I, \pi(x), y : O \vdash R(x, y) \; prop \qquad\qquad \mathbf{R_1}$$

$$\forall x : I \cdot \forall y : O \cdot \pi(x) \to (\phi[x, y] \to R(x, y)) \qquad\qquad \mathbf{R_2}$$

$$\forall x : I \cdot \forall y : O \cdot \pi(x) \to (R(x, y) \to \phi[x, y]) \qquad\qquad \mathbf{R_3}$$

Let $\mathbf{T^R}$ *be the theory obtained from* **T** *by the addition of a new relation symbol (R) that is governed by these axioms.*

The new relation is not Σ unless both π and ϕ are. However, the addition of such relations is still conservative, and the proof is identical.

Theorem 254 *Suppose that* Γ, Θ *do not contain R. Then*

$$\Gamma \vdash_{\mathbf{TR}} \Theta \; implies \; \Gamma \vdash_{\mathbf{T}} \Theta$$

Our definitions of totality and functionality extend to definitions without change. Moreover, for those relations F that are functional, we can conservatively add application, i.e., $app(F, a)$. Indeed, the whole development proceeds as before.

We now provide some simple examples of schema definitions. These are instances where, arguably, the obvious definition is not Σ. The first is the one already alluded to; it is the standard definition of the greatest common divisor.

Example 255 (GCD)

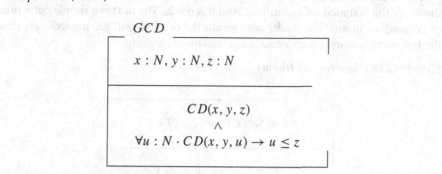

$$GCD$$

$$x : N, y : N, z : N$$

$$CD(x, y, z)$$
$$\wedge$$
$$\forall u : N \cdot CD(x, y, u) \rightarrow u \leq z$$

This seems like the natural way of writing the GCD of two numbers. It simply states that z is a common divisor of x and y and that any other CD is less than or equal to z. However, it is not Σ.

Our next example is along similar lines, but it is a little more complicated. It involves the concept of a *Hamming number*.

Example 256 (Hamming Numbers)

$$Ham(n)$$

$$n : N$$

$$\forall x : N \cdot (Prime(x) \wedge Divides(x, n)) \rightarrow x = 2 \vee x = 3 \vee x = 5$$

In number theory, these numbers are called *5-smooth* because they can be characterized as having only 2, 3, or 5 as prime factors. They are a specific case of what are called k smooth numbers, those sets of numbers that have no prime factors greater than k. Again, this is a schema definition that is not a specification.

Our next few examples are taken from finite set theory.

Example 257 (Subset)

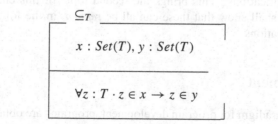

$$\subseteq_T$$

$$x : Set(T), y : Set(T)$$

$$\forall z : T \cdot z \in x \rightarrow z \in y$$

This is the standard definition and the only one that could be expressed without the use of the bounded set quantifiers. And it is not Σ. The next is a simple definition of generalized union. The reader who recalls the original will see immediately that the following is standard, more succinct, and more elegant.

Example 258 (Generalized Union)

$$
\begin{array}{|l}
\hline
\cup_T \\
\hline
u : Set(Set(T)), w : Set(T) \\
\hline
\forall x : T \cdot x \in w \leftrightarrow \exists v \in u \cdot x \in v \\
\hline
\end{array}
$$

The last is even more convincing in terms of its relative simplicity. Indeed, it is the normal definition of power set; i.e., a set is in the power set of another iff it is a subset of it. You will recall that the original was an inductive definition that followed the inductive structure of the underlying set.

Example 259 (Power Set)

$$
\begin{array}{|l}
\hline
Pow \\
\hline
x : Set(T), y : Set(Set(T)) \\
\hline
\forall z : Set(T) \cdot z \in y \leftrightarrow z \subseteq x \\
\hline
\end{array}
$$

A number of other examples may be marshalled to demonstrate the need for non-Σ specifications [4]. Some are subtly different in nature to those presented here. However, they all succume to the analysis we shall offer. Some of the replacements suggested here can be found in [2], [3]. In these papers, one can also find some further discussion of the issues.

While these definitions are not Σ, they have the merit of requiring little knowledge of the underlying theories of numbers/sets. But how exactly are they related to schema specifications? This brings the second topic of this chapter into play: Eventually, we shall show that these can all be *refined*, in the following sense, to schema specifications.

17.2 Refinement

In the formal paradigm for program development, programs are obtained from specifications via refinement, in the sense of [7], [6]. Via a sequence of refinement steps, a specification is massaged into a program. However, this process does not necessarily begin with schema specifications: It may begin with schema definitions; i.e., arbitrary propositions are permitted in definitions and the refinement process moves them closer and closer to actual implementations [5].

Fortunately, we are not concerned with the whole gambit of the process from definition to program, but only with the move from schema definitions to schema specifications. That is, we are interested in how refinement can be employed to bridge the gap between schema definitions and specifications. Theoretically, this is a crucial step.

We begin with the general notion of refinement. According to the following, a relation S, viewed as an operation, is a *refinement* of another R if

(i) when R is applicable, so is S,
(ii) when R is applicable but S is applied, the result is consistent with R being applied.

Definition 260 *Let R and S be two schema definitions with preconditions*

$$R \triangleq [x : I, y : O \mid \pi[x]; \phi[x, y]]$$
$$S \triangleq \left[x : I, y : O \mid \pi'[x]; \phi'[x, y]\right]$$

*Then we shall say that S is a **weak refinement** of R iff*

$$\forall x : I \cdot \pi[x] \to \pi'[x] \tag{1}$$
$$\forall x : I \cdot \forall y : O \cdot \phi'[x, y] \to \phi[x, y] \tag{2}$$

*We shall say that S is a **strong refinement** of R, written as $R \sqsubseteq_s S$, iff it is a weak refinement and*

$$\forall x : I \cdot \forall y : O \cdot \phi[x, y] \to \phi'[x, y] \tag{3}$$

Refinement encapsulates the standard ideas of *weakening the precondition* and *strengthening the postcondition;* i.e., where applicable, the postcondition of the new relation implies the postcondition of the old. We may extend the definition to definitions without preconditions by taking the precondition to be a tautology; i.e., $x =_I x$.

Lemma 261 *Refinement and strong refinement are reflexive and transitive.*

Refinement also supplies us with a notion of schema equivalence; i.e., equivalent relations refine each other.

Definition 262 *Let R and S be two schema definitions where*

$$R \triangleq [x : I, y : O \mid \pi[x]; \phi[x, y]]$$
$$S \triangleq [x : I, y : O \mid \pi'[x]; \phi'[x, y]]$$

*We shall say that R and S are **equivalent**, written $R \equiv S$, iff $R \sqsubseteq S$ and $S \sqsubseteq R$.*

This goes beyond strong refinement in that it demands that both the preconditions and postconditions are logically equivalent. The following tells us that schema equivalence can function as a notion of equality for schemata.

Proposition 263 *Let R and S be two schema definitions where*

$$R \triangleq [x : I, y : O \mid \pi[x]; \phi[x, y]]$$
$$S \triangleq \left[x : I, y : O \mid \pi'[x]; \phi'[x, y]\right]$$

Then

$$\frac{\psi[S] \; prop \qquad\qquad R \equiv S \qquad\qquad \psi[R]}{\psi[S]}$$

is derivable.

Proof Assume that $R \equiv S$ and $\phi[R]$. Then, by equivalence, we know that the preconditions of R and S are logically equivalent as are their postconditions. It follows, by induction on the structure of ϕ, that R and S are interchangeable. ∎

This notion of equivalence will play a role shortly; i.e., many of our schema definitions are equivalent to their original schema specifications. We first observe that there are some general aspects that relate the notions of totality and functionality to refinement.

Proposition 264 *Assume that*

$$R \triangleq [x : I, y : O \mid \pi[x]; \phi[x, y]]$$
$$S \triangleq \left[x : I, y : O \mid \pi'[x]; \phi'[x, y]\right]$$

Then we have the following.

1. *If* $\forall x : I \cdot \pi[x] \leftrightarrow \pi'[x]$, *then if* $R \sqsubseteq S$ *and S is total, then so is R.*
2. *If* $\forall x : I \cdot \pi[x] \leftrightarrow \pi'[x]$, *then if* $R \sqsubseteq S$ *and R is functional, then so is S.*

Proof They are both immediate from the definitions. ∎

Where there are no explicit preconditions, there is an alternative way of defining refinement: We employ the domain of the relations as the precondition.

Definition 265

$$R \triangleq [x : I, y : O \mid \phi[x, y]]$$
$$S \triangleq \left[x : I, y : O \mid \phi'[x, y]\right]$$

*Then we may take S to be a **domain refinement** of R iff* $\widehat{R} \sqsubseteq \widehat{S}$

This unpacks to the following.

$$\forall x : I \cdot Dom R(x) \rightarrow Dom S(x)[x]$$
$$\forall x : I \cdot Dom R(x) \rightarrow \forall y : O \cdot \phi'[x, y] \rightarrow \phi[x, y]$$

And this agrees with the definition of refinement for schemata given in [6].

17.3 Implementable Definitions

We can now use refinement to connect our notions of schema definition and schema specification. The basic idea is clear: Starting with a schema definition, via refinement, we need to end up with a schema specification. This is captured in the following.

Definition 266 *We shall say that a schema definition*

$$R \triangleq [x : I, y : O \mid \pi[x]; \phi[x, y]]$$

is **implementable** *iff it can be strongly refined to a schema specification.*

Implementable relations, restricted to their pre-conditions, are logically equivalent to schema specifications. We demonstrate that the examples, marshalled to indicate the need for schema definitions, are all, in the above sense, implementable.

Example 267 (Greatest Common Divisor)

$$\begin{array}{|l|}
\hline
GCD \\
\hline
x : N, y : N, z : N \\
\hline
\forall u < Min(x, y) \cdot CD(u, x, y) \rightarrow u \le z \\
\hline
\end{array}$$

The relation $CD(u, x, y)$ is Δ. So the implication $CD(u, x, y) \rightarrow u \le z$ can be replaced by $\neg CD(u, x, y) \vee u \le z$. Hence, the definition is equivalent to a Σ one. The observation that makes this work is that any common divisor must be smaller than the minimum of x, y. Thus, the two predicates are equivalent in arithmetic. But one needs to know a little bit about number theory (or maybe just about numbers) to make this observation. On the other hand, presumably, one has to know this much in order to implement it correctly.

Example 268 (Hamming)

$$
\begin{array}{|l}
\hline
\;Ham(n) \underline{\hspace{11cm}} \\[1ex]
\quad n : N \\[1ex]
\underline{\hspace{9cm}} \\[1ex]
\quad \forall k < 6 \cdot (Prime(k) \wedge Divides(k, n)) \rightarrow k = 2, 3, 5 \\[1ex]
\hline
\end{array}
$$

This is a specification of the *Hamming numbers*. The obvious numerical knowledge enables one to reduce the definition to a specification.

We have already seen that each of the set-theoretic examples is implementable. However, to draw out some issues, consider again the original specification of power set.

Example 269 (Power Set)

$$
\begin{array}{|l}
\hline
\;Pow \underline{\hspace{8cm}} \\[1ex]
\quad x? : Set(T), \; y! : Set(Set(T)) \\[1ex]
\underline{\hspace{7cm}} \\[1ex]
\quad \forall x \in v \cdot u \circledast x \in z \\
\quad \wedge \\
\quad \forall y \in z \cdot \exists x \in v \cdot y = u \circledast x \\[1ex]
\hline
\end{array}
$$

This does indeed demand some knowledge of the theory of sets, specifically, that it is an inductive theory generated by adding an element to an existing set. But it is certainly not the standard definition. It only works because the set theory is an inductive theory.

Although most of these examples can be quite straightforwardly rewritten as Σ specifications, the rewriting does require some knowledge of the underlying base theory, e.g., some knowledge of number theory or set theory.

17.4 The Limits of Refinement

Of course, not all schema definitions are implementable. Although it could be more precisely coded, it should be clear that if the following were implementable, we would be able to effectively solve the halting problem [1].

Example 270 (Halting Problem)

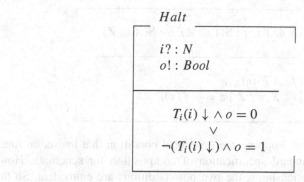

$$Halt$$
$$i? : N$$
$$o! : Bool$$

$$T_i(i) \downarrow \wedge o = 0$$
$$\vee$$
$$\neg(T_i(i) \downarrow) \wedge o = 1$$

where $T_i(i) \downarrow$ says the Turing machine with code i halts on input i.

Let $Halt$ be implementable via S. Since the precondition of $Halt$ is true, we cannot weaken it. Hence, being Σ, we may use S to enumerate the pairs $i : N, o : Bool$ that satisfy the postconditions of $S/Halt$. For any pair, eventually it will appear, and so we have a decision procedure, i.e., a solution to the halting problem. And so the assumption that $Halt$ is implementable must be false.

17.5 Properties of Schemata

Some properties of schemata do not determine the input/output of a program; they articulate properties of the relation determined by the input/output pairing. The following are the familiar definitions of functionality and totality cast as schema definitions.

Definition 271 (Functionality)

$$Fun_{XY}$$
$$\triangleq$$

$$[f : S(X \otimes Y) \mid \forall x : X \cdot \forall y : Y \cdot \forall z : Y \cdot f(x, y) \wedge f(x, z) \rightarrow y = z]$$
$$Tot_{XY} \triangleq [f : S(X \otimes Y) \mid \forall x : X \cdot \exists y : Y \cdot f(x, y)]$$
$$TF_{XY} \triangleq [f : S(X \otimes Y) \mid \forall x : X \cdot \exists! y : Y \cdot f(x, y)]$$

These properties are now more elegantly expressed. They may well enter into schema definitions in that we may wish to impose the constraint that a particular relation preserve them; i.e., although they are not Σ, they do seem to be something we may wish to employ in the process of specification. However, they need to be appropriately placed in the process. To illustrate matters, consider the following definition of functional composition.

Definition 272 (Functional Composition)

$$^{\circ}Fun$$

$$f : S(X \otimes Y), g : S(Y \otimes Z), h : S(X \otimes Z)$$

$$Fun(f) \wedge Fun(g);$$
$$h = [x : X, z : Z \mid z = g(f(x))]$$

This may be refined by dropping the functional condition that insists on functionality, i.e., by the standard specification of composition for schemata. However, where the precondition bites, the two postconditions are equivalent. So the schematic version strongly refines the functional one. We shall see another example of this later.

Of course, not all schema definitions are for the purposes of program specification. Some are there to state properties of schema that are to be used for mathematical purposes. The following are some examples of properties or relations on schemata that are clearly not intended to form part of any program specification. They are the schema definition versions of schema inclusion, monotonicity, and compactness. Their role is mathematical.

Definition 273 (Monotonicity and Compactness)

$$\subseteq_X \triangleq [f, g : S(X) \mid \forall x : X \cdot f(x) \to g(x)]$$
$$Mon_X \triangleq [h : S(S((X)) \mid \forall f : S(X) \cdot \forall g : S(X) \cdot f \subseteq g \to h(f) \subseteq h(g)]$$
$$Com_X \triangleq [h : S(S(X)) \mid \forall f : S(S(X)) \cdot h(\cup f) \subseteq \cup h(f)]$$

While schema definitions are a mathematical luxury rather than a necessity, they do clarify, and facilitate, the use and role of noncomputable properties in specification.

References

1. Cutland, N. Computability: An Introduction to Recursive Function Theory. Cambridge university Press, Cambridge, 1990.
2. Fuchs, N.E. Specifications are (preferably) Executable. Software Eng. J., 7(5): 323–334, 1992.
3. Gravell, A., and Nederson, P. Executing formal specifications need not be Harmful (1996). Software Eng. J., 11(2): 104–110.
4. Hayes, I.J., and Jones. C.B. Specifications are not (necessarily) harmful. Software Eng. J., 4(6): 330–339.
5. Morgan. C.C. Programming from Specifications. Prentice Hall, Inc., Englewood Cliffs, 1994.
6. Potter, B. Sinclair, J. and Till, D. An introduction to formal specification and Z. Prentice Hall, Inc., Englewood Cliffs, 1991.
7. Woodcock, J., and Davies, J. Using Z, Specifications, Refinement and Proof. Prentice Hall, Inc., Englewood Cliffs, 1996.

Chapter 18
Computable Ontology

So far, our only explicitly declared example of a computable model involved the specification of a simple software system. This kind of structure consists of little more than a suite of interconnected specifications. While an example of what we mean by a computable model, it is not a very theoretically exciting one. The specifications are mathematically rather parochial. And although such systems may employ some variation on our notion of schema definition, they rarely have much theoretical interest. Our objective in this chapter is to take us a little beyond such systems. More exactly, we shall provide a more theoretically demanding and interesting example of a computable model.

In particular, thus far we have not examined any models that are not normally subject to computable modeling. Many of these employ some portion of set theory. And, on the face of it, many are not obviously capable of being given a computational makeover. For example, a standard approach to the mathematical representation of *time* and *events* employs an underlying set-theoretic foundation in which instants are modeled as infinite sets of overlapping events. While there are many other examples where set theory underlies the mathematics, and we shall provide a few more as we proceed through the book, this one is relatively easy to reproduce. In this chapter we shall study this application not just for its own sake, but as an illustration of the construction of more theoretically thrilling instances of the computable modeling process.

18.1 Implementable Models

In particular, by extending the idea of implementation to include schema definitions that can be refined to schema specifications, we induce a corresponding generalization of the notion of a computable model, a generalization that includes collections of scheme definitions, each of which is implementable

In this extended guise, an *implementable model* is to consist of the following:

- a collection of schema definitions and specifications;
- a collection of refinements and their associated proofs that link each schema definition with its corresponding implementing specification.

R. Turner, *Computable Models*, DOI 10.1007/978-1-84882-052-4_18,
© Springer-Verlag London Limited 2009

This structure will be found in all of our examples. So, even at the level of the model description, there is some mathematical work to be done; i.e., proofs of refinement have to be provided.

18.2 A Type of Events

We shall illustrate this structure in the following simple case study in *computable ontology* in which we develop a computable model of *events* and *time*. We begin with the data type of events. Although there are many possible ways of introducing events, the following is quite elegant [1], [3], [2]. Our goal here is to explore some of the consequences of a computational makeover of this standard theory of events and time.

To begin with, we introduce a basic type of *events*, **E**. This is given with two basic relations:

- $\prec$ an ordering of temporal precedence on events: $e_1 \prec e_2$ asserts that e_1 happens before e_2;
- $\bigcirc$ a relation of temporal overlap: $e_1 \bigcirc e_2$ asserts that e_1 overlaps e_2.

The data type of events is then determined by the following rules.

Definition 274 (Events)

$$\mathbf{V_1} \quad \mathbf{E}\ type \qquad \mathbf{V_2} \quad \frac{e_1 : \mathbf{E} \quad e_2 : \mathbf{E}}{e_1 \prec e_2\ prop}$$

$$\mathbf{V_3} \quad \frac{e_1 : \mathbf{E} \quad e_2 : \mathbf{E}}{e_1 \bigcirc e_2\ prop} \qquad \mathbf{V_4} \quad \frac{e_1 \prec e_2}{\neg(e_2 \prec e_1)}$$

$$\mathbf{V_5} \quad \frac{e_1 \prec e_2 \quad e_2 \prec e_3}{e_1 \prec e_3} \qquad \mathbf{V_6} \quad \frac{e_1 \bigcirc e_2}{e_2 \bigcirc e_1}$$

$$\mathbf{V_7} \quad e_1 \bigcirc e_1 \qquad \mathbf{V_8} \quad \frac{e_1 \prec e_2}{\neg(e_1 \bigcirc e_2)}$$

$$\mathbf{V_9} \quad \frac{e_1 \prec e_2 \quad e_2 \bigcirc e_3 \quad e_3 \prec e_4}{e_1 \prec e_4}$$

These postulates are the obvious ones for any notion of event with temporal operators for precedence and overlap. The rules $(\mathbf{V_1})$ guarantee that **E** is a type and $(\mathbf{V_2}, \mathbf{V_3})$ that temporal precedence and overlap form propositions over events. $\mathbf{V_4}$ demands that precedence is not symmetric, while $\mathbf{V_5}$ insists that it is transitive. On the other hand, $\mathbf{V_6}$ insists that overlap is symmetric, $\mathbf{V_7}$ that it is reflexive, and $\mathbf{V_8}$

that precedence precludes overlap. The last relates the two relations: Precedence is still transitive when it is interrupted by an overlap.

Both relations are taken to be decidable in the resulting theory. So we also have the following rules.

$$\mathbf{V_{10}} \; \frac{e_1 : \mathbf{E} \quad e_2 : \mathbf{E}}{e_1 \not\prec e_2 \; prop} \qquad \mathbf{V_{11}} \; \frac{e_1 : \mathbf{E} \quad e_2 : \mathbf{E}}{e_1 \not\prec e_2 \leftrightarrow \neg(e_1 \prec e_2)}$$

$$\mathbf{V_{12}} \; \frac{e_1 : \mathbf{E} \quad e_2 : \mathbf{E}}{e_1 \ominus e_2 \; prop} \qquad \mathbf{V_{13}} \; \frac{e_1 : \mathbf{E} \quad e_2 : \mathbf{E}}{e_1 \ominus e_2 \leftrightarrow \neg(e_1 \bigcirc e_2)}$$

The type of events $\mathbf{E}$ is thus given by rules $\mathbf{V_1}$-$\mathbf{V_{13}}$. This gives us a minimal theory of events.[1]

Definition 275 (Theory of Events) *This is the theory whose basic type is* $\mathbf{E}$ *and that is closed under products and schema formation, i.e., the theory*

$$\mathbf{Th(E, \otimes, S)}$$

This is our basic framework and it will be enough to illustrate some of the issues involving refinement in model construction. But first we must check that there is an arithmetic interpretation.

18.3 Arithmetic Interpretation

There are standard arithmetic models of this structure. For example, events may be modeled as ordered pairs of numbers

$$[n, m]$$

where $n \leq m$. The ordering and overlap relations on events may then be defined as

$$[n, m] \prec [n', m'] \triangleq m < n'$$
$$[n, m] \bigcirc [n', m'] \triangleq (n \leq n' \leq m) \vee (n' \leq n \leq m')$$

It is straightforward to check the rules.

---

[1] It can be extended with axioms such as the following.

$$\frac{e_1 : \mathbf{E} \qquad e_2 : \mathbf{E} \qquad e_3 : \mathbf{E}}{e_1 \prec e_2 \vee e_1 \bigcirc e_2 \vee e_2 \prec e_1}$$

But this is more controversial. It is argued in that it is not always possible to delineate events precisely enough to guarantee its truth. In any case, whatever decision is taken over this, it is not relevant to the present reconstruction.

18.4 Instants

The second notion of our ontology (*instants*) is not primitive but is defined. It is here where our treatment differs from the set-theoretic one. In the traditional approach, *instants* are introduced as maximally overlapping sets of events. We aim to mimic this construction. We do so using the data type of events and schemata. We introduce instants as properties of events that are *maximally overlapping*.

Definition 276 (Instants)

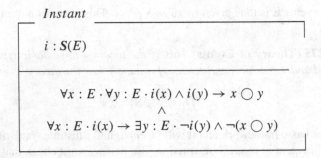

This is a schema definition; instants are not Σ properties of events. We shall return to its implementation later. For the moment, we push the theory forward and introduce a temporal ordering on instants. The following is the schema definition of the ordering.

Definition 277 (Ordering)

$$
\boxed{
\begin{array}{l}
< \\[4pt]
\hline
i : S(E) \\
j : S(E) \\[4pt]
\hline
Instant(i) \wedge Instant(j); \\
\exists x : E \cdot \exists y : E \cdot i(x) \wedge i(y) \wedge x \prec y
\end{array}
}
$$

Instants are introduced as preconditions. According to the above, one instant precedes another if there exist two event members of the corresponding instants that precede each other; i.e., the instant ordering is defined in terms of the event ordering. Note that this is an ordering on instants and their specification is not Σ. Consequently, this is not a Σ specification.

It is then easy enough to show simple properties such as the transitivity of this relation.

18.5 Implementation

The only notions that are not Σ are the definitions of *instant* and *instant ordering*. However, we can implement IO by dropping the precondition requirement in the specification of instants.

Example 278 (Ordering)

$$\begin{array}{|l}
\hline
\quad < \\
\hline
\quad i : S(E) \\
\quad j : S(E) \\
\hline
\quad \exists x : E \cdot \exists y : E \cdot i(x) \wedge i(y) \wedge x \prec y \\
\hline
\end{array} \qquad (IIO)$$

This new relation is Σ and is a refinement of the original, and so the latter is implementable.

All this is a sketch of a computational theory of events and time. It has a very different flavor to the early theories of intervals and time that found their way into the literature on artificial intelligence. These theories were based upon standard data structures but with no axiomatization. [2] provides a rich source for formal theories of periods, events, and points. Indeed, a topic of some interest might be to develop a more complete *formal ontology*. For example, we might add a type of Individuals **I** and a type of propositions **P**

$$\mathbf{Th}(\mathbf{I}, \mathbf{P}, \mathbf{E}, \otimes, \mathbf{S})$$

where presumably **I** is a basic type and **P** is taken to be closed under the logical connectives and quantifiers. But we shall pursue this on another occasion.

This case study illustrates how noncomputational properties of data items, in collaboration with refinement, can play a role in computational modeling. There is much more to say on this topic, and especially with regard to the applications of these issues to computational real analysis and programming language semantics. And we shall get to them later.

References

1. Russell, B.A.W. Our Knowledge of the External World. Allen and Unwin, London, 1914.
2. Van Benthem, J. Tense logic and time. Notre Dame J. Formal Log. 25(1): 1–16, 1984.
3. Whitehead, A.N. Process and Reality. An Essay in Cosmology. Macmillan. New York, 1929.

Chapter 19
Classes

Classes form a natural accompaniment of schema definitions.[1] They extend the separation constructor to arbitrary propositions. In particular, they support the definition of a class of functions. This will facilitate the direct specification of operations on functions. And, even though in the end we will shall have to furnish an implementation, classes will greatly increase the range and application of our notion of computable model.

Of course, classes cannot be taken as types since the latter are required to have an interpretation as recursively enumerable sets. Consequently, classes must be added as a new layer of objects. Moreover, we shall require classes to combine with the other classes to form new ones. This has some impact upon the underlying framework of the theory. However, although there is a substantial increase in expressive power, the addition of classes is conservative. So we gain expressive power but maintain our recursive models.

19.1 Classes and Judgments

To facilitate the expression of these ideas, we must add a new judgment to the effect that something is a *class*, i.e.,

$$C\ class$$

The new judgment is governed by the following rules.

$$C_1 \ \frac{T\ type}{T\ class} \qquad C_2 \ \frac{T_1\ class,\ ...,\ T_n\ class}{O_i(T_1,\ ...,\ T_n)\ class}$$

---

[1] This use of the term *class* follows the standard terminology for naming notions that stand on top of other notions of classification [2], [1]. It is not to be confused with the classes of object-oriented programming languages.

R. Turner, *Computable Models*, DOI 10.1007/978-1-84882-052-4_19,
© Springer-Verlag London Limited 2009

where O_i is any type operator of the background theory $\mathbf{Th}(O_1, ..., O_k)$. C_1 guarantees that any type is a class and C_2 insists that classes are closed under the type constructors of the given background theory. Of course, such a judgment would be vacuous without the presence of a constructor that generates classes in the first place. Here we employ separation for arbitrary propositions. This is governed by the normal rules for separation, the ones we introduced for separation types, but now the propositions are not restricted to Σ ones. For convenience, we keep the same names as before.

$$\mathbf{Sep_0} \quad \frac{x : T \vdash \phi \; prop}{\{x : T \mid \phi\} \; class}$$

$$\mathbf{Sep_1} \quad \frac{x : T \vdash \phi \; prop \qquad a : T \qquad \phi[a/x]}{a : \{x : T \mid \phi\}}$$

$$\mathbf{Sep_2} \quad \frac{a : \{x : T \mid \phi\}}{a : T}$$

$$\mathbf{Sep_3} \quad \frac{a : \{x : T \mid \phi\}}{\phi[a/x]}$$

In addition, we have to extend our other rules to allow for classes. To begin with, we need to generalize the structural rules. They are identical to the type rules, which are now special cases.

$$\mathbf{A_1} \quad \frac{\Gamma \vdash C \; class}{\Gamma, x : C \vdash x : C}$$

$$\mathbf{W_1} \quad \frac{\Gamma, \Delta \vdash \Theta \qquad \Gamma \vdash C \; class}{\Gamma, x : T, \Delta \vdash \Theta}$$

$$\mathbf{W_2} \quad \frac{\Gamma, \Delta \vdash \Theta \qquad \Gamma \vdash \phi \; prop}{\Gamma, \phi, \Delta \vdash \Theta}$$

Many of the other rules also need to be extended. The relevant ones are the following.

$$\mathbf{E_1} \quad \frac{\Gamma \vdash t : C \qquad \Gamma \vdash s : C}{\Gamma \vdash t =_c s \; prop} \qquad \mathbf{E_2} \quad \frac{\Gamma \vdash t : C}{\Gamma \vdash t =_c t}$$

$$\mathbf{E_3} \quad \frac{\Gamma \vdash t =_c s \qquad \Gamma \vdash \Theta[t/x]}{\Gamma \vdash \Theta[s/x]}$$

$$\mathbf{L_{18}} \quad \frac{\Gamma, x : C \vdash \phi \; prop}{\Gamma \vdash \exists x : C \cdot \phi \; prop}$$

$$L_{19} \quad \frac{\Gamma \vdash \phi[t/x] \quad \Gamma \vdash t : C \qquad \Gamma, x : C \vdash \phi \; prop}{\Gamma \vdash \exists x : C \cdot \phi}$$

$$L_{20} \quad \frac{\Gamma \vdash \exists x : C \cdot \phi \qquad \Gamma, x : C, \phi \vdash \eta}{\Gamma \vdash \eta} \qquad L_{21} \quad \frac{\Gamma, x : C \vdash \phi \; prop}{\Gamma \vdash \forall x : C \cdot \phi \; prop}$$

$$L_{22} \quad \frac{\Gamma, x : C \vdash \phi}{\Gamma \vdash \forall x : C \cdot \phi} \qquad L_{23} \quad \frac{\Gamma \vdash \forall x : C \cdot \phi \quad \Gamma \vdash t : C}{\Gamma \vdash \phi[t/x]}$$

Given the background theory $\mathbf{Th}(O_1, ..., O_k)$, we shall call the resulting class theory

$$\mathbf{Thclass}(O_1, ..., O_k)$$

Our first and most important example of class formation is determined by the functions of the theory. This class is given as follows.

Example 279 (Function Class) In the theory

$$\mathbf{Thclass}(\mathbf{N}, \mathbf{DP}, \mathbf{S}, \mathbf{type})$$

let C and D be classes. We define the **class of functions** from C to D as follows.

$$C \Rightarrow D \triangleq \{ f : \mathbf{S}(C \otimes D) \mid \forall x : C \cdot \exists ! y : D \cdot f(x, y) \}$$

We shall study this example in some detail in the next chapter. And in a later one, the following class of computable real numbers will take center stage.

Example 280 (Computable Reals)

$$\mathfrak{R} \triangleq \{ f : N \Rightarrow Q \cdot \exists z : N \cdot \forall y \geqslant z \cdot \forall x \geqslant z \cdot |f(x) - f(y)| \leq 1/z \}$$

But, for the present, we put a little more formal flesh on our notion of class. We shall assume that all the formal notions such as *inclusion* are extended to classes in the exactly analogous way. We assume that we are working in the theory

$$\mathbf{Thclass}(O_1, ..., O_k)$$

Definition 281 *For classes C, D, we define*

$$C \subseteq D \triangleq \forall x : C \cdot \exists y : D \cdot x = y$$

We also need to examine the impact of classes on our notion of refinement. We shall ignore preconditions since these can be expressed using separation types, which are special cases of classes.

Definition 282 *Let R and S be two schema definitions, where in the following C, D, E are classes.*

$$R \triangleq [x : C, y : E \mid \phi[x, y]]$$
$$S \triangleq \left[x : D, y : E \mid \phi'[x, y]\right]$$

*S is a **weak refinement** of R, written as $R \sqsubseteq S$, iff*

$$C \subseteq D \tag{1}$$
$$\forall x : C \cdot \forall y : E \cdot \phi'[x, y] \to \phi[x, y] \tag{2}$$

This subsumes our notion of refinement since the class can now contain the precondition.

19.2 Class Elimination

Classes are meant to be a luxury rather than a necessity. However complex the resulting treatment, we must be able to get by without them. Of course, this is a matter of taste and judgment: We would not want to get by with just numbers. Nevertheless, technically it is essential that we have a recursive model. And this is indirectly guaranteed by the following result. We show that any such theory is a conservative extension of the base theory.

In the following we abbreviate

$$\mathbf{ThC} = \mathbf{Thclass}(O_1, ..., O_k)$$
$$\mathbf{Th} = \mathbf{Th}(O_1, ..., O_k)$$

Lemma 283 *For each judgment of **Thclass**, there are judgments of **Th** such that*

1. *if $\Gamma \vdash_{\mathbf{ThC}} C$ class, then $\Gamma^* \vdash_{\mathbf{Th}} C^+$ class and $\Gamma^* \vdash_{\mathbf{Th}} C^-(x)$ prop,*
2. *if $\Gamma \vdash_{\mathbf{ThC}} \phi$ prop, then $\Gamma^* \vdash_{\mathbf{Th}} \phi^*$ prop and, if ϕ is Σ, so is ϕ^*,*
3. *if $\Gamma \vdash_{\mathbf{ThC}} t : C$, then $\Gamma^* \vdash_{\mathbf{Th}} t^* : C^+$ and $\Gamma^* \vdash_{\mathbf{Th}} C^-(t^*)$,*
4. *if $\Gamma \vdash_{\mathbf{ThC}} \phi$, then $\Gamma^* \vdash_{\mathbf{Th}} \phi^*$,*
5. *if $\Gamma \vdash_{\mathbf{Th}} T$ type, then $\Gamma \vdash_{\mathbf{Th}} t : T$ iff $\Gamma \vdash_{\mathbf{Th}} t^* : T^+$,*
6. *if $\Gamma \vdash_{\mathbf{Th}} \phi$ prop, then $\Gamma \vdash_{\mathbf{Th}} \phi^*$ iff $\Gamma \vdash_{\mathbf{Th}} \phi$.*

Proof We proceed as with the removal of separation types. The transformation removes classes by removing the predicate information and places it in the predicate of the schema definition. In particular, the classes are transformed in the same way as separation types; i.e.,

$$C^* \triangleq (C^+, C^-) \quad where$$
$$\{x : C \cdot \phi\}^+ \triangleq C^+$$
$$\{x : C \cdot \phi\}^- (x) \triangleq C^-(x) \wedge \phi^*[x]$$

And, for the propositions, we need to say how quantification over classes is removed, and this also follows the pattern of separation types.

$$(\exists x : C \cdot \phi)^* \triangleq \exists x : C^+ \cdot C^-(x) \wedge \phi^*$$
$$(\forall x : C \cdot \phi)^* \triangleq \forall x : C^+ \cdot C^-(x) \rightarrow \phi^*$$

This removes all references to classes.∎

Classes are a fiction, but a useful one. In particular, as we shall see, they play a central role in our accounts of computable analysis and the definition of programming languages.

References

1. Krivine, J.L. Introduction to Axiomatic Set Theory. Springer-Verlag, New York, 1971.
2. Potter, M.D. Sets: An Introduction. Clarendon Press, Oxford, 1990

Chapter 20
Classes of Functions

In certain applications it is natural to work with the subclass of relations that are functions, especially where the standard development of the theory employs functions. Real analysis and functional programming are obvious examples. In this chapter we consider a constructor that supports this, i.e., the class of functions from one type to another. However, this constructor is not a type constructor but a class generator. Consequently, it cannot enter into schema specifications; we may only employ it in schema definitions. And it cannot be a member of **type**.

Fortunately, we have a technique for massaging such schema definitions into specifications. More exactly, specifications involving the corresponding schema type will emerge via class elimination and refinement. In particular, operations over functions will be refined to operations acting over the whole of the containing schema type.

We shall develop several computable models to illustrate this technique. One will involve the specification of the computable real numbers and some of its associated operations, specifically, real addition and multiplication. This will yield a class of computable real numbers and initiate a version of computable analysis. In another application we shall examine the semantics of programming languages. More exactly, we shall treat the specification of a programming language as the construction of a computable model.

These two applications will occupy the next two chapters. In this one we concentrate on putting the class constructor in place.

20.1 Function Application

Throughout this chapter we shall work in the theories

$$\text{Th}(\mathbf{N}, \mathbf{DP}, \mathbf{S}, \mathbf{type})$$

$$\text{ThC} = \text{Thclass}(\mathbf{N}, \mathbf{DP}, \mathbf{S}, \mathbf{type})$$

i.e., the where the base theory is generated by numbers, dependent products, schemata, and a type of types. Within this framework we define the class of functions from one class to a second. Once in place, we shall explore the addition of application as a built-in operator. Recall the following definition from the last chapter.

Definition 284 (Function Class) *Let C and D be classes in* **ThC**. *We define the class of total functions from C to D as follows.*

$$C \Rightarrow D \triangleq \{F : \mathbf{S}(C \otimes D) \mid \forall x : C \cdot \exists ! y : D \cdot F(x, y)\}$$

In itself, this constructor is not that useful. It only becomes so when we add application. Consequently, we enrich the theory **ThC** by the addition of application that is taken to satisfy the following rules.

$$\mathbf{App_1} \quad \frac{F : C \Rightarrow D \qquad a : C}{apply(F, a) : D} \qquad\qquad \mathbf{App_2} \quad \frac{F : C \Rightarrow D \qquad a : C}{F(a, apply(f, a))}$$

The first is the standard application rule and the second insists that, together, the input and the result of the application satisfy the function when understood as a relation. We shall call this theory **ThC^{apply}**.

Proposition 285 *In* **ThC^{apply}** *the following holds.*

$$\frac{F : A \Rightarrow B \qquad\qquad a : A \qquad\qquad b : B \qquad\qquad F(a, b)}{b =_B apply(F, a)}$$

Proof We know there is only one such $b : B$ such that $F(a, b)$; and by App$_2$, we know that it is $apply(F, a)$.∎

More importantly, we know that adding application for functions is conservative.

Theorem 286 ThC^{apply} *is a conservative extension of* **ThC**.

Proof We appeal to our original conservative extension result for the removal of application. We have to take care of the presence of the type **type** and of the fact that schemata are variable binders i.e., the cases where application occurs in class/type terms and in schemata, but the same technique and argument work as in the theory without the classes.∎

Moreover, given the conservative nature of class addition, we have

Corollary 287 *The Theory* **ThC^{apply}** *is a conservative extension of* **Th**.

From now on we shall drop the decoration and assume that **ThC** has application built in. The following will prove useful.

Lemma 288 *Let*

$$R \triangleq [x : C, y : T \mid \phi]$$

be any schema definition in **ThC^{apply}** *where ϕ is Σ. Then R is implementable.*

Proof By definition of refinement for schema definitions involving classes (i.e., by weakening the contained precondition), we have that

$$[x : \{x : C^+ \cdot C^-(x)\}, y : T \mid \phi[x, y]]$$

is refined by

$$[x : C^+, y : T \mid \phi[x, y]]$$

This is a schema. It implements R.∎

20.2 Specifications and Function Classes

We shall now provide a sequence of simple examples to illustrate the use of such function classes. The early ones are familiar from our treatment of schemata. As we proceed, we shall indicate their implementations.

Our first is a new definition of functional composition using classes. It is more elegant than the one that employs preconditions.

Definition 289 (Functional Composition)

$$
\begin{array}{|l}
\hline
{}^\circ Fun \\
\hline
u : \textbf{type}, v : \textbf{type}, w : \textbf{type} \\
f : u \Rrightarrow v, g : v \Rrightarrow w, h : u \Rrightarrow w \\
\hline
h = [x : u, z : w \mid z = g(f(x))] \\
\hline
\end{array}
$$

If this is to form part of a computable model, we need to indicate how to implement it. But that is easy enough: We replace the classes by their underlying base types and remove application.

Example 290 (Relational Composition)

$$
\begin{array}{|l}
\hline
{}^\circ Rel \\
\hline
u : \textbf{type}, v : \textbf{type}, w : \textbf{type} \\
f : \mathsf{S}(u \otimes v), g : \mathsf{S}(v \otimes w), h : \mathsf{S}(u \otimes w) \\
\hline
h = [x : u, z : w \mid \exists y : v \cdot f(x, y) \wedge g(y, z)] \\
\hline
\end{array}
$$

We demonstrate that this is an implementation of functional composition. We first remove the function classes. Notice we have not included the fact that the output is functional, since this is derivable. We have to check that when the inputs are functions, the predicate of $\circ_{Rel}$ is equivalent to that of $\circ_{Fun'}$. Assume $TF(f, u, w)$ and $TF(g, v, w)$ and there is an h such that $TF(h, u, w)$, which is their composition. The following holds.

$$\forall x : u \cdot \forall z : w \cdot ((\exists y : v \cdot f(x, y) \wedge g(y, z)) \leftrightarrow z = apply(g, apply(f, x)))$$

This is immediate from the uniqueness properties of functions. The result now follows from the definition of refinement.■

Such examples involve only one level of function class construction. We now consider cases that illustrate the use of higher-order function classes. The following are some of the central combinators of combinatorial logic, which we have already seen in relational form.

Example 291 (The Combinator S)

S_{Fun}

---

u : **type**, v : **type**, w : **type**
$f : u \Rightarrow (v \Rightarrow w)$
$g : u \Rightarrow v$
$h : u \Rightarrow w$

$$h = [x : u, y : w \mid y = fx(gx)]$$

This is implemented by the following schema specification: To get to it, we first remove the function spaces. We then refine to the following specification, by removing application.

Example 292 (An Implementation of S)

S_{Rel}

---

u : **type**, v : **type**, w : **type**
$f : S(u \otimes S(v \otimes w))$
$g : S(u \otimes v)$
$h : S(u \otimes w)$

$$h$$
$$=$$
$$[x : u, z : w \mid \exists y : v \cdot \exists w : S(v \otimes w) \cdot f(x, w) \wedge g(x, y) \wedge w(y, z)]$$

Our last two examples are the standard Currying operation and its inverse, together with their refinements.

Example 293 (Currying)

Curry

u : **type**, v : **type**, w : **type**
$f : (u \otimes v) \Rrightarrow w$
$g : u \Rrightarrow (v \Rrightarrow w)$

$g = [x : u, h : (v \Rrightarrow w) \mid h = [y : v, z : w \mid z = f(x, y)]]$

This may be implemented as the following schema specification.

Example 294 (An Implementation of Currying)

Curryspec

u : **type**, v : **type**, w : **type**
$f : \mathbf{S}((u \otimes v) \otimes w)$
$g : \mathbf{S}(u \otimes \mathbf{S}(v \otimes w))$

$g = [x : u, h : \mathbf{S}(v \otimes w) \mid h = [y : v, z : w \mid f(x, y, z)]]$

The inverse operation and its specification are given as follows.

Example 295 (UnCurrying)

UnCurry

u : **type**, v : **type**, w : **type**
$f : u \Rrightarrow (v \Rrightarrow w)$
$g : (u \otimes v) \Rrightarrow w$

$g = [x : u \otimes v, z : w \mid z = f(x_1, x_2)]$

This is refined by the following, where the function spaces are replaced with the corresponding schema types.

Example 296 (Implementation)

```
┌─ UnCurryspec ──────────────────────────────────────────────┐
│                                                              │
│   u : type, v : type, w : type                               │
│   g : S(u ⊗ S(v ⊗ w))                                        │
│   f : S((u ⊗ v) ⊗ w)                                         │
│  ─────────────────────────────────────────────────────────  │
│                                                              │
│   f = [x : u ⊗ v, z : w | ∃h : S(v ⊗ w) · g(x₁, h) ∧ h(x₂, z)]│
│                                                              │
└──────────────────────────────────────────────────────────────┘
```

$$u : \textbf{type}, v : \textbf{type}, w : \textbf{type}$$
$$g : \mathbf{S}(u \otimes \mathbf{S}(v \otimes w))$$
$$f : \mathbf{S}((u \otimes v) \otimes w)$$

$$f = [x : u \otimes v, z : w \mid \exists h : \mathbf{S}(v \otimes w) \cdot g(x_1, h) \wedge h(x_2, z)]$$

These examples clearly illustrate the implementation relationship between functional definitions and their relational refinements. They demonstrate how operations that are restricted to functions can be extended to operations that operate over the whole of their containing schema type. But we do not lose anything in the process since the operations preserve functions; i.e., functions in, functions out.

20.3 Partial Functions

We now bring partial functions into the picture. This will prove necessary for our treatment of programming language semantics. Specifically, the following class of functions will prove essential to the latter.

Definition 297 *Let C and D be classes in* **ThC**. *We define the* **class of partial functions** *from C to D as follows.*

$$C \twoheadrightarrow D \triangleq \{F : \mathbf{S}(C \otimes D) \mid \forall x : C \cdot \forall y : D \cdot \forall z : D \cdot F(x, y) \wedge F(x, z) \rightarrow y = z\}$$

Application is now taken to satisfy the following rules.

$$\textbf{App}_1 \ \frac{F : C \twoheadrightarrow D \quad Dom(F)(a)}{apply(F, a) : D} \qquad\qquad \textbf{App}_2 \ \frac{F : C \twoheadrightarrow D \quad Dom(F)(a)}{F(a, apply(f, a))}$$

Of course, this is a special case where the precondition is taken to be the domain of the relation. This extension is also conservative, and the same argument works. The following illustrates the application of this notion.

Example 298 (Generalized Composition)

$\circ_{Fun}$

$$f : B \otimes C \twoheadrightarrow D$$
$$g : A \twoheadrightarrow B$$
$$h : A \twoheadrightarrow C$$
$$w : A \twoheadrightarrow D$$

$$\frac{w}{\cdot} =$$
$$[z : A \otimes D \cdot \exists x : B \cdot \exists y : C \cdot g(z_0, x) \wedge h(z_0, y) \wedge f(x, y, z_1)]$$

The result w is clearly functional. The schema definition may be implemented by removing the function spaces in favor of the corresponding schema types, i.e.

$\circ$

$$f : S(B \otimes C, D)$$
$$g : S(A \otimes B)$$
$$h : S(A \otimes C)$$
$$w : S(A \otimes D)$$

$$\frac{w}{=}$$
$$[z : A \otimes D \cdot \exists x : B \cdot \exists y : C \cdot g(z_0, x) \wedge h(z_0, y) \wedge f(x, y, z_1)]$$

20.4 Polymorphism

Polymorphism in its most famous guise is to be found in the second-order lambda calculus. And this has two sources: theoretical computer science and mathematical logic. Within the former, Reynolds [2] introduced it to formalize the kind of uniform polymorphism implicit in much programming practice. It was independently introduced by Girard (see [1]) to provide a consistency proof for classical analysis. While few programming languages support the full impredicative polymorphism of the Second Order Calculus, some form of polymorphism is supported by most current programming languages. We explore its role in specification.

Our present treatment of function types is limited in that they cannot represent any form of dependency. The alert reader will have noticed that, while we have generic functional schema, where the type is supplied as part of the declaration, we have not discussed its class. For this we require a more standard representation of polymorphic functions. Consider the following schema definition.

Example 299 (Functional Composition)

$$
\boxed{
\begin{array}{l}
^\circ Fun \\[6pt]
\hline \\[-4pt]
u : \textbf{type}, v : \textbf{type}, w : \textbf{type} \\
f : u \Rightarrow v, g : v \Rightarrow w, h : u \Rightarrow w \\[6pt]
\hline \\[-4pt]
h = [x : u, z : w \mid z = g(f(x))]
\end{array}
}
$$

This is clearly functional. But how do we assign a class to it? The class of h depends upon the class of the inputs, so that the class of the definition cannot be expressed in the form

$$\textbf{type} \Rightarrow (\textbf{type} \Rightarrow (\textbf{type} \Rightarrow \ldots$$

To express it, we need to incorporate dependency into the class itself. This motivates the following class constructor.

Definition 300 (Polymorphic Function Class) *Assume that in* **ThC**

$$C \; class \;\; and \;\; x : c \vdash D[x] \; Class$$

*We define the **class of dependent functions** from C to D as follows.*

$$\Pi x : C \cdot D \triangleq \{F : S(\Sigma x : C \cdot D) \mid \forall x : C \cdot \exists! y : D[x] \cdot F(x, y)\}$$

As before, we enrich the theory **ThC** by the addition of application that is taken to satisfy the following rules.

$$\textbf{App}_1 \; \frac{F : \Pi x : C \cdot D \quad a : C}{apply(F, a) : D[a/x]} \qquad \textbf{App}_2 \; \frac{F : \Pi x : C \cdot D \quad a : C}{F(a, apply(f, a))}$$

These are the dependent versions of the rules. The proof of the following is the same as the simple functional case.

Theorem 301 *The addition of application yields a conservative extension of* **ThC**.

We may now return to our example: Functional composition has the following class structure.

Example 302 (Composition)

$$\circ : \Pi u : \textbf{type} \cdot \Pi v : \textbf{type} \cdot \Pi w : \textbf{type} \cdot ((u \Rightarrow v) \otimes (v \Rightarrow w)) \Rightarrow (u \Rightarrow w)$$

Consequently, we can now assign a class to such generic schemata. And it can be implemented as follows.

Example 303 (○ Implemented)

$\circ_{Fun}$

$u : \textbf{type}, v : \textbf{type}, w : \textbf{type}$
$f : S(u \otimes v), g : S(v \otimes w), h : S(u \otimes w)$

$$h = [x : u, z : w \mid \exists y : v \cdot g(x, y) \wedge g(y, z)]$$

This completes our brief introduction to function classes. We have considered a class of functions and two variations that allow for partiality and polymorphism. We now turn to the application of these notions. We begin with the case of simple functions.

References

1. Girard, L. Taylor, P. Proofs and Types. Cambridge University Press, Cambridge, 1989.
2. Reynolds, J.C. Introduction to polymorphic lambda-calculus. In: G. Huet (Ed.), Logical Foundations of Functional Programming, pp. 77–86. Addison-Wesley, Reading, MA, 1990.

Chapter 21
Computable Analysis

This chapter is devoted to the construction of a computable model that involves the use of function types. Specifically, we carry out a small case study in the representation of the *computable real numbers* and their associated operations [2, 1]. This is a reasonable test bed for our theories. For one thing, the notions of function and function space are central to the constructions. More explicitly, any representation of the real numbers takes them to be infinite sequences of some sort. In our case we shall employ a version of Cauchy sequences. But a further step is often taken where these sequences are given a set-theoretic makeover; i.e., Cauchy sequences are interpreted as set-theoretic functions. But we shall not take this step. Instead, we shall employ the notion of function of the present theories, i.e., single-valued schema relations. The actual development of the theory will look much like its classical set-theoretic analogue, but its underlying mathematical foundations will be different.

Once our basic notion of real number is in place, we shall enrich the theory with notions of real equality, addition, and multiplication, and thus initiate a version of computational real analysis. But we shall not go much further. Our objective is only to demonstrate how the computable model is constructed and implemented.

21.1 Cauchy Sequences

As we indicated, we shall base the representation on *Cauchy sequences*. We shall work in the theory developed in the last chapter.

$$\textbf{Thclass(N, DP, S, type)}$$

In this theory, the class of Cauchy real numbers is defined as follows.

Definition 304 (Cauchy Reals)

$$\mathfrak{R} \triangleq \{f : N \Rightarrow Q \cdot \exists z : N \cdot \forall y \geqslant z \cdot \forall x \geqslant z \cdot |f(x) - f(y)| \leq 1/z\}$$

The real numbers are functions from numbers to rationals, where for large enough natural numbers, the absolute difference between them is as small as

R. Turner, *Computable Models*, DOI 10.1007/978-1-84882-052-4_21,
© Springer-Verlag London Limited 2009

required. This is the classical definition of the real numbers (or one of them) in terms of Cauchy sequences. Of course, this is not a type but a class. However, the real numbers as data items are treated as the intensions of Cauchy sequences and as schemata are computable objects. We shall first provide some simple examples and then look at the development of the elementary theory.   •

Definition 305 (Identity and Zero)

$$1_\Re(x) \triangleq \lambda x : \Re \cdot x$$
$$0_\Re(x) \triangleq \lambda x : \Re \cdot 0_\varrho$$

Here we use the lambda notation for explicitly specified functions. To facilitate some of our later definitions, we define the following.

Definition 306 (Canonical Bound) *Let* $f : \Re$. *Define the canonical bound of* f *as follows.*

$$B_f \triangleq [z : N \mid (z > f(1) + 2) \wedge \forall u > f(1) + 2 \cdot u \geq z]$$

B_f applies to only one number and we shall use B_f to refer to it; i.e., we conservatively add a constant (constant function with value B_f applied to any number) with value B_f.

With these notions in play, we can move on to a standard definition of equality for the real numbers i.e., two reals are the same if, for large enough inputs, the difference between them is as small as needed.

Definition 307 (Real Equality)

$$=_\Re$$

$f : \Re, g : \Re$
$\exists x : N \cdot \lvert f(x) - g(x) \rvert \leq_\varrho 2/x$

The following shows that real equality is an equivalence relation. The proofs are standard and the present context changes little about them.

Proposition 308 *The following properties of real equality are provable*

1. $\forall f : \Re \cdot f =_\Re f$.
2. $\forall f : \Re \cdot \forall g : \Re \cdot f =_\Re g \rightarrow g =_\Re f$.
3. $\forall f : \Re \cdot \forall g : \Re \cdot \forall h : \Re \cdot f =_\Re g \wedge g =_\Re h \rightarrow f =_\Re h$.

Proof We illustrate with property 3. Assume that

$$\exists x : N \cdot \lvert f(x) - g(x) \rvert \leq_\varrho 2/x$$
$$\exists y : N \cdot \lvert g(y) - h(y) \rvert \leq_\varrho 2/y$$

Then let z be the maximum of the guaranteed x and y and their respective convergence numbers. Observe that

$$|f(z) - h(z)| \leq_Q |f(z) - g(z) + g(z) - h(z)|$$
$$\leq |f(z) - g(z)| + |g(z) - h(z)|$$
$$\leq 2/z + 2/z \leq_Q 4/z.$$

Hence, $f = h$. ∎

21.2 Operations on the Real Numbers

We now turn to the standard operations of addition and multiplication for the Cauchy real numbers. We take them in turn. Again, the definitions are fairly standard.

Definition 309 (Addition)

$$+_\mathfrak{R}$$

$f : \mathfrak{R}, g : \mathfrak{R}, h : \mathfrak{R}$
$h = [(x, y) : N \otimes Q \mid y = f(2x) +_Q g(2x)]$

We need to establish that this definition preserves real numbers. We shall do this in conjunction with the properties of multiplication. The latter is specified as follows.

Definition 310 (Multiplication)

$$\times_\mathfrak{R}$$

$f : \mathfrak{R}, g : \mathfrak{R}, h : \mathfrak{R}$
h $=$

$x : N, y : Q$
$y =_Q f(2x \times max(B_f, B_g)) \times_Q g(2x \times max(B_f, B_g))$

These specifications preserve the real numbers, and they are functional. This is the content of the following.

Proposition 311 (Functionality) *Addition and multiplication are total functions on* $\mathfrak{R}$*; i.e.,*

$$+ : \mathfrak{R} \otimes \mathfrak{R} \Rightarrow \mathfrak{R}$$

$$\times : \mathfrak{R} \otimes \mathfrak{R} \Rightarrow \mathfrak{R}$$

Proof We illustrate with +. The totality and functionality are clear. This leaves us to show that addition preserves the Cauchy condition. Suppose

$$\forall y \geqslant z' \cdot \forall x \geqslant z' \cdot |f(x) - g(y)| \leq 1/z'$$

and

$$\forall y \geqslant z'' \cdot \forall x \geqslant z'' \cdot |f(x) - g(y)| \leq 1/z''$$

Let z be the maximum of z', z'' and suppose $y \geqslant z$ and $x \geqslant z$. Then we have

$$
\begin{aligned}
|(f + g)(x) - (f + g)(y)| &= |f(2x) + g(2x) - f(2y) + g(2y)| \\
&\leq |f(2x) - f(2y)| + |g(2x) - g(2y)| \\
&\leq 1/z + 1/z = 2/z \qquad \blacksquare
\end{aligned}
$$

The proofs of the following are also standard.

1. $\forall f : \mathfrak{R} \cdot \forall g : \mathfrak{R} \cdot \forall h : \mathfrak{R} \cdot (f + g) + h =_{\mathfrak{R}} f + (g + h)$.
2. $\forall f : \mathfrak{R} \cdot \forall g : \mathfrak{R} \cdot f + g =_{\mathfrak{R}} g + f$.
3. $\forall f : \mathfrak{R} \cdot (f + 0) =_{\mathfrak{R}} f$.
4. $\forall f : \mathfrak{R} \cdot \exists! g : \mathfrak{R} \cdot (f + g) =_{\mathfrak{R}} 0$.
5. $\forall f : \mathfrak{R} \cdot \forall g : \mathfrak{R} \cdot f \times g =_{\mathfrak{R}} g \times f$.
6. $\forall f : \mathfrak{R} \cdot \forall g : \mathfrak{R} \cdot \forall h : \mathfrak{R} \cdot (f \times g) \times h =_{\mathfrak{R}} f \times (g \times h)$.
7. $\forall f : \mathfrak{R} \cdot \forall g : \mathfrak{R} \cdot \forall h : \mathfrak{R} \cdot (f + g) \times h =_{\mathfrak{R}} (f \times h) + (g \times h)$.
8. $1 \neq_{\mathfrak{R}} 0 \wedge \forall g : \mathfrak{R} \cdot 1 \times g =_{\mathfrak{R}} g$.
9. $\forall f : \mathfrak{R} \cdot \exists! g : (f \times g) =_{\mathfrak{R}} 1$.

This concludes our very brief introduction to our version of the computable real numbers. It should be clear that it takes on much the same structure as ordinary analysis based upon Cauchy sequences. But we have the following additional checks to carry out.

21.3 Implementation

Since not all the information in these definitions is computable, computation cannot proceed on their basis. We cannot compute with objects if the computation needs the information that they are real numbers. However, our definitions are all implementable. Although the general technique for the following was outlined in the last chapter, it will be instructive to carry out the analysis on these examples.

Proposition 312 *Equality, addition, and multiplication on the real numbers are all implementable.*

Proof The schema specifications are obtained by replacing the type of real numbers by the corresponding schema type. For equality, we simply replace matters as follows.

$$=_{S(N \otimes Q)}$$

$$f : S(N \otimes Q), g : S(N \otimes Q)$$

$$\exists x : N \cdot \exists y : Q \cdot \exists y : Q \cdot f(x, y) \wedge g(x, z) \wedge |x - y| \leq_Q 2/x$$

This is an implementation of the original. The following implements addition.

$$+_{\mathfrak{R}}$$

$$f : S(N \otimes Q), g : S(N \otimes Q), h : S(N \otimes Q)$$

$$h = [(x, y) : N \otimes Q \cdot$$
$$\exists z_1 : Q \cdot \exists z_2 : Q \cdot f(2x, z_1) \wedge g(2x, z_2) \wedge y = z_1 +_Q z_2]$$

And the following implements multiplication.

$$\times_{\mathfrak{R}}$$

$$f : S(N \otimes Q), g : S(N \otimes Q), h : S(N \otimes Q)$$

$$h = \{(x, y) : N \otimes Q \cdot \exists z_1 : Q \cdot \exists z_2 : Q \cdot$$

$$f(2x \times max(b_f, b_g), z_1)$$
$$\wedge$$
$$g(2x \times max(b_U, b_V), z_2)$$
$$\wedge$$
$$y = z_1 \times_Q z_2\}$$

This completes the proof.∎

This model of *computable real numbers* is a more conceptually interesting example of a computable model than those generally provided by software specification.

It employs separation, refinement, and function spaces. Of course, we could spend an almost endless amount of time developing this approach to analysis, but we have probably done enough to indicate its nature and how it functions as a computable model. Our objective is not to provide an in-depth analysis of any such model but rather to indicate the range of the notion. We now turn to another example of a computable makeover of a set-theoretic model.

References

1. Turing, A.M. On computable numbers, with an application to the Entscheidungsproblem. Proceedings of the London Math. Soc., 42(2), 230–265; correction ibid. 43, 544–546 (1937).
2. Weihrauch, K. Computable Analysis. Springer-Verlag, Berlin, 2000.

Chapter 22
Programming Language Specification

There are various semantic accounts of programming languages. Two that are taken to be different, but complementary, are the operational [3, 7, 8] and denotational approaches [9, 1, 2, 12, 10]. One characterization of the former is that it provides an interpretation in terms of some abstract machine. In apparent contrast, a denotational semantics provides the semantic account in terms of some more traditional mathematical objects such as sets or categories. However, the distinction between these two semantic forms is not hard and fast [11]. An operational semantics, given in terms of an abstract machine, may still be mathematical in the sense that the machine is given via some semantic or axiomatic account. And most denotational definitions, indeed all if the notion of machine is taken liberally enough, involve the specification of an underlying abstract machine.[1] It is just that it is expressed in terms of sets or whatever else the basic mathematical building blocks of the semantics are taken to be. Indeed, any legitimate semantic account of a programming language must, in some way, make reference to some model of its intended underlying abstract machine. Moreover, a semantics might be denotational while being fully abstract [5].

As a further example of computable modeling we develop an approach to semantics that is best described by the title of this chapter; i.e., we construct computable models that are *specifications of programming languages*.

22.1 The Abstract Machine

To begin with, we develop a simple abstract machine that will provide the mathematical building blocks of the semantics. We shall work in the theory

$$\text{ThC}(\mathbf{N}, \mathbf{DP}, \mathbf{type}, \mathbf{S})$$

---

[1] Perhaps the use of extensional and infinite sets in some denotational approaches marks the deeper difference.

R. Turner, *Computable Models*, DOI 10.1007/978-1-84882-052-4_22,
© Springer-Verlag London Limited 2009

We shall also admit some basic types. In particular, our formal notion of state builds upon a type of identifiers (**Ide**) that we include as a basic type. States are then taken to be mappings from **Ide** to values, which here, for simplicity of exposition, are taken to be numbers.

Example 313 (State)

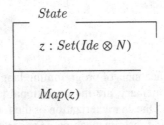

Presumably, an identifier is associated with just one value, hence the use of maps. Using separation, we may consider these as types, and this will help us to express our account of the abstract machine in a slightly more elegant way. Indeed, given the conservative nature of separation, classes, and application, we shall use them freely.

Upon this notion of state we can specify operations that make up the abstract machine. The first is the operation that retrieves the value associated with a given identifier; i.e., given that states are maps, we may employ map application.

Example 314 (Retrieve)

$$
\boxed{\begin{array}{l}
\textit{Retrieve} \\[4pt]
\hline
u : State, x! : Ide, y? : N \\[4pt]
\hline
x \in Dom(u); u(x) = y
\end{array}}
$$

This is a partial function in the following sense. The proof is clear.

Lemma 315 *Retrieve* : $(State \otimes Ide) \rightarrow\!\!\!\!\rightarrow N$.

Our second abstract machine operation is the standard update operation on states. This takes a pair consisting of an identifier and a value and generates a state-to-state transformation.

Example 316 (Update)

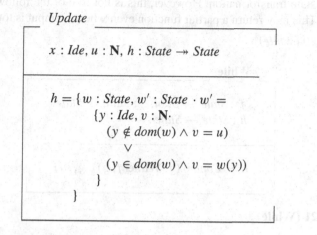

Update

$x : Ide, u : \mathbf{N}, h : State \twoheadrightarrow State$

$h = \{w : State, w' : State \cdot w' =$
$\quad \{y : Ide, v : \mathbf{N}\cdot$
$\qquad (y \notin dom(w) \land v = u)$
$\qquad \lor$
$\qquad (y \in dom(w) \land v = w(y))$
$\quad \}$
$\}$

It has the following functionality.

Lemma 317 *Update* $: Id \otimes \mathbf{N} \Rightarrow (State \twoheadrightarrow State)$, $i = 1, 2$.

Proof The first part of its functionality is easy to see. So is the second. It is functional because it is explicitly defined.∎

Actually, it is total in its second argument; i.e.,

$$z : Id \otimes \mathbf{N} \vdash Update(z) : (State \Rightarrow State)$$

The next operation is a version of conditional that operates on state transformations.

Example 318 (Conditional)

$Cond_{Fun}$

$f : State \twoheadrightarrow Bool$
$g : State \twoheadrightarrow State$
$h : State \twoheadrightarrow State$
$w : State \twoheadrightarrow State$

$w = Cond \circ (f, g, h)$

This has the following class structure; this is self-evident from the definitions.

Lemma 319 (Conditional)

$$Cond_{Fun} : ((State \twoheadrightarrow Bool) \otimes (State \twoheadrightarrow State)^2) \twoheadrightarrow (State \twoheadrightarrow State)$$

It is also clear that if the input state transformations are total functions, then so is the output state transformation. However, this is not true of the following iterative operation. This may return a partial function even when the input is total.

Example 320 (While)

While

$$f : State \twoheadrightarrow Bool, g : State \twoheadrightarrow State$$
$$h : State \twoheadrightarrow State$$

$$h = Cond \circ (f, \textbf{While}(f, g) \circ g, id)$$

Lemma 321 (While)

$$\textbf{While} : ((State \twoheadrightarrow Bool) \otimes (State \twoheadrightarrow State)) \twoheadrightarrow (State \twoheadrightarrow State)$$

Proof We employ the induction principle provided by the recursive definition of **While**. For the induction to work, we have to show that the predicate preserves functionality; i.e., we have to show that if

$$F : ((State \twoheadrightarrow Bool) \otimes (State \twoheadrightarrow State)) \twoheadrightarrow (State \twoheadrightarrow State)$$
$$f : State \twoheadrightarrow Bool$$
$$g : (State \twoheadrightarrow State)$$

then

$$Cond \circ (f, F(f, g) \circ g, id) : State \twoheadrightarrow State$$

But given the assumptions, this is clear. ∎

This completes the definition of our underlying abstract machine. Of course, it is simplistic in that it takes no account of types, procedures, and declarations, etc., but our aim is only to introduce the general idea of a specification semantics for programming languages.

22.2 A Programming Language and Its Specification

We shall illustrate matters with the semantics for a rather simple imperative programming language [1]. It has three syntactic categories: Boolean expressions (B), expressions (E), and commands (C). We shall describe these as structural types, where these types are given by the following BNF grammar. We have already seen how to view this as a simultaneous schema recursive specification.

$$B ::= true \mid false \mid E < E \mid \textbf{if } B \textbf{ then } B \textbf{ else } B$$
$$E ::= 0 \mid Ide \mid E^+$$
$$C ::= Ide := E \mid \textbf{if } B \textbf{ then } C \textbf{ else } C \mid C;C \mid \textbf{While } B \textbf{ do } C$$

Booleans are generated from *true* and *false* by the less-than relation ($<$) between expressions and the conditional. The expression language contains zero and identifiers and is closed under successor operation. The language of commands is generated by simple assignment statements, conditionals, sequencing, and a while loop.

We require the following semantic functions for the various syntactic types.

$$\mathcal{B} : B \Rightarrow (State \rightarrow Bool)$$
$$\mathcal{E} : E \Rightarrow (State \rightarrow \mathbf{N})$$
$$\mathcal{C} : C \Rightarrow (State \rightarrow State)$$

These semantic functions are then given recursively as follows. Their existence as functions in the theory is guaranteed by the existence of such recursive functions on these recursive types. We deal with the three functions in turn. The Boolean function is straightforward.

$$\mathcal{B}[true] = \lambda s : State \cdot true$$
$$\mathcal{B}[false] = \lambda s : State \cdot false$$
$$\mathcal{B}[e_1 < e_2] = \quad \lambda s : State \cdot \mathcal{E}[e_1]s < \mathcal{E}[e_2]s$$
$$\mathcal{B}[\textbf{if } b \textbf{ then } b_1 \textbf{ else } b_2] = \textbf{Cond} \circ (\mathcal{B}[b], \mathcal{C}[b_1], \mathcal{C}[b_2])$$

And the expression semantic function is equally predictable. In particular, the variables obtain their values from the state. The rest is as expected.

$$\mathcal{E}[x] = \lambda s : State \cdot Retrieve(s, x)$$
$$\mathcal{E}[0] = \lambda s : State \cdot \mathbf{0}$$
$$\mathcal{E}[e^+] = \lambda s : State \cdot (\mathcal{E}[e]s)^+$$

The meat of the definition is the semantic function for commands, but we have done all the hard work in defining the abstract machine.

$$\mathcal{C}[x := e] = \lambda s : State \cdot Update(x, \mathcal{E}[e]s)$$
$$\mathcal{C}[\textbf{if } b \textbf{ then } c_1 \textbf{ else } c_2] = \textbf{Cond} \circ (\mathcal{B}[b], \mathcal{C}[c_1], \mathcal{C}[c_2])$$
$$\mathcal{C}[c_1; c_2] = \mathcal{C}[c_2] \circ \mathcal{C}[c_1]$$
$$\mathcal{C}[\textbf{while } b \textbf{ do } c] = \textbf{While}(\mathcal{B}[b], \mathcal{C}[c])$$

The assignment command is interpreted using the update function, the clause for the conditional uses the conditional, sequencing is interpreted as relational composition, and the **while** loop is unpacked in terms of the **While** transformation on the state.

Now observe the following. This is a consequence of the properties of the abstract machine.

Theorem 322 *For each expression, Boolean expression, and command, t, $\mathcal{E}[t]$, $\mathcal{B}[t]$, and $C[t]$ are partial functions.*

Proof We use structural induction over the types of the grammar. We have to show by induction that each stage preserves the functionality. For example, one part of the induction will involve showing that

$$(f : State \rightarrowtail State \wedge g : State \rightarrowtail State) \rightarrow f \circ g : State \rightarrowtail State$$

And we have already done the hard work in the analysis of the abstract machine. And this applies to all cases. ∎

22.3 Implementation

The semantics has been given in terms of partial functions. To implement matters, we need to generalize to the underlying relational representations. We take each of our abstract machine operations in turn.

For the conditional, the corresponding schema specification is given as follows.

Example 323 (Relational Conditional)

$$
\begin{array}{l}
\underline{\ Cond_{Rel}\ } \\
\quad f : \mathbf{S}(State \otimes Bool),\ g : \mathbf{S}(State \otimes State), \\
\quad h : \mathbf{S}(State \otimes State),\ w : \mathbf{S}(State \otimes State) \\
\hline
\\
\qquad\qquad w \\
\qquad\qquad = \\
\quad \left[\begin{array}{l} (s, s') : State \otimes State \mid \\ (f(s, true) \wedge g(s, s')) \vee (f(s, false) \wedge h(s, s')) \end{array} \right]
\end{array}
$$

Lemma 324 *$Cond_{Rel}$ is an implementation of $Cond_{Fun}$.*

Our next specification is the iterative operation on the state. This is implemented as follows.

Example 325 (Implementation of While)

$While_{Rel}$

$f : \mathbf{S}(State \otimes Bool), g : \mathbf{S}(State \otimes State)$
$h : \mathbf{S}(State \otimes State)$

$$h = \begin{bmatrix} u : State, v : State \mid \\ (f(u, true) \wedge \exists z : \mathbf{S}(State \otimes State) \cdot \exists y : State \cdot g(u, y) \cdot \\ \mathbf{While}(f, g, z) \wedge z(u, v) \\ \vee \\ (f(u, false) \wedge v = u) \end{bmatrix}$$

Proposition 326 While$_{Rel}$ *implements* **While**

This completes our rather brief account of language specification. The above should provide enough of the flavor for the reader to see how one might extend matters to more complex language features. The above is merely a taster; but it is enough to provide the flavour of the modeling.

References

1. Gordon, J.C. The Denotational Semantics of Programming Languages. Springer-Verlag, New York, 1970.
2. Gunter, C. Semantics of Programming Languages: Structures and Techniques. MIT Press, Cambridge, MA, 1992.
3. Landin, P. The mechanical evaluation of expressions. The Comp. J. 6(4):308–320, 1964.
4. Milne, R. and Strachey, C. A Theory of Programming Language Semantics, Halsted Press, New York, 1977.
5. Mulmuley, K. Full Abstraction and Semantic Equivalence. MIT Press, Cambridge, MA, 1986.
6. Pierce, B.C. Types and Programming Languages. MIT Press, Cambridge, MA, 2002.
7. Plotkin, G.D. G. Tech. Rep. DAIMI FN-19, Computer Science Department, Aarhus University, Aarhus, Denmark. Reprinted with corrections in J. Log. Algebr. Program. 60–61: 17-139, 2004.
8. Plotkin, G.D. The Origins of structural operational semantics. J. Log. Algebra. Program. 60–61:3–15, 2004.
9. Stoy, J.E. Denotational Semantics: The Scott Strachey Approach to Programming Language Theory. MIT Press, Cambridge, MA, 1977.
10. Tennent, R.D. Denotational semantics. In: Handbook of Logic in Computer Science, vol. 3, pp. 169–322. Oxford University Press, Oxford, 1994.
11. Turner, R. Understanding programming languages. Minds and Machines. 17(2) 2: 203–216 . 2007.
12. Winskel, G. Formal Semantics of Programming Languages. MIT Press, Cambridge, MA, 1993.

Chapter 23
Abstract Types

Computer science is centrally concerned with the invention and application of mechanisms for abstraction and information hiding. Examples include interfaces, modules, libraries, classes and abstract data types. Such mechanisms are essential for specification and design. They enable a level of design and specification where the accessibility and visibility of implementation details are limited. In addition, they facilitate the reuse and redesign of software components.

In this chapter we bring together several type constructors and illustrate their use in the representation of *abstract data types*. The latter provide a powerful tool of abstraction in computational modeling [2, 6, 3]. As we shall see, in various ways they hide information and thus enable a variety of possible implementations.

In our approach, which has its origins in the treatment of [4] and [5], we shall demonstrate how the dependent product type constructor, in conjunction with the type of types and the polymorphic class constructor, provides an analogue of the standard treatment of abstract types, cast within the following theory and its conservative extensions.

$$\text{ThC}(\mathbf{N}, \mathbf{DP}, \mathbf{type}, \mathbf{S}).$$

Within this setting are several layers of abstraction; we shall gradually pick our way through them.

23.1 Axiomatic Specifications

Consider again the specification of the real numbers and their associated operations and relations. In particular, you will recall that the class of real numbers was defined as

$$\mathfrak{R} \triangleq \{ f : N \Rightarrow Q \cdot \exists z : N \cdot \forall y \geqslant z \cdot \forall x \geqslant z \cdot |f(x) - f(y)| \leq 1/z \}$$

where real addition is specified as follows.

R. Turner, *Computable Models*, DOI 10.1007/978-1-84882-052-4_23,
© Springer-Verlag London Limited 2009

$$+_\Re$$

$$f : \Re, g : \Re, h : \Re$$

$$h = [(x, y) : N \otimes Q \mid y = f(2x) +_Q g(2x)]$$

A similar specification determined multiplication.

$$\times_\Re$$

$$f : \Re, g : \Re, h : \Re$$

$$h$$
$$=$$
$$[(x, y) : N \otimes Q \mid$$
$$y =_Q f(2x \times max(B_f, B_g)) \times_Q g(2x \times max(B_f, B_g))]$$

The real numbers are given a concrete representation in terms of functions operating on the natural numbers and returning rational ones. The operations of addition and multiplication for the real numbers are defined in terms of the corresponding operations on the rationals. And any implementation will employ the implementations of these operations.

But this is not an abstract characterization of the real numbers. It is a concrete representation in terms of existing notions. For an abstract account we need to get away from such concrete representations. The following pair of specifications do so: They introduce different levels of abstract type for the real numbers.

Example 327 (Abstract Reals I)

$\mathfrak{R} : N \Rightarrow Q$
$+ : \mathfrak{R} \otimes \mathfrak{R} \Rightarrow \mathfrak{R}$
$\times : \mathfrak{R} \otimes \mathfrak{R} \Rightarrow \mathfrak{R}$

$\forall f : \mathfrak{R} \cdot \forall g : \mathfrak{R} \cdot \forall h : \mathfrak{R} \cdot (f + g) + h =_{\mathfrak{R}} f + (g + h)$
$\forall f : \mathfrak{R} \cdot \forall g : \mathfrak{R} \cdot f + g =_{\mathfrak{R}} g + f$
$\forall f : \mathfrak{R} \cdot (f + 0) =_{\mathfrak{R}} f$
$\forall f : \mathfrak{R} \cdot \forall g : \mathfrak{R} \cdot \forall h : \mathfrak{R} \cdot (f + g) + h =_{\mathfrak{R}} f + (g + h)$
$\forall f : \mathfrak{R} \cdot \forall g : \mathfrak{R} \cdot f + g =_{\mathfrak{R}} g + f$
$\forall f : \mathfrak{R} \cdot (f + 0) =_{\mathfrak{R}} f$
$\forall f : \mathfrak{R} \cdot \forall g : \mathfrak{R} \cdot f \times g =_{\mathfrak{R}} g \times f$
$\forall f : \mathfrak{R} \cdot \forall g : \mathfrak{R} \cdot \forall h : \mathfrak{R} \cdot (f \times g) \times h =_{\mathfrak{R}} f \times (g \times h)$
$\forall f : \mathfrak{R} \cdot \forall g : \mathfrak{R} \cdot \forall h : \mathfrak{R} \cdot (f + g) \times h =_{\mathfrak{R}} (f \times h) + (g \times h$
$1 \neq_{\mathfrak{R}} 0 \wedge \forall g : \mathfrak{R} \cdot 1 \times g =_{\mathfrak{R}} g$
$\forall f : \mathfrak{R} \cdot \exists! g : (f \times g) =_{\mathfrak{R}} 1$

Example 328 (Abstract Reals II)

Reals

$u : \textbf{type}$
$+ : u \otimes u \Rightarrow u$
$\times : u \otimes u \Rightarrow u$

$\forall f : u \cdot \forall g : u \cdot \forall h : u \cdot (f + g) + h =_u f + (g + h)$
$\forall f : u \cdot \forall g : u \cdot f + g =_u g + f$
$\forall f : u \cdot (f + 0) =_u f$
$\forall f : u \cdot \forall g : u \cdot \forall h : u \cdot (f + g) + h =_u f + (g + h)$
$\forall f : u \cdot \forall g : u \cdot f + g =_u g + f$
$\forall f : u \cdot (f + 0) =_u f$
$\forall f : u \cdot \forall g : u \cdot f \times g =_u g \times f$
$\forall f : u \cdot \forall g : u \cdot \forall h : u \cdot (f \times g) \times h =_u f \times (g \times h)$
$\forall f : u \cdot \forall g : u \cdot \forall h : u \cdot (f + g) \times h =_u (f \times h) + (g \times h)$
$1 \neq_u 0 \wedge \forall g : u \cdot 1 \times g =_u g$
$\forall f : u \cdot \exists! g : (f \times g) =_u 1$

The first does not tell us how to implement the operations. It is an axiomatic definition of these operations where the scheme definition has two declarations (+ and ×) of functional operations, but the actual operations are not given explicitly but circumscribed by the axiomatic conditions that express the standard properties.[1]. We know that the actual given representation satisfies the requirement of this schema. The second example take matters a stage further by abstracting on the actual class of real numbers.

This is about as far as we can go with this example. To illustrate the full expressive power of data abstraction, we need to consider a type constructor rather than a single type.

23.2 Polymorphism and Data Abstraction

We shall employ the stack type constructor. If you recall, the type constructor for stacks was given as follows, where, for pedagogical reasons, we have simplified matters. The abstract type abstracts away by using type variables and, at the same time, packages the whole axiomatic bundle together in the form of schema. But first recall the rules for stacks.

$$\frac{T\ type}{Stack(T)\ type}$$

$$\frac{a:T \quad b:Stack(T)}{push_T(a,b):Stack(T)} \qquad \frac{b:Stack(T)}{top_T(b):T}$$

$$\frac{b:Stack(T)}{pop_T(b):Stack(T)} \qquad \frac{a:T \quad b:Stack(T)}{pop_T(push_T(a,b))=b}$$

$$\frac{a:T \qquad b:Stack(T)}{top_T(push_T(a,b))=a}$$

The schema describes the classes and the equations they are to satisfy, e.g.,

$$pop(push(element, stack)) = stack$$
$$top(push(element, stack)) = element$$

---

[1] Here we are not claiming that the following is all we need for mathematical purposes; we are only illustrating the different levels of abstraction.

This leads to the following abstract notion of stack. The idea is that the formation rules for stacks are captured by the functionality of the operations in the new schema. The remainder of the rules are reflected in its predicate.

Example 329 (Stacks)

$$
\begin{array}{|l}
\hline
\textit{Stacks} \\
\quad stack : \textbf{type} \Rrightarrow \textbf{type} \\
\quad push : \Pi u : \textbf{type} \cdot (u \otimes stack(u)) \Rrightarrow stack(u) \\
\quad top : \Pi u : \textbf{type} \cdot stack(u) \Rrightarrow u \\
\quad pop : \Pi u : \textbf{type} \cdot stack(u) \Rrightarrow stack(u) \\
\hline
\\
\quad \forall u : type \cdot \forall x : u \cdot \forall y : Stack(u) \cdot top(u)(push(u)(x, y)) = x \\
\quad \forall u : type \cdot \forall x : u \cdot \forall y : Stack(u) \cdot pop(u)(push(u)(x, y)) = y \\
\\
\hline
\end{array}
$$

Here v is the actual stack and u is the type of its elements.

Note that the predicate can be unpacked without universal quantification. For example,

$$[u : type, x : u, y : stack(u), z : u \mid top(u)(push(u)(x, y))]$$

$$=$$

$$[u : type, x : u, y : stack(u), z : u \mid z = x]$$

This provides a description of the notion of stack at a very abstract level. The only information supplied is the relationships between the classes and operations. It does not specify the operations.

But specifications previously given provide the basis for an implementation of this schema definition; i.e., in any such implementation we need to replace the function spaces by schema types

$$
\begin{aligned}
&stack : \textbf{S}(\textbf{type} \otimes \textbf{type}) \\
&push : \textbf{S}(\Sigma u : \textbf{type} \cdot \textbf{S}(u \otimes stack(u)) \otimes stack(u)) \\
&top : \textbf{S}(\Sigma u : \textbf{type} \cdot \textbf{S}(stack(u) \otimes u)) \\
&pop : \textbf{S}(\Sigma u : \textbf{type} \cdot \textbf{S}(stack(u) \otimes stack(u)))
\end{aligned}
$$

and then we remove the applications from the predicates.

We could muster many more examples, but we should have sufficiently whetted the reader's appetite for a more detailed investigation of both the present topic and the topic of the whole book.

References

1. Barendregt, H.P. Lambda calculus with types. In S. Abramsky, D.M. Gabbay, and T.S.E. Maibaum, (Eds), Handbook of Logic in Computer Science. Oxford Science Publications. Abramsky, S., Gabbay, D.M. and Maibaum, T.S.E., pp. 118-310, Oxford University Press, Oxford, 1992.
2. Dale 1996 : Dale, N., and Dale, H.M.W., Abstract Data Types: Specifications, Implementations, and Applications. Jones and Bartlett Publishers, Boston, 1996.
3. Pierce, B.C. Types and Programming Languages. MIT Press, Cambridge, MA, 2002.
4. Mitchell, J.C. Plotkin. G.D. Abstract types have existential type. ACM Trans. Program. Lang. Sys. (TOPLAS) 10(3): 470 – 502, 988.
5. Reynolds, J.C. Introduction to polymorphic lambda-calculus. In: G. Huet (Ed.), Logical Foundations of Functional Programming, pp. 77–86. Addison-Wesley, Reading, MA, 1990..
6. Thomas, P., Robinson, H. and Emms, J. Abstract Data Types: Their Specification, Representation. Oxford University Press, Oxford, 1988.

Chapter 24
Conclusion

We have covered a fair amount of ground. We have provided a basic logical framework (typed predicate logic) within which we have articulated a rich variety of theories of data types. The latter have been constructed from a wide range of types and type constructors. In particular, we introduced types and type constructors for the natural numbers, finite sets, schemata, a type of types, subtypes, dependent products, and abstract types. Moreover, each of these theories was shown to have an arithmetic interpretation, i.e., a recursive model. We have simultaneously developed a general theory of specification/computable models. Our notion of specification applies to any **TDT**. Our case studies of computable models included examples from theoretical computer science, computable real analysis, philosophical logic, and formal ontology. Moreover, all of the theories and the models constructed have recursive interpretations. Furthermore, we extended the basic notions of specification to include those that were not computable and used the notion of refinement to justify them.

Despite this coverage, there are some major omissions. To begin with, some of the topics covered deserve more attention. In particular, the chapter on programming language specification could easily have taken a good portion of the book. Many of the central issues of semantics were left untouched. Much the same could be said for all the case studies of computable models; each could have been extended considerably.

In addition, several important topics were not even mentioned. Some more investigation of the connection between the present approach to specification and that of constructive type theory would have been pleasant. This would seem appropriate given the nearness of our formal setting to that of constructive type theory. A chapter on the topic was planned. Unfortunately, one chapter turned out to be insufficient to do justice to the material. We had also planned a chapter on the development of a **TDT** aimed at object-oriented specification. But again, time and space prevented a detailed development of the theory. Some of this material will be presented elsewhere.

R. Turner, *Computable Models*, DOI 10.1007/978-1-84882-052-4_24,
© Springer-Verlag London Limited 2009

Index